" . . . The Great Work is
the raising of the whole man in
perfect balance to the power of infinity."

~ ALEISTER CROWLEY

TAROT

for the

NEW AEON

Tarot
for the
New Aeon

*A Practical Guide
to the Power and Wisdom
of the Thoth Tarot*

P. C. Tarantino

ALTERNATIVE INSIGHTS
PUBLISHING

Published by:

ALTERNATIVE INSIGHTS PUBLISHING
P. O. B. 1519
Pebble Beach, California 93953 U.S.A.
Tel. 800 • 768-6821   Fax: 831 • 626-7360
email: Insights@AlternativeInsightsPublishing.com
www.AlternativeInsightsPublishing.com

Design: Kedron Bryson
Set in Apollo

ISBN: 0-9766184-0-0
ISBN 13: 978-0-9766184-0-9

Library of Congress Control Number: 2005907097

1. Tarot   2. Mysticism   3. Metaphysics
4. Aleister Crowley   5. Thoth Tarot   I. Title

Printed in Canada

*Dedicated to Kristin, James,
Nichole and Aiden.*

THE CARDS OF THE THOTH TAROT

Major Arcana

0	The Fool	XI	Lust
I	The Magus	XII	The Hanged Man
II	The Priestess	XIII	Death
III	The Empress	XIV	Art
IV	The Emperor	XV	The Devil
V	The Hierophant	XVI	The Tower
VI	The Lovers	XVII	The Star
VII	The Chariot	XVIII	The Moon
VIII	Adjustment	XIX	The Sun
IX	The Hermit	XX	The Aeon
X	Fortune	XXI	The Universe

Minor Arcana · THE SMALL CARDS

Wands Suit

Ace of Wands
Two of Wands (Dominion)
Three of Wands (Virtue)
Four of Wands (Completion)
Five of Wands (Strife)
Six of Wands (Victory)
Seven of Wands (Valour)
Eight of Wands (Swiftness)
Nine of Wands (Strength)
Ten of Wands (Oppression)

Swords Suit

Ace of Swords
Two of Swords (Peace)
Three of Swords (Sorrow)
Four of Swords (Truce)
Five of Swords (Defeat)
Six of Swords (Science)
Seven of Swords (Futility)
Eight of Swords (Interference)
Nine of Swords (Cruelty)
Ten of Swords (Ruin)

Cups Suit

Ace of Cups
Two of Cups (Love)
Three of Cups (Abundance)
Four of Cups (Luxury)
Five of Cups (Disappointment)
Six of Cups (Pleasure)
Seven of Cups (Debauch)
Eight of Cups (Indolence)
Nine of Cups (Happiness)
Ten of Cups (Satiety)

Disks Suit

Ace of Disks
Two of Disks (Change)
Three of Disks (Work)
Four of Disks (Power)
Five of Disks (Worry)
Six of Disks (Success)
Seven of Disks (Failure)
Eight of Disks (Prudence)
Nine of Disks (Gain)
Ten of Disks (Wealth)

Minor Arcana · THE COURT CARDS

Wands Suit
Knight / Queen
Prince / Princess

Swords Suit
Knight / Queen
Prince / Princess

Cups Suit
Knight / Queen
Prince / Princess

Disks Suit
Knight / Queen
Prince / Princess

CONTENTS

CONTENTS continued

Preface

My initiation into the world of Aleister Crowley took place in 1979 in Carmel, California. At 36 years of age, I was at a crossroads: trying to make the desperate decision of whether to stay in an unhappy relationship, or move out in the world on my own as a single parent with two children.

In a local bookstore, I noticed a flyer for a tarot class that was to begin that very evening. I surprised myself by enrolling. Little did I know that this class, taught by Dr. James Wanless, would mark a dramatic transformation in my life. At first, I was just fascinated by the breadth of the tarot cards, so rich in imagery, symbols and magical instruction. I would soon learn that the Thoth deck is a limitless wellspring of guidance and personal revelation.

Working with the Thoth Tarot, I began to envision my situation from a different perspective. Anticipation replaced anxiety; pessimism and despair gave way to optimism and hope. Before long I felt empowered to make the choices for myself and to know the responsibility—and delight—of creating the life I desired.

My fascination with tarot in general, and Aleister Crowley's Thoth Tarot in particular, has continued to grow over the last twenty-eight years. In 1984 I was encouraged to teach my own tarot class. As I began teaching, I concentrated on empowering students to use the tarot for personal advice and direction. It didn't take long to realize that people may have come to my classes for private guidance, but left with a passion for the Thoth Tarot and a desire to use it to explore all of life's treasures.

I had two main thoughts in mind while writing this book. The first was to give you a simple way to do an instant tarot reading for yourself or friends, using the Thoth Tarot Advisor (Section I). The second thought was to pique your interest in this remarkable deck so you would want to learn more about it. Section II—Symbols of the Thoth Tarot—explains the meaning of the cards in a down-to-earth way. Section III of the book— Personal Guidance Cards—shows you how to find even more specific direction, inspiration, and revelation for your life journey.

I believe the wisdom of the Thoth Tarot offers us everything we need to know to live a full, happy and productive life. I hope this book will deepen your respect for the magnificence of life and the divine power of magick inherent within your being.

~ P. C. TARANTINO

INTRODUCTION

Overview

Tarot for the New Aeon is a practical, no-nonsense manual that opens a portal into the magical world of Aleister Crowley's Thoth Tarot.

Here you will find a common sense guide to using the Thoth Tarot for an instant reading, as well as detailed interpretations of the compelling symbology in the cards. While this book respects the original spirit of Crowley's work, it has been crafted to make his timeless illuminations readily accessible to the modern reader.

Tarot for the New Aeon is in four parts.

In this **Overview**, you'll find:

- A short background on the tarot.
- A brief description of how and why the cards work.
- The basic structure of the Thoth deck.
- Instructions on how to do readings with the Thoth Tarot.

Section I, Thoth Tarot Advisor, gives an interpretation of all 78 cards for your instant advice reading. The cards are shown in their upright and inverted positions, giving a total of 156 possible responses to your queries.

Section II, Symbols of the Thoth Tarot, covers the meaning of each card's symbols, to enhance their messages for you.

Section III, Personal Guidance Cards, offers you ways to illuminate your lifetime path using the symbols of the deck.

Consulting the Oracle

Buried deep within the collective human psyche is the aspiration to seek purpose and meaning in life. Human beings have throughout history sought knowledge of the unknown by consulting many different types of oracles. Everything—tea leaves, crystals, stones, coins, sticks, and even bones—has been used for the art of divination and spiritual communication. The tarot cards, I-Ching, runes, and other forms of revelation provide a way for people to use symbols to gain profound insight and a sense of continuity for life experiences.

The tarot in particular has caught our attention because it is a timeless oracle whose messages are as compelling and true today as they were in the first century of its use. Tarot can be seen as an ancient book of wisdom encoded, through pictures and symbols, on 78 cards that hold the key to our understanding of the universal principles of life and the laws in play creating our reality. Use of the cards in readings unlocks our inner knowledge. Tarot is an Egyptian word meaning "Royal Road" and represents the journey we take through life uncovering the timeless wisdom deep within us.

Emergence of Tarot

The origin of the tarot is shrouded in mystery. There are as many theories about its genesis as there are experts to address them. Tarot at one time or another has been thought to originate in such diverse places as ancient Egypt, China, Morocco, or India. Some theories claim the tarot was taken from Egypt by Gypsies fleeing the country, or was simply the encoded teachings of some secret society. These and other ideas about the tarot's beginnings are romantic, but lack hard evidence to support them.

The current view of the tarot's history places its creation in fifteenth century Italy, an era that saw a growing interest in the study of alchemy, astrology and magic. Italy played a major role by producing the deck as a game of playing cards called *Tarocchi*. The tarot that is familiar to us today was uncovered when the deck, waning in popularity as a game, came to be seen in another light.

Antoine Court de Gébelin, a French occultist, recognized the depth of the tarot images, their structure and their esoteric aspects. He believed the tarot to be an ancient Egyptian book of wisdom, and brought it into use as a divinatory tool in the latter part of the 18th century.

The tarot's emergence as a tool of magic gained impetus when, in reaction to 19th century materialism, an interest in the occult resurfaced in Europe. Secret societies were formed, and as esoteric ideas rode the wave of enthusiasm, students of the mystic arts were increasingly attracted to the tarot's intriguing images. One interpreter was Eliphas Levi (a pseudonym of Alphonse Louis Constant). He saw a connection between the tarot and the ancient Hebrew mystical system called the *Qabalah* (also *Kabbahla* or *Cabala*). Levi called attention to the relationship between the 22 letters of the Hebrew alphabet and the 22 trumps of the tarot. He was also responsible for bringing the concept of "human will" into play in relation to the tarot's hidden messages. He considered the human will to be a material force that played a major role in the creation of life as we know it.

The twentieth century saw the formation of the secret society of the Hermetic Order of the Golden Dawn, founded by Samuel Liddell Mathers, Wynn Westcott and W. K. Woodman. The Golden Dawn came to be the central source of interpretive wisdom about the tarot in the early 1900s. Arthur Edward Waite, head of the London Temple of the Golden Dawn, created the Rider-Waite Tarot deck, the first to gain wide use as an oracular instrument, and still widely popular.

It was as an initiate of the Golden Dawn that Aleister Crowley, at 23 years of age, began his career in ritual magic. In 1938, Crowley, with the help of Lady Frieda Harris, would begin to create a magnificent and powerful deck of tarot cards, based on Egyptian, Christian, Greek and Eastern symbols. This diversity accounts for the richness of symbolism and the scope of its wisdom.

Six decades later, Crowley's tarot cards and accompanying writings are widely used in every country.

But what can the Tarot, a collection of ancient, occult symbols, hold for us in this day of psychological sophistication? The Tarot's powerful images have long held interest for a certain group of psychologists, and are now being seen even in the business world. The eminent psychologist Carl Jung mentioned the tarot in his writings, and his work with universal symbols and images influenced broader exploration of the deck's symbols. Jung understood that at a deep level we are all interconnected and that we share the same basic instinctual forces or drives no matter what our cultural make-up. He referred to these forces as "archetypes"— primitive images or templates of behavior passed down from our ancestors, engraved in our consciousness and rooted in the collective unconscious. These archetypes are visible in the symbols and pictures of the Thoth Tarot.

The tarot and its remarkable imagery has come to be used in settings far from the esoteric milieu of secret societies, in ways that include dream analysis, cognitive and behavioral therapies, and couples counseling. It is currently to be seen on the tables of think tanks in many corporations, a somewhat surprising recognition of how the tarot can reveal and catalyze new perspectives and understanding of the deepest dynamics of human experience.

The value of tarot is unmistakable. Tarot is everything we thought it was. It embraces a philosophy of life, and lights the path to self knowledge and transformation. It is a map of the unseen inner realms, a representation of the natural forces of nature and a book of ancient wisdom. The tarot cards contain images that represent a myriad of human possibilities as well as illustrating the different aspects of our psyche. It seduces our imagination, and can be used to divine our fortune . . . determine our psychological states . . . or uncover our subconscious needs and desires. It is a finely tuned instrument for the practice of self discovery. As the origin of tarot becomes clearer, how much more will we discover? I believe that our journey with the tarot has only just begun to unfold.

Aleister Crowley
and The Thoth Tarot

Edward Alexander Crowley was born on October 12, 1875 in England, at the height of the Victorian age. Born into a family of financial privilege, he was well educated and enjoyed the advantages of their social class. His parents, Edward and Emily Crowley, were members of an evangelical sect called the Plymouth Brethren. They raised their son in an atmosphere of strict Christian fundamentalism. Alix (as he was called) had a deep attachment toward his father. When he was eleven years old he lost his beloved father to cancer. After this loss, everything changed for young Alix. His already strained relationship with his mother deteriorated further as he began to question the religious doctrines he had been taught.

Crowley's early academic career was one of Victorian corporal punishment, struggle, and isolation. At age twenty he became heir to a large sum of money through his father's estate, and found himself free to experience life on his own terms. To go along with this new sense of freedom he changed his name to Aleister Crowley. He entered Trinity College, Cambridge, and there discovered a love of poetry and literature, as well as his skill as a writer. As he matured, Crowley developed an interest in tarot and alchemy as well as other metaphysical pursuits. He began his magical career in earnest at twenty-three when he joined the Hermetic Order of the Golden Dawn. Crowley grew to adulthood with considerable talents: he became a fine poet, novelist, theatrical producer, mountain climber, artist and magus.

In 1904, following the instructions of what he termed a discarnate voice, Crowley transcribed the Book of the Law over 3 days in April. The Book of the Law announced the closing of the current era and a new millennium—beginning on March 20, 1904. The philosophy and teachings of this New Aeon were to become the compelling focus of Crowley's life. He believed this coming age would usher in a time of expanded awareness; a time when the individual would come to understand his position as the creator of his personal universe. He understood that, as human beings, we were in the infantile stage of our development; moving into the New Aeon, we would be able to access more of our potential. Each person would have the opportunity to come to know his or her true nature and develop an ability to consciously direct individual will and imagination.

Since Crowley considered himself to be the Prophet of the New Aeon, he accepted the responsibility of sharing his knowledge with the world. He professed the use of certain practices as the way to create change according to one's will, he referred to these practices as "Magick." By discovering one's authentic nature (our link with the divine), and living in alignment with this nature, we would be able to determine the correct path for ourselves.

There are three basic messages contained within The Book of the Law that influenced Crowley's teachings:

> Do What Thou Wilt Shall Be the Whole of the Law
> Love Is the Law, Love Under Will
> Every Man and Every Woman Is a Star

> (*The Book of the Law*, 1976 edition, Samuel Weiser Inc.)

Crowley cautioned that the Book of the Law should not be taught by anyone but himself. In this way he hoped that the teachings would not become rigid and dogmatic, but be a guide to facilitating each individual's knowledge of the sacred through direct, personal experience. He therefore suggested that you read the text and draw your own conclusions.

To say the least, Aleister Crowley has had a lot of "bad press." Some of it deserved, some slanderous—some orchestrated by Mr. Crowley himself. His writing spoke his truth, but his books were often misunderstood by the critics. He was often referred to as The Wickedest Man on Earth, and seemed to instill fear in the hearts of total strangers by his eccentricities. Crowley did nothing to counter this image; in fact, he enjoyed playing to the crowd.

He was notorious for his manner of dress, and loved wearing turbans and Indian caftans whenever possible. He could also appear, if he so desired, in full formal attire and look much the gentleman. He was a man on a mission and that mission was to offer others the tools to uncover their own spiritual nature and begin the journey toward conscious direction of one's will and imagination. He was driven to communicate this message at all costs to himself or to others; for that reason, his words and actions were at times brutal.

At other times he could be kind and compassionate. Whatever you believe about the man Aleister Crowley doesn't affect the validity of the message he delivered. Once you experience the beauty and wisdom expressed in his Thoth Tarot, all other decks will pale in comparison.

The magnificent artwork on the tarot cards was painted by Lady Frieda Harris and took five years to produce (1938–1943). Crowley had originally wanted to update an existing tarot deck. It was Lady Harris who convinced him to create a new one based on his understanding of the New Aeon. They worked closely together on this project, with Crowley explaining every detail and symbol to be illustrated on the cards. Crowley published *The Book of Thoth: A Short Essay on the Tarot of the Egyptians* in 1944, three years before his death. It was written as a companion book to shed light on the Thoth Tarot cards. It is a demanding manuscript, since Crowley expected that the reader would know as much as he did about the arcane study of tarot. Nonetheless, it is an important book for anyone seeking a deeper understanding of Crowley and of the Thoth Tarot. Crowley's Tarot deck, as we know it today, did not receive worldwide distribution until Grady L. McMurtry had the paintings photographed and the cards produced in color in 1969. To this day they have never been out of print.

There have been many biographies written that will help you to explore the paradox of Aleister Crowley. You may agree or disagree with his tenets, like or dislike the man, but if you're willing to separate the man from the message there is a world of wisdom to acquire from his extraordinary works.

A Note
on Thoth

Aeons in the past, people of the Nile River valley created a rich and beautiful civilization, for amongst them moved luminous beings with powers to guide the human race to Paradise. The deities of the ancient Egyptians dwelt invisibly in their world, and in timeless dimensions of mind and spirit as well. We find, amidst the compelling remains of that lost age, that they revered Thoth as the God of Writing, Lord of the Moon, and Master of Time.

Thoth was the wisest of the gods, a powerful deity of wisdom and magic, learning and medicine who protected and guided those working with knowledge and the word—scribes, teachers, and writers. Thoth was also the patron of astronomy, languages, mathematics and accounting—major arts in that sophisticated culture so remote in time.

Egyptians portrayed Thoth with the head of an ibis, a bird that, dwelling on the shore between deep water and the land, symbolizes communion between the conscious and subconscious minds. Other representations show Thoth as a lunar deity with a moon headdress, and also as a wise-looking baboon.

The Egyptians considered their system of writing to be of divine origin—the gift of gods to humanity. "Hieroglyph" means "god's word," and scribes were accorded high status in the culture's religious sphere. Thoth would have guided them in creating the sophisticated symbols so complex and layered that modern scholars are still decoding their meaning.

The Grecian deity Hermes (Mercury to the Romans) is a counterpart to the Egyptians' Thoth. The Greeks revered Hermes as the god of communication, an intermediary between deities and mortals. Hermes was invested with strong magic, and bore the caduceus, a staff with intertwined snakes symbolizing the power to unite those divided by conflict. As with Thoth, his domain was that of words and writing, when to capture ideas and thoughts in symbols was still a mysterious, even divine act.

The powers of Thoth were so great that legends tell of a book of secret wisdom, written by the god himself, which would allow a person who read it to become the most powerful magician in the world. In The Book of Thoth, one could learn "the language of the beasts, how to see the wind and how to hear the sun, the secrets of the gods and the songs of the stars."

Aleister Crowley studied the occult knowledge of the ancient Egyptians, perceiving the illumination of inner realms and "all that is hidden in the stars." After creating the Thoth Tarot deck, a path to self knowledge and transformation, Crowley wrote *The Book of Thoth—A Short Essay on the Tarot of the Egyptians.*

The Tarot for the New Aeon brings the skills of Thoth into the 21st Century, by offering you a method to illuminate your thoughts, understand your emotions, and consciously clarify your will and intent.

Tarot: A Tool for Self-Empowerment

The tarot cards function as an extension of your psychic awareness. The wisdom and energy used to move the cards and their seemingly random choice is a direct result of your inner knowledge.

Everything you need to know is within the grasp of your mind. It is a normal function of your brain to process data from all dimensions of your experience simultaneously. For instance, when you walk into a room full of strangers, your five senses immediately register hundreds of details, and your rational mind processes the information so you can respond to this new situation. But *extra-sensory* perception is also allowing you to perceive beyond the senses, even beyond the rational mind. Your intuition knows what's happening at the deepest levels and also serves to guide you.

As a psychic tool, tarot helps you to temporarily bypass reason and listen to intuition. It operates as a catalyst to bring deep, innate wisdom into your consciousness. Using the tarot cards, in fact, makes it possible for you to advise yourself. By asking a question and randomly selecting a card from the deck, you're able to see reflected in the pictures and symbols of tarot the answer that you already sense intuitively at the subconscious level.

The tarot cards help you to see how you subjectively participate in the creation of your everyday life through your thoughts, beliefs, and attitudes. As an oracle, the tarot is neither absolute nor fatalistic. The message it reveals to you today may be different tomorrow if you've changed your ideas, attitudes or beliefs. The very fact that you stopped and examined your situation will alter the circumstances. Every time you acquire new knowledge, you have a decision to make: you can choose either to learn and grow—or to protect and defend the status quo. The choice is always yours to make. As your awareness expands more choices become available. And let's face it, the more choice you have, the more fulfilled your life will be.

Structure of the Thoth Tarot

The Thoth Tarot deck totals 78 cards, and is divided into two main parts, the Major Arcana and the Minor Arcana. While the Minor Arcana includes the Court cards, in this book the Court cards are treated separately for their distinctive attributes.

The Major Arcana

The book of the Major Arcana consists of 22 separate cards—called Atu, trumps or keys—each with particular images, special colors and powerful symbols that evoke a particular archetype. The 22 Major Arcana cards profoundly represent the cyclic phases of birth, death, and subsequent rebirth that we experience throughout our lifetime.

The Minor Arcana

The book of the Minor Arcana consists of a total of 56 cards, which are divided into 40 numbered cards (Ace through Ten—called "pips" or small cards) and the 16 Court cards. Each pip or small card in the Minor Arcana represents a particular test, challenge, or opportunity that feeds your life with experience.

The Court Cards

Part of the Minor Arcana, the Court cards number 16 in all. There are 4 of these "Royalty" cards— Knight, Queen, Prince, Princess—in each of the 4 suits: Wands, Cups, Swords, Disks. The Court cards represent 16 different personas or masks that we may choose to wear when we interact with the outer world. The Court cards can signify other people as well as certain aspects of our own personality, and our qualities, talents and abilities.

Suits of the Minor Arcana

The Minor Arcana is divided into 4 suits, symbolized as Wands, Cups, Swords, and Disks. They each have their own attributes as per Suit, as well as the attribute of the designated number of the card (Ace through Ten).

Wands

This suit addresses the Spirit of *Will* as it functions in the world around us. It represents the power of our desire and intent. Anything we choose to create begins with will. It takes a strong will to generate the courage and motivation needed to make things happen in the physical world. Wands symbolically represent our will, intent, and passion. Without tempering, they depict arrogance, selfishness and ruthlessness.

Cups

This suit portrays the Spirit of our *Understanding*. Expressing feelings of joy, love, and compassion helps us to focus energy on what we desire. How we feel about a particular circumstance will influence its physical manifestation. Cups symbolically represent our feelings, understanding, perception and intuition. Without surrender to a higher purpose, they portray self-delusion and self-indulgence.

Swords

This suit deals with the Spirit of *Reason*. It is within the Swords suit that we find the most cards with a seemingly negative connotation. This is because it is within the mind that we become either burdened by or released from our ideals, dogmas, and beliefs— the mind can be a crucible of chaos or an engine of creation. Swords symbolize our intellect—how we think, plan, and organize our priorities. They free our perception from emotions, and enable us to be objective. Swords symbolically represent judgment, analysis and communication. Without objectivity, the mind becomes enmeshed in confusion, conflict and indecision.

Disks

This suit represents the Spirit of *Matter*, expressed in our day-to-day physical reality. The Disks focus on relationships, family, career, health and financial possibilities. They speak of tradition, structure, and self-discipline. The Disks symbolize integrity, loyalty and pragmatism. Without flexibility, however, they become symbols of dullness, pessimism, and stubbornness.

How to use
Tarot for the New Aeon

Anyone can use the Thoth Tarot cards to increase awareness and understanding, help make decisions, and find assistance in resolving particular issues, situations or problems. When you ask a question about a situation or issue in your life, the card you draw, seemingly at random, reflects the answer and reveals specific guidance for you as you study it. With the help of *Tarot for the New Aeon*, you can form questions regarding everything from business to relationships, from family to career, from love to finance, from domestic life to the soul's journey. *Tarot for the New Aeon* then helps you interpret the card's meaning as you consult each section of the book.

In the three sections of the book you will find:

I.)   advice based on the cards in your readings
II.)   details and definitions of the meaning of the symbols
III.) reading the cards from a lifetime path perspective

For a quick reference with concise advice about the situation in question, you'll find the *Bottom Line Card Interpretations* in Appendix II, at the end of the book.

I. Thoth Tarot Advisor

With the help of the Advisor, you'll be able to do a reading for yourself or your friends in a matter of minutes. This section interprets the esoteric meanings of the 78 cards in the Thoth Tarot deck in a down-to-earth, practical way. There's a list of the cards and their page numbers at the beginning of the section. The Tarot Advisor employs an easygoing, dialogue-type style that, when read aloud, is like having your own "tarot reader" with you. The cards have been interpreted in both the upright and inverted positions, presenting 156 potential responses to each and every question you may choose to ask. While answering your questions, *Tarot for the New Aeon* also asks you questions to help you see your situation from many different angles.

This section is simple, straightforward advice based on the esoteric meaning of each card that will enable you to do a reading for yourself or your friends without having to study the Thoth Tarot directly. My hope is that "playing" with the cards in this manner will pique your interest and entice you into learning more about the Thoth Tarot.

II. Symbols of the Thoth Tarot

This section explains each of the 78 cards and provides an interpretation of the deck's rich symbology. After you've worked with the tarot a bit, you'll want to explore this section to enhance your understanding of the images of each card you draw.

III. Personal Guidance Cards

This section helps you uncover your personal life path. Based on your birth date, this array of cards illumine your basic personality traits, as well as inherent characteristics that underlie your behavior.

- *Personality Card* represents your innate character traits, and the "persona" or face you turn toward the world.
- *Soul Card* depicts the deepest essence of your nature. It shows where your heart is, and what feeds your soul.
- *Challenge and Opportunity Cards* illustrate the situations that present themselves for your consideration. They point out what comes easy to you, and what may be more difficult for you to come to terms with.

- *Inner Teacher Card* depicts where your priorities are and what you are committed to accomplish.
- *Growth Year Card* explains the energy patterns you will encounter in the coming year as well as the resources you'll have at your disposal.
- *Lifetime Collage.* This comprehensive "mandala" of your life is created by bringing all your Personal Guidance Cards together and reading them as a composite. Together they tell the story of who you are in this life experience, what you seek to achieve, and the direction your life will take.

Appendix I and II

Appendix I gives a brief overview of the Qabalah, astrology and alchemy as they relate to the depth and scope of the Thoth Tarot. Patterns that appear in your readings are also detailed.

Bottom Line Card Interpretations are found in Appendix II. This is a quick reference that you can consult for an instant reading, or as a reminder of each card's overall message.

Working with the Cards

Make it easy for yourself! If you're a person who needs peace and quiet to concentrate, by all means set aside a quiet time to read the cards when you know you won't be disturbed. If you love the hustle and bustle of life, you can read the cards in a train station or a coffee house—it won't matter.

If ritual is important to you, create a ritual for working with the cards. Ritual will help to solidify intent by focusing your energy on the process of reading the cards. Let the experience be a sacred one. Wrap your cards in silk cloth and store them in a beautiful box. Meditate before reading the cards to quiet your mind. Play soft music. Have a special table or surface to lay the cards on. Select the card with your left hand (your receptive side). Have your favorite incense burning and light candles.

If ritual isn't your thing, make it simple, and ask the question respectfully, then draw the card.

It's not how you store the cards, where or when you read them that matters, but that you listen with your heart to the guidance given you. Take time to allow the images to communicate their message.

Wisdom comes from knowledge plus experience, therefore tread lightly with the guidance you're given. Ask yourself, "How do I feel about this advice? Am I comfortable with these suggestions? Does it makes sense in the larger context of my life? What are the ramifications of following this guidance? Am I willing to make the changes indicated?" Think the situation through before you act.

There are many different ways to read the cards. You can ask a single question and pick one card for a reading, or you can ask several questions and draw an arrangement of cards known as "spreads." A spread is a group of related questions that are arranged so that they tell the story surrounding your project or situation. A spread can range from two cards to the entire deck.

Reading the Cards

This practice is the same for every type of reading. Just follow these simple directions and you're minutes away from your first Thoth Tarot reading!

- Determine the question or questions you want to ask. Refer to the List of Sample Questions below for your basic Single Card Reading. The more specific your question, the more direct the answer will be. It is preferable to not ask questions with a simple Yes or No answer.
- Shuffle the cards with your query in mind.
- When you've completed shuffling the cards, fan them out face down on a flat surface in front of you.
- Randomly select a card to represent the answer to your question. Place the card face down in front of you. Set the deck aside.
- Repeat the question, and turn the card face up.
- Turn to The Tarot Advisor—Section I, and find the upright or inverted description of the card.

- With your question in mind—read the answer.

If you do not readily understand the answer you are given, select another card from the deck. The new card will explain the previous one from a different angle.

Upright and Inverted Positions

The cards are drawn in either the upright or inverted (upside down) positions. When a card appears in an upright position, it generally means that you're expressing in your day-to-day life the aspects represented by that particular card. Generally, when a card comes to you in an inverted position, you are being shown the *potential* for creative response within the situation. This potential is released when you confront the challenges created by your thoughts, attitudes, or behaviors as they relate to the card you selected.

Negative Cards

Certain cards in the tarot have a seemingly negative connotation—Disappointment, Sorrow, Strife for example. These cards reflect the pitfalls in the path you have chosen. Yet they simultaneously herald a new wave of possibility for the project or situation. The simple act of selecting a card from the deck and reading the answer begins to change the way you perceive your circumstances. As you see the situation from a different angle, you will never be able to see it in quite the same way you did before. Like it or not: your perception has changed.

Whether you choose to act on the new data is another story altogether. Keep in mind that if you don't like where the situation is headed you can always try a new approach. All you need to do is to step back, take a look at your situation, then choose another direction.

When the Answer Doesn't Seem to Make Sense

There are times when the cards may not shed any light on your situation. This is rare, but it does happen. If this occurs, you're being asked to rely on what you consciously know already. Sometimes you need to respect the mystery of life and just stay with whatever is happening. Eventually, time will bring the answer.

Single Card Reading

Good for anything, any time. Use the list of Sample Questions, or create your own.

Sample Questions

You can gather information about your specific circumstances by using a single question from the following list. Begin by looking at the list below, and seeing which query is appropriate to your situation. If you're not comfortable with the answer, repeat the question, and select a second card to help explain the previous answer from a different angle.

What is the best course of action to take regarding_____?

At this time, what do I need to know about _____?

Regarding _____, what is the nature of my problem?

How can I improve my relationship with _____?

What advice do I need concerning _____?

What can I do to improve _____?

What do I need to do to bring harmony into my _____?

What do I need to do to improve my self-esteem?

How best can I nurture my _____ at this time?

How can I best deal with the changes that are occurring in my _____?

What adjustments regarding _____ do I need to make?

The main thing I need to remember about _____ is.

Concerning _____, what can I do to find emotional security?

How am I sabotaging my _____?

What is the best way to express myself regarding _____?

In regard to _____, how can I best assert myself at the moment?

Relating to _____, how can I best shine a light on any secrets and hidden matters?

Concerning _____, what do I need to understand?

Pertaining to _____, how can I best communicate my thoughts?

With regard to _____, what do I need to do to get the recognition I deserve?

As regards _____, what is the best way for me to transform the situation?

What do I need to do to get a promotion?

What can I do to improve my chances of finding a good job?

What is the main thing I need to remember about job-hunting?

Example of a Single Card Reading with Sample Questions:

Jennifer has one week to decide between taking a job as a stockbroker, or eking out a promising but, at the moment, less lucrative career as a writer. She decides to compare both options by consulting the Thoth Tarot before making her decision. She chooses the following question from the preceding **List of Sample Questions** and poses this question for both choices.

She begins with the job as a stockbroker and asks, "At this time, what do I need to know about my job as a stockbroker?" She pulls the Five of Cups, upright, from the deck, and looks up the advice in the Advisor section. She learns the Five of Cups indicates "unfulfilled expectations followed by disappointment."

She asks the same question concerning her career as a writer; "At this time, what do I need to know about my career as a writer?" She pulls the Prince of Wands. The Prince of Wands says "trust yourself as you move full speed ahead to accomplish your goals."

After examining these two options, if she were to choose the job as a stockbroker she would be disappointed with her choice. A career as a writer would take courage on her part—however, she would achieve a sense of personal fulfillment, as well as reap the rewards of her effort.

Spreads

A spread or a layout is a group of cards relating to a particular theme. A spread will enlarge the scope of a single-card inquiry. The questions have a relationship to each other, in that each one contributes a paragraph to your story. You can create a personal spread for yourself by listing the questions you have regarding a specific theme. Use a choice of questions from the list of Sample Questions.

For example: "I am having problems finding a job and need assistance." You may choose to ask the following three questions:

What can I do to improve my chances of finding a good job?

What is the main thing I need to remember about job hunting?

What can I do to improve my self-esteem?

You've just created a specific personal spread!

Basic 3-Card Spread

This basic spread can be used to gather information about any subject you want. You may ask questions about a specific project or situation, a family matter, a relationship, job prospect etc.

Questions for the 3-Card Spread:

What are the present implications of _____?

What do I need to do to obtain the results I desire?

What opportunities or challenges will I encounter along the way?

Example of a Reading using the Basic 3-Card Spread:

John and his father haven't spoken to each other in years. What began as just a misunderstanding has escalated into a rigid estrangement—neither will give an inch. The rift has affected the whole family. John's mother is caught between her husband and her son; his wife worries that their children are losing precious time with their grandfather. John realizes that he misses his father and the time has come for him to make the first move in getting together again—yet he has no idea of how to begin. John turns to the Thoth Tarot for direction, working with the Basic 3-Card Spread.

John selects a card after asking the first question. **What are the implications of my situation?** He draws The Aeon card, advising him to learn from his past so that he does not make the same mistake again. Rather than judge his father, he needs to look deeply into his own behavior and take responsibility for his part in that ancient misunderstanding. The Aeon card indicates that John is being given a *second chance* to develop a strong, loving relationship with his dad—he needs to use it wisely.

What do I need to do to obtain the results I desire? John pulls the Death card inverted, representing "transformation that has been blocked." John has spent years resisting any attempt at reconciliation, immersed in denial of his true feelings. The results of breaking through that resistance will far outweigh his present anxiety. The Death card shows the possibility for new beginnings—this is the time to make the much longed for reconnection with his father.

What opportunities or challenges will I encounter along the way? The Moon card inverted holds John's answer: One of the most difficult phases of your life is over. This card reveals that the most significant battles we will ever fight are the ones that rage within us, deeply personal yet driving our outward behavior. John can let go of the turmoil now. Indeed, The Moon card urges him to see that the darkness has passed, and the horizon is already lightening with the sun's rays.

When we take all three cards into consideration we see that as John acknowledges his participation, he gains a liberating insight. The power of transformation is on his side as he reaches out to his father; the rewards will far outweigh his apprehension. He can end the old, wearying inner struggles, as he and his father move forward with a clean slate.

While it's ultimately up to John to follow his intuition, the Thoth Tarot's counsel for him reveals the opportunity to reforge a strong relationship and bring harmony back to the family.

Relationship Spread

This 6-card spread will help you evaluate any relationship: romance, friendship, business, career, parent and child.

Questions for the Relationship Spread:

In regard to this relationship:

What is the current issue for me?

What is being tested or challenged within me?

What thoughts or feelings do I have that I am not conscious of regarding this relationship?

What can I do to find the emotional security I desire within this relationship?

What can I do to improve this relationship?

What behavior will help me realize the full potential of this relationship?

New Year's Spread

Spreading the cards in this manner can be used to evaluate the coming calendar year, or the year beginning with your birthday. This spread can help to alert you to significant challenges or opportunities coming your way.

Questions for the New Year's Spread:

In regard to this coming year:

How do I make the most out of the coming year?

What opportunities or challenges present themselves?

What do I need to know about my family?

What issues influence my relationships?

What circumstances surround my career?

What do I need to do to get my financial situation in order?

How can I best improve my health?

Past, Present & Future Spread

Here's a useful 3-card spread that provides a quick and easy look at where you've been, where you are now, and where you're going.

Questions for the Past, Present & Future Spread:

Past: What have I resolved?

Present: What am I working on now?

Future: What new beginnings are coming to me?

Illumination Spread

When you're not sure about a situation, you can use this revealing 7-card spread to shed light on the subject.

Questions for the Illumination Spread:

What is my basic situation?

What is influencing this situation?

What is really driving me in this situation?

How can I improve my circumstances?

What is my greatest fear?

What is my greatest hope?

What is coming toward me in the near future?

Morning Spread

You can do a simple spread in the morning while you're having breakfast to help you see the energies that will be in play for the day ahead.

Questions for the Morning Spread:

What do I need to be the most aware of today?

What do I need to communicate today?

What do I need to do today to nourish my soul?

Before going to bed that evening, review the day and see how timely your answers were.

An Important Note

Honor Your Intuition

When using the Thoth Tarot Advisor, it's important that you remain the final judge of what is best for you. The suggestions made in this section are given to help you understand the forces at work in your life, to expand your options, and simply to enjoy and have fun with. When you understand the guidance you've been given, use the sword of your mind to cut through the information in an objective way so that you balance your heart and thinking mind. Don't accept the information you're given unconditionally. It's not meant to be blindly accepted as the final and absolute truth about how you should live! If you read something that doesn't feel right to you, by all means question it! When in doubt, honor your own feelings and let your intuition and common sense have the final word.

Section I

Thoth Tarot
ADVISOR

ADVISOR CARDS

The Major Arcana

The Minor Arcana   The Small Cards

The Court Cards

For Bottom Line Card Interpretations, please see Page 383.

• 0 •
The Fool

The appearance of The Fool card suggests you abandon any further attempt to orchestrate this situation, and instead trust the natural unfolding of a new experience. If you go with the flow, the potential for this endeavor will far exceed your initial limited expectations.

When you listen to your heart and trust your instincts, the floodgates of your imagination will open and breathe new life into your endeavor. A fresh, innovative approach is called for. The Fool assures you that this is the perfect time to open your mind to new visions instead of shrinking back into conservative caution.

Short-term goals may change as you move forward. Trust your instinctive response to these shifts in direction, though they may be viewed as inconsistency. Peers will insist that you're making a big mistake. Can you stand your ground and not be swayed by other people's opinions? Ask yourself, "Can I march to my own music? Am I willing to throw caution to the winds and even risk appearing foolish? Can I allow myself to 'color outside the lines'—if it feels like the correct thing to do?"

Each moment is a new beginning. If you stay in the moment, you'll discover a sense of liberation greater than you ever thought possible. It's never too late to lighten up. When you honor The Fool within your own psyche, you revitalize your spirit of adventure, and that alone will have a profound effect on the circumstances.

Don't be so concerned with the end results. Let go of what you think you know and take a blind leap of faith into the unknown.

· 0 ·
The Fool
Inverted

Drawing The Fool inverted urges you to stop acting like a perpetual "Peter Pan." Get your head out of the clouds and grow up!

By not taking your circumstances seriously enough you've made some foolish choices. Stop and analyze the situation before deciding on a plan of action; this is not the time to take a blind leap of faith. If you act impulsively you may have to backtrack.

By taking unnecessary risks you'll place this enterprise in jeopardy. Don't be naïve and assume the situation will just take care of itself—it will not. You need to develop boundaries and structure, not only within the situation, but within yourself as well.

You have a lot of potential. Nevertheless, until you express this potential in well-considered action, it's worthless. You seem to be open-minded, innovative and extremely creative. Why not use these talents to your advantage? If you would structure your circumstances with a little planning and some discipline, the sky could be the limit.

To have the success you want, be willing to take full responsibility for the consequences of your behavior. By keeping your commitments, paying attention to details and completing what you start, not only do you experience success, but you also find the ultimate freedom you seek.

· I ·
The Magus

When you draw The Magus card, you're being asked to stay focused on the outcome you wish to produce, while remaining flexible as to how it's achieved.

As you approach this project or situation, take into account that you are a unique individual. No one else has your special talent or exact set of resources. Your particular attitudes, beliefs, likes, and dislikes shape the world you live in. Your thoughts give voice to what you believe is possible by supplying meaning to the events in your life. Through *your* imagination, your dreams have the potential to become reality.

As a true magician, it is important that you keep all lines of communication open. Ask yourself: "What are my thoughts regarding this endeavor? Is there something about this situation that I've wanted to communicate? If there is, now is the time to do it."

Listen closely to your internal dialogue (self-talk). Does your inner voice enhance the project or situation, or does it undermine it? Self-talk is powerful—choose productive inner dialogue that will support your goals.

You may have to revise your plans several times before reaching your final destination. Be flexible; if you can't do it one way, you can always do it another.

If you believe in yourself and your ability to create what you want, you'll be able to pull the rabbit out of the hat any time you're ready. Remember when all is said and done, you are the magic!

• I •
The Magus
Inverted

When you select The Magus inverted, it's reminding you that you must take full responsibility for your situation, as it is, before you'll have the power to change it!

When you see yourself as victimized and powerless, you cease to imagine any magic in your life. Without imagination life can seem hopeless. Be mindful that how you choose to perceive the current situation will influence your behavior and therefore affect the outcome of your endeavor. If you see yourself as ineffectual and the current circumstances as impossible, you lower your expectations, take fewer risks . . . and before long fulfill your own prophecy. As you create less of what you want, your self-confidence will diminish, your motivation will decline, and your commitment will weaken. Ask yourself: "What do I really think about this project or situation? How are my thoughts, beliefs and attitudes driving my actions?

Take into account that without imagination, there is no creativity. Magic exists within the power of your mind to consciously manipulate the beliefs and attitudes that underlie your behavior. You're not as powerless as you've led yourself to believe.

Program your mind to see not only the challenges in your path, but the possibilities for success within the situation as well. If you're able to do that, you will know how to proceed.

Consider the fact that you create what you can imagine. If you can imagine your success, you're already halfway there. Think positively; then *act* creatively. What have you got to lose?

· II ·
The Priestess

Drawing The Priestess card counsels that regarding this particular situation, you're going to have to trust your intuition whether you like it or not.

The fact remains that you intuitively know more than you think you do! The knowledge contained within your intuition, however, is not always readily available to your conscious mind. To access this knowledge you need to take the time to reflect on your present circumstances.

Ask yourself, "What's my hunch about this situation?" The voice of intuition speaks very softly; therefore, you must stop long enough to listen. Your intuition will speak to you when you're willing to let go of the illusion of control. The answers will come to you when, where and how you least expect them.

Give special notice to your dreams, because dreams reflect your underlying feelings and thoughts about the project or situation. They can carry hidden messages from your unconscious mind. What are your dreams telling you? Pay attention to your daydreams as well—they will alert you to any unrevealed desires you harbor concerning this endeavor. Monitor the coincidences and twists of fate that occur in your everyday life. Your unconscious can send you messages this way. As more information is revealed, the choices about this situation will become more apparent.

For the time being, adopt a "wait-and-see" attitude. At this particular time in your life, trust your inner knowing and remember that you are your own best counsel.

• II •
The Priestess
Inverted

The Priestess inverted is asking you to be honest with yourself about your actual feelings in this matter. This is not a time to turn away from yourself, but a time to look deeper into your emotions.

When you don't acknowledge your true feelings, you lose your sense of integrity; when you lose your sense of integrity, you diminish your personal power. Ask yourself: "What do I know about myself and this situation that I'm unwilling to face? Am I paying close enough attention to the messages I'm being given? What does my intuition tell me?"

There are deep currents below the surface appearance of this situation. Don't push for a resolution until you have further information and are able to understand the long term consequences of any action you may choose to take.

At this moment, there's so much going on inside of you that it's difficult to be quiet and listen. Remember: You'll learn more by listening than talking. Start by listening to your own intuition rather than being influenced by the ideas and beliefs of others. You've gathered their opinions only to become increasingly confused; everyone's advice has been different. This is a time to trust your native instincts.

Sit still, be quiet, listen to your hunches. If you follow them you won't go wrong.

· III ·
The Empress

Selecting The Empress card tells you that you're moving way too fast. Hold on a minute, take a deep breath, and slow down.

Because your imagination has worked overtime and filled you with so many good ideas, you're anxious to get started. Take into account, however, that it's not to your benefit to rush this stage of the creative process. This new undertaking will require time and patience on your part. A period of gestation is absolutely necessary to allow the seeds of your vision to blossom into their full potential.

All good things will come to you if you have a little patience. You certainly have the skill and talent to sustain this endeavor through every level of its development. Time itself will take care of the details. Meanwhile, nurture yourself; it will increase your creativity and sustain your energy for this project.

By the way, where did you get the idea that you have to do everything yourself? Your situation doesn't rely so heavily on what you do, as it does on how you do it. Regarding your current venture, you intuitively know what to do, and who you can get to help you do it. Be willing to delegate authority to those who are ready, willing, and able to assist you.

The best thing you can do for yourself and your situation at this time is relax and be gracious. What's the rush? Take the time you need to wind down and enjoy the process. You'll be a lot more effective that way.

· III ·
The Empress
Inverted

The Empress inverted states that you risk destroying the situation in question if you continue to smother it with your attention.

By constantly obsessing over the outcome you could inadvertently get in your own way. When experiencing high levels of stress, you can easily create more problems for yourself if you attack the very people who are trying to help you.

The insecurity you've experienced lately accounts for your present state of anxiety. To feel more in control of the situation, it seems that you've attempted to do everything by yourself. It's obvious you can't: Why would you even want to try?

Push yourself too hard, and you'll become physically exhausted and emotionally drained. You'll be left feeling angry and frustrated. What good are you then to either yourself or your situation?

Until you're willing to take better care of yourself, it will be difficult for you to nurture anyone else. Remember, no one is willing to do for you what you're unwilling to do for yourself! If you don't take care of you—who will? Without self-nurturing you risk total burnout. Neglect yourself and you're sure to lose heart; as you lose heart your creative vision will begin to fade. The situation itself will be destroyed if your "vision" dies.

If you want things to work out, stop trying to manipulate the circumstances, take care of yourself, and allow the situation to grow at its own pace.

· IV ·
The Emperor

The possibility of starting a new project or creating a new set of circumstances in your life is at an all-time high. The Emperor recommends that you begin thinking in terms of leadership, risk taking, and above all—action. Everyone will profit if you take charge of the situation and put your organizational skills to work. The appearance of The Emperor indicates that the decisions you make and the actions you take need to be based on the common good of those involved.

In regard to the enterprise in question: timing is of the essence, so take advantage of your impulse to act. Ask yourself: "What have I wanted to do for some time now? Am I willing to throw caution to the wind and take the initiative and just do it?" At this particular time, the greatest risk for you is not to take any risk at all.

Once you have an organized plan of action in place, don't second-guess yourself. Be confident enough to trust your own judgment. When you have the courage to participate actively in life by taking the necessary actions to fulfill your ambitions, you'll experience success. It can be very boring if you never take a chance, and you've come far enough to realize that life is much too short to waste time in boredom.

Because people are depending on you, the sooner you begin the better. If you allow yourself to be bold, courageous, and daring with regard to the future of this endeavor, whatever you attempt at this time will succeed.

· IV ·
The Emperor
Inverted

Drawing The Emperor inverted indicates that lately you've been experiencing some difficulty getting things done.

You seem to be wasting a lot of effort spinning your wheels and not following through with your plans. It's time to determine what you really want, so you can start to take the necessary steps toward materializing those goals. Begin by organizing your resources; then create a simple basic schedule for yourself with your goals in mind.

Be aware that at this time in your life your actions will speak louder than your doubts! You must be willing to take a chance on yourself. What's stopping you? Could it be that you're trying to follow when what you need to do is lead?

Keep in mind that the first step of any new project or situation is always the most difficult. After you determine what the first step is, ask yourself, "Am I willing to take that step right now? Am I ready to accept the personal responsibility I need to finish what I started?"

You've done enough procrastinating. What could you do at this very moment that would help you begin the journey toward your goals?

Whatever you've wanted to do—now is the time to do it. It will be difficult for you to realize your full potential without taking a risk; therefore, throw caution to the wind and "jump." Don't worry—you'll land on your feet.

The Hierophant

· V ·
The Hierophant

The Hierophant puts you on notice that at this point the very foundation of your project or situation is being tested and challenged.

The circumstances that surround this endeavor have been difficult, to say the least. Nonetheless, you can be proud of the fact that by working through the obstacles in your path, you've grown in wisdom. If you feel a need for guidance at this time in your life, seek it directly within your own knowledge and experience.

This is not a time for innovative strategies. It will be to your benefit to take a conservative approach to the situation. In these circumstances there's an advantage to be gained from tradition, convention and structure. It is suggested that you play by the rules and operate from within well-established guidelines.

When The Hierophant appears he signals a new phase of education in your life. Before you start the next facet of this venture, it is essential to have a well-thought-out plan of action in place.

Ask yourself: "To facilitate the situation in question, what do I need to learn? What can the others involved in this situation learn from me?" In this particular situation, when you share your experience and acquired knowledge with others, your own path becomes illuminated.

Look for the practical or homespun wisdom within your day-to-day experiences; they will give you information that will contribute directly to a successful outcome.

· V ·
The Hierophant
Inverted

The Hierophant inverted draws your attention to the fact that the time has come to re-evaluate your initial plan.

It's important that you begin to listen to the voice of your own experience so you can do things in your own way. At the moment, you seem to be drowning in a sea of "should" and "ought to."

What's worked for other people in similar situations won't necessarily work for you. You might want to consider a more innovative, less conventional approach than you've been willing to try in the past.

You can begin by questioning the values and beliefs you've been taught. Which of these are true for you today and which no longer apply? It's important that you understand what you *personally* believe about your situation. Examine beliefs, particularly the cultural or family beliefs, that could be holding you back. Create a list of these beliefs and, if necessary, let go of the ones that don't support your current situation. Remember beliefs are tools of your mind, and can be used to help direct your actions.

You've overcome many tests and challenges and have thus acquired a personal treasury of first-hand knowledge. Use it! Ask yourself: "What have my particular experiences taught me?" This knowledge will be beneficial to you and to the outcome of this endeavor.

Trust yourself to do what you personally feel you need to do, and want to do; not what you think you should do!

• VI •
The Lovers

The Lovers card depicts a union of seemingly opposed forces within our psyches.

We are all saints and sinners, constructive and destructive, nurturing and distant. Within our nature we contain the whole spectrum of human potential. It is through our interaction with other people that we begin to discover who we are and come to understand how we fit into the world. Unrealistic expectations of your partner can destroy the possibility for a meaningful relationship. We need to accept each other as we are before our relationship will deepen and move forward. It is within relationships that we come face to face with our own vulnerability. Ask yourself: "Can I let go of my defenses and be open to my partner? How successful have my relationships been? What can I do to improve the situation?"

At this time in your life you are either creating a new union, or experiencing the deepening of a relationship, project, or situation in which you are currently involved. This relationship, project, or situation will allow you total freedom to express yourself. You will therefore come to know your personal wants, needs and desires.

Through cooperative endeavor, you can acquire the ability to work with other people without losing vital aspects of yourself in the process.

While enjoying relationships with others, always remember— the greatest gift of all is the relationship you develop with yourself.

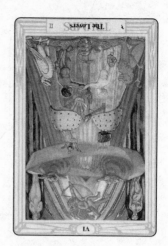

· VI ·
The Lovers
Inverted

Selecting The Lovers card inverted addresses the possibility that you're repressing your own needs and desires while attempting to lose yourself in a project, situation or relationship.

Whether you maintain your individuality within the present circumstances, and not be consumed by them, will determine what happens in the future. Ultimately, you will create a predicament that is less than harmonious if you expect someone to do for you what you've been unwilling to do for yourself.

If you want this particular relationship to continue or your project to evolve, you need to take full responsibility for your own behavior. You must be willing to nurture and care for yourself. Bear in mind that any relationship or situation in which you are involved will, in the end, be as healthy as you are.

Before you proceed with the current circumstances, ask yourself: "Am I ready to take responsibility for my own needs? What adjustments do I need to make to move forward with this relationship?"

If you're unwilling to change the structure of your relationship or circumstances to accommodate new growth, the union or situation will become brittle enough to break under the strain.

The Chariot

• VII •
The Chariot

This has been an extremely difficult time for you; when The Chariot card appears you can pause, take a deep breath and put down your tools of battle. The breakthrough you've been hoping for is at hand.

You'll soon be given the opportunity to embark on a wonderful new project or situation. Be prepared to enjoy one of the most exciting times of your life. With a new sense of self-confidence, you'll be able to easily access your personal power. In so doing, you're prepared to open up to more possibilities and take more risks. This then is a perfect time to initiate any major lifestyle change you may be considering. Ask yourself: "Am I willing to trust this new situation and accept the wonderful adventure I'm being offered?"

Start your journey by exploring all the possibilities that the current situation makes available. Within your new venture there will be many exciting turns in the road—stay awake so that you don't miss any of them.

Your life is moving too fast and changing too quickly for you to entertain any long-term plans; therefore, don't waste time trying to create tightly structured goals. Remain flexible, put short term goals in place and see what happens. Take the time to experiment with the numerous opportunities that will cross your path.

Your hard work has already guaranteed a successful outcome; why not just sit back, relax, and enjoy the ride?

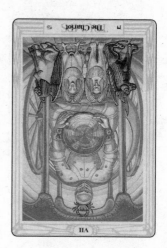

· VII ·
The Chariot
Inverted

T he Chariot inverted reminds you that your situation is unpredictable and can easily get out of control.

At this time in your life you feel you lack the self-confidence and autonomy necessary to ensure your victory. You think that hiding your true desires and ambitions can protect your emotional vulnerability. Guess again! Hiding your needs only contributes to your feeling like a victim—caught in a battle between the part of you that wants to change, and the part that wants everything to remain the same. Remember that it's impossible for you to be out in the world and safe at home at the same moment in time.

To achieve the breakthrough you desire, it is mandatory that you increase your interaction with other people. Let the present circumstances move you away from home base and out into the world again. Focus on what is really important. Listen to reason, trust your instincts, but—above all else—follow your heart.

The time has arrived for you to become truly independent; therefore, you must accept complete responsibility for keeping focused on your goals. Through self-discipline you will be able to attain the ultimate freedom you long for.

With every action you take, ask yourself: "Is this action moving me toward my goals or further away from them?" Then act accordingly.

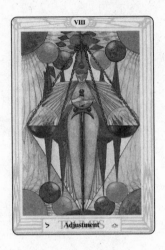

• VIII •
Adjustment

The Adjustment card suggests that you postpone making any further plans until you've had a chance to judiciously weigh all the pros and cons of the situation. You need to allow yourself enough time to adjust to the changes that have already occurred before you take the next step.

In the meantime, try to look at the situation from as many different angles as possible. You will find it easier to adapt to new circumstances if you remain flexible in your thinking. Ask yourself: "Am I willing to stay open to new possibilities and stop myself from rushing to premature conclusions? When new information presents itself, will I keep an open mind . . . will I be flexible enough to re-evaluate the situation or endeavor?"

The more you know about this particular enterprise, the better. Don't be surprised if you have to change course several times before your project or situation is complete. It will take a little doing, but eventually everything will settle down.

Nonetheless, you'll experience more harmony and balance in your life if you're willing to find stability within yourself, rather than in the outside world. When you can let go of your expectations, you'll feel a sense of relief and a calm inner peace.

The Justice aspect of this card can specifically relate to legal affairs. Be sure to consider the legalities of the situation before you act; then make an effort to stay within these guidelines.

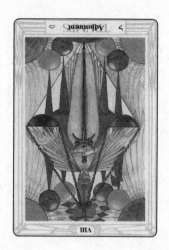

· VIII ·
Adjustment
Inverted

The Adjustment card inverted counsels that you may temporarily be caught in an unjust situation.

In the short term, there seems to be nothing you can do but sit back and accept the circumstances as they are. In the long run, however, justice will prevail and the present circumstances will resolve themselves in your favor.

At the moment, your life may seem more chaotic than usual; you may feel that you're involved in a constant juggling act; if you move too much in one direction or another you'll lose equilibrium. That's because you've been trying to fit the situation to your expectations— whether it fits or not.

Ask yourself: "Do I have all the information I need to make a reasonable decision? Have I weighed all the pros and cons? Am I truly willing to consider some alternative ways to obtain the results I desire?"

Being more resilient in your approach to the project or situation will help to restore a sense of balance and harmony. Remember that with regard to this situation, when emotional tensions build, you can become inflexible and get thrown off balance.

Concentrate your energy on the present moment, without seeking immediate resolution, and everything will fall into place.

· IX ·
The Hermit

The Hermit cautions you to slow down and re-group before attempting to complete the next phase of this project or situation.

In order to give your full attention to the present endeavor, it's appropriate that you withdraw from the task at hand long enough to sort through the information you've gathered and determine where you are at this point.

Drawing The Hermit may indicate the necessity to take time for solitude and introspection. Sometimes you need to turn your back to the outside world, and go deep within your own heart and mind to discover what is of value to you. When you're able to examine the situation more closely, you can decide what's important and let go of the rest. It will be easier for you to navigate new terrain and explore new areas of creativity if you're unencumbered by the past.

Ask yourself: "What excess baggage am I carrying with me? How can I tie up loose ends? What do I need to let go of to be completely focused on the present moment?"

A temporary delay will serve to clarify your vision, re-establish your initial goals, and reinforce your commitment to completing the project or situation at hand.

Be willing to focus your awareness on the current moment— the light cast by your present vision will be the only lamp required to illuminate your path.

· IX ·
The Hermit

Inverted

Be advised that it will be impossible to move freely if you continue to drag the past with you like a ball and chain.

Selecting The Hermit card inverted serves as a warning that the time has come to confront the past and resolve any conflicting circumstances. When you have unfinished business, the energy devoted to it can cloud your thinking and divert your attention from the situation at hand.

However, you don't have all the information you need at the moment to figure things out on your own. Can you see where you need help?

Separating yourself from other people will not benefit either you or the situation in question. Your seclusion, which began as an aid to your healing, now contributes to your loneliness and isolation.

Fear of repeating mistakes keeps you in a state of paralysis. Remember that failure can help you to progress toward your goals if you use your mistakes as lessons to help you move ahead, not as weapons to annihilate yourself. Examine the past so you can learn from mistakes, and get on with your life. What's done is done. Give it up! You're a lot smarter now than you were then.

Move back into the world and the flow of everyday experiences will allow you to confront your fears and move through them, into the bright future waiting for you.

· X ·
Fortune

When the Fortune card appears, you're being informed that you're approaching a major turning point in your life.

The breakthrough you've been waiting for is at hand. You're about to experience an unexpected turn of fate and a windfall of good luck. If you're willing to take a chance on yourself, you can turn any situation to your favor.

The time for contemplation has passed. What is being called for is your immediate, active participation in this project or situation. It is imperative for you to realize that as you move through this journey of life, nothing stays the same. Life is continuously evolving. It is inevitable that in time your present circumstances will also change.

The Wheel of Fortune is spinning: make the most out of this period of good fortune by being open to all possibilities. This way you will be sure not to miss anything. Stay wide awake, for at a moment's notice, the circumstances surrounding your situation may shift and new opportunities may surface.

Ask yourself: "How can I best capitalize on the possibilities this situation offers me?" Remember that you must become actively involved. You can't sit passively by and expect the prize to be handed to you.

On the merry-go-round of life, you have a chance to reach out and grab a brass ring: if you are willing to take a chance, success is yours.

· X ·
Fortune
Inverted

The Fortune card inverted signifies that you're stuck in a rut and don't feel you have the necessary vitality to pull out of it.

Although this period of your life may be extremely uncomfortable, it's to your advantage to accept the circumstances as a challenge.

When you're willing to see your present discomfort as temporary rather than a permanent state of affairs, you're ready to begin the process of turning the situation around. Remember that *inherent in every problem is a creative solution*; you just haven't found it yet.

Ask yourself: "What are the main changes that are occurring? How can I use these changes to my best advantage?"

You've got to help yourself out of this rut because no one is going to do it for you. Don't waste any time: start right now by getting yourself up off the couch.

When you make a commitment to yourself, your personal universe immediately begins to attract the opportunities you need. It is not opportunities alone, but how you use these prospects and resources that become available, that will guarantee your success.

At this time in your life, opportunity keeps knocking; isn't it time you got up and answered the door?

· XI ·
Lust

The Lust card indicates just how excited you are about this situation and how important the outcome is to you. Your desire to succeed empowers you by supplying the ambition you need to accomplish your goals. Pure determination will supply the stamina necessary to work through any difficulties that may arise. Ask yourself: "Am I willing to stay with this endeavor even when it seems that the odds are stacked against me?" If you don't give up, you have a good chance to be successful.

What you're driven to do now may not seem reasonable to you. Do it anyway—it's right for you. It's the passion you feel about this project or situation that will help you achieve the summit of your desires. The more challenged you are, the more you'll be committed to carry your project through to a successful conclusion.

When your fears and anxieties surface, have the courage to override their negative effects and forge ahead. When you confront past conditioning and move beyond its influence, you not only increase your ability to succeed, but you also gain access to your personal power. Personal power is the capacity to appreciate all facets of life and consequently to find pleasure and joy in everything you do.

Your enthusiasm will carry you into the next phase of your project or situation as it moves you toward the ultimate result you desire.

· XI ·
Lust
Inverted

The Lust card inverted pictures life as a gift. However, the way in which you choose to live that life is completely up to you.

It looks as though you've allowed yourself to become cynical and overwhelmed by your dilemma. Be advised that you use up a lot of vital energy and creativity maintaining useless cynicism. The joy and passion you once felt for this project or situation seems to have almost disappeared. It's no wonder you seem to lack motivation to get the job done.

Keep in mind that your emotions only express what you think and feel at the time; they cloud your perception of the true nature of the situation.

You're projecting your fears and anxieties onto your current situation, which in turn prevent you from acting productively. Listen to your needs and desires rather than worrying about appearing unreasonable.

There was a time when you felt strongly about this endeavor: what can you do now to help yourself rediscover that initial passion? Is it really that you don't care—or is it that you're repressing your feelings because you care too much? Sometimes our feelings of disappointment and sorrow are nothing more than the price we pay for the gift of being fully alive.

When you re-establish a firm commitment to follow your dream, the desire and enthusiasm for your project or situation will return and once again you'll feel inspired to move forward.

· XII ·
The Hanged Man

Acceptance and surrender are attributes of The Hanged Man. Drawing this card indicates that you are involved in circumstances that are temporarily beyond your control.

The best thing you can do at the moment is to relax and "hang in there" (pardon the pun). The way things are going, you might as well give up any preconceived ideas you have about this situation. Your expectations will only keep you stuck and help to prolong your discomfort.

When all is said and done, you may have to sacrifice some long-held dream or desire. The time will come when you find yourself with nowhere to turn and your back against the wall. Consider the fact that you may eventually have to change your approach. So, why wait—prepare to do it now!

There are many ways to resolve this situation that you have not even considered yet. You may need to broaden your perspective before further progress can be made. Within your current state of affairs is the groundwork for this new perspective. Consider it a gift. Forced inactivity can be extremely frustrating; nevertheless, it will force you to see your situation in an entirely different way.

You've entered an initiation phase that precedes an important transition in your circumstances. You will be given an opportunity to redeem yourself and turn this situation around. Then you'll be able to act in a manner that allows your endeavor to prosper. Success will follow if you're willing to release your illusion of control and allow the process to take its course.

· XII ·
The Hanged Man
Inverted

Taking into account the difficulties of your present circumstances, The Hanged Man inverted is asking you: "In the name of progress, why are you so unwilling to try a new approach? If you still want this project or situation to succeed, when are you going to give up and stop hitting your head against the wall?"

There are certain times in our lives when we may have to yield in order to overcome. For you, this is one of those times. Recognize the fact that the harder you fight to maintain your illusion of control, the more isolated and frustrated you will become. Manipulation and coercion have not affected your present circumstances; however, surrender will.

Sometimes it's necessary for us to hit rock bottom before we're willing to see things in a different way. Fate has had a hand in pulling the rug out from under your feet; you might as well acknowledge it and get on with life.

There's nothing you can do at the moment except graciously embrace this period of inactivity. A delay now will create the environment you need to help you see things in a totally new way.

Keep in mind that this situation is not permanent. Your feelings of isolation and frustration will soon end and before you know it, you'll find yourself back in the mainstream of life—ready to take on the world again.

· XIII ·
Death

Choosing the Death card represents death not in a literal sense, but as transformation, rebirth and regeneration.

We experience a sense of crisis in our lives when a significant change is about to occur. Your situation or project is falling apart in front of your eyes. It's time to ask: "Have I had enough of the status quo? Am I ready to embrace the changes that are inevitable and long overdue?"

Remember that life moves in cycles: to allow for new beginnings, some things must come to an end. If you want the endeavor in question to endure, you must remain flexible enough to adapt to the shifts that occur from moment to moment.

The pain and struggle you've recently experienced will certainly help motivate you to accept the changes that are about to occur.

What is called for now is a deliberate "cutting to the very core of your situation." Keep what works and get rid of the rest. When you're ready to discard outworn attitudes, ideas and beliefs, you'll make way for all kinds of new possibilities. When you let go of the old, you create space for the new to manifest.

Be willing to embrace the changes that appear in your life, because they're necessary for your progress and imperative to your happiness.

Celebrate! The time has come to let go of the old ways and move forward with the new.

· XIII ·
Death

Inverted

The Death card inverted illustrates what comes to pass when you stay in a situation long after it is productive to do so.

You're being forewarned that if you choose to ignore the need for change and continue to maintain your present position, you'll experience stagnation, followed by frustration and conflict. When resisted, transition can be a slow and painful process.

The situation in question needs to undergo a major transformation. Why are you so unwilling to allow that to happen? What do you think you're holding on to? Why do you think you're holding on to it?

If you look closely at your life, you'll notice that your project or relationship has been "dead" for a long time now. The circumstances surrounding this situation have been extremely painful for you. For that reason, life is being kind to you by taking this endeavor out of your hands and insisting that you let go.

You've no choice but to good-naturedly allow the changes that are already in progress. Rest assured that these changes will liberate you and facilitate the unfolding of new life.

If necessary, take whatever time you need to mourn your loss; then take a deep breath and immerse yourself in life. You have many new chapters to write; chapters filled with love, joy, and adventure. What are you waiting for? Turn the page, pick up your pen and get started!

• XIV •
Art

The Art card brings you to the realization that the circumstances of your project or situation are not as clear-cut as you thought. You may have to demonstrate a bit of patience before your situation becomes clear enough to proceed.

Your ideas, beliefs, and attitudes have undergone major changes. Ask yourself: "What do I desire at this time from the present situation? How do I feel about it?" Look for the answer to come to you in a unique way. The answer may come through your intuition, be revealed in your dreams, or appear as nothing more than coincidence (synchronicity). Pay attention to the twists of fate that occur —they will supply the information you need to move forward.

It takes a while to come to know yourself, to understand what you truly want. When new ideas are taking shape, give them time to surface at their own rate, before you begin to develop and act on newly baked strategies. A delay at this time benefits your situation.

Be prepared to have your situation change radically from one form to another before it finally calms down. Even though this endeavor calls for elaborate maneuvering, rest assured that success will follow.

Remember: being given a totally clean slate does not mean you need to immediately write on it. Be patient as you experiment combining your resources in different, imaginative ways. Your life is full of glorious possibilities. Therefore, this is a great time to mix a little of this and a little of that, and see what develops.

· XIV ·
Art
Inverted

The Art card inverted implies that at this time in your life, nothing seems to be working out as you planned. Are you trying to put things together that just don't fit? To achieve the success you want, you may have to proceed in a totally different way. As for the situation in question, sheer willpower will not create the results you desire.

To achieve your goals, it is important that you try to resolve discord. Have you examined your situation lately to see whether your methods have been too radical, excessive or inflexible for the people around you? You need to consider modifying your strategy by slowing down, avoiding extremes, and learning to compromise.

Stay alert; don't venture where wise men fear to tread. Bear in mind that if you are prudent and think before you speak, you are less likely to end up with your foot in your mouth.

Your circumstances have changed radically. Act accordingly. Let your behavior reflect your current thoughts and ideas. Keep a check on yourself to make sure that you're not acting in outmoded ways.

Let moderation be the rule of the day. With compromise and negotiation, you can recreate your situation to your desire.

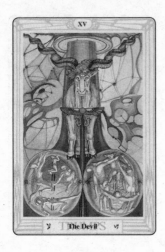

· XV ·
The Devil

Lighten up! Drawing The Devil card puts you on notice that you've lost your sense of humor and, at the moment, seem to be taking yourself and your situation much too seriously. It seems all the fun has gone out of your life, leaving only a heavy sense of duty, obligation and drudgery. How did you become so grim? Can you even recall the last time you did anything for the sheer pleasure of it?

The Devil card invites you to take the time to go and play a little. Relax and enjoy yourself: it nourishes your soul. Do something that you've wanted to do just for the fun of it.

You feel trapped in your present situation, but look closely: there are no locks on the doors. You can let yourself out any time you want.

A good place to start is to learn to laugh at yourself because laughter liberates the human spirit. If you could find the humorous side of your circumstances (and believe me they are there), it would help bring your situation into perspective.

There was a time you had such enthusiasm about this venture. What happened? If you lighten up, you'll be able to recapture that wonderful sense of excitement. You can begin to resolve the present circumstances by realizing that things are not as bad as they seem. Decide what you want to do and then—above all else—do it for the fun of it.

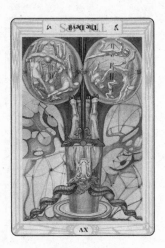

· XV ·
The Devil
Inverted

The Devil card inverted cautions that the situation is doomed to fail unless you start telling yourself the truth about what you're feeling.

As children we're taught which emotions are acceptable and which are not. You have learned to conceal the feelings you deem unacceptable. The more feelings you deny. the more you lose touch with the joy and pleasures of life. Have you noticed that when you least expect them to, your feelings seem to sneak out anyhow and surprise you?

Maintaining a state of denial can be difficult and leave you feeling trapped. Suppressing your true feelings about this matter is taking vital energy—energy that could be put to better use. Denial is a no-win situation. You're afraid of being yourself because others may not approve, but when you're not yourself, *you* don't approve.

You act as though you desire freedom but continually imprison yourself by allowing fear of rejection to make decisions for you. Ask yourself: "If I feel trapped at the moment, how could I be creating this feeling? How do I really feel about this situation? What do I want to do about it? What am I afraid will happen if I express my true feelings?"

Level with yourself: you'll not only feel better, but you'll also know instinctively what you want to do next.

• XVI •
The Tower

When The Tower card shows itself, expect the earth to tremble beneath your feet and lightning to strike. Hold on! You're about to experience a totally unexpected shift of circumstances that will rearrange the very foundation upon which your enterprise has been built.

This process will occur so quickly that you'll be unable to stop it. You may discover that it will necessitate abandoning your current plans for the time being and completely shifting your direction.

There are now powerful elements of change at work. The tension within your situation will soon increase to breaking point. When you least expect it, it's going to blow.

As strange as it may sound, when "the tower" falls it could be a blessing in disguise. If you want to be totally honest with yourself, the circumstances that have surrounded this endeavor have not been that great to begin with. Why not consider this a chance to rebuild from the ground up?

The course of events will clear the playing field and give you the opportunity to make a clean break with the past. It is in the midst of turmoil that we often discover what's really important to us.

Here's your chance to go back to step one and start fresh. It's about time you admit (at least to yourself) that this is what you've wanted to do for a long time now.

· XVI ·
The Tower
Inverted

The Tower card inverted says that you can avoid misfortune, but only if you get your head out of the clouds. You can start by coming down to earth and planting your feet firmly on the ground. You need to be completely honest with yourself. If you aren't, when the reality of your situation hits, you're going to be jolted out of your self-delusion.

The Tower card indicates that on some level you know exactly what's happening and yet you choose to do nothing about it. Until you acknowledge just how angry you are about the circumstances in question, you'll feel powerless to do anything to change them.

Don't allow yourself to entertain illusions about this situation; it won't help. Ignorance is no excuse either. When all is said and done, your habit of selective seeing and hearing has complicated the matter. Tell yourself the truth to see clearly what needs to be done. Ask yourself: "What's really going on here? How have I entrapped myself in this unpleasant situation? What can I do to turn the situation around?"

Consider the possibility of initiating damage control so that your project or situation will not have to end in total devastation. Don't be complacent; if you see a problem starting, take care of it immediately. Stay ahead of the game—you can avert misfortune if you're well prepared.

· XVII ·
The Star

The Star card signifies that each of us is a star that shines brightly in his or her personal universe. Each and every one of us has unique talents and resources that set us apart from every other person. The circumstances, in question, will benefit from your particular talents and resources. Ask yourself: "What can I contribute to the present situation? What assets can I bring to the table?"

Take full advantage of this period of heightened creativity. Your insights into this endeavor will enable you to see clearly the possibility for creating something extraordinary. It's important that you pay attention to the thoughts that come to you at this time in your life. Your best ideas will show up when you least expect them. Trust your judgment—it will lead you to the recognition and success for which you have worked so hard.

Don't be afraid to express your hopes, dreams and visions to anyone who will listen. Communicating your innermost thoughts and desires will not only prove to be inspiring for you, but will also help you turn your dreams into reality.

Give yourself the credit you deserve, and do it often. Have faith in yourself; do whatever you're inspired to do, and the situation or project will benefit.

You deserve to be happy. The spotlight is on you, so let your enthusiasm carry you forward to center stage. Go ahead; don't be afraid to shine. The time has come to act like the true "star" you are!

· XVII ·
The Star
Inverted

The Star card inverted calls your attention to the fact that your lack of confidence has been undermining the successful resolution of the project or situation.

The circumstances surrounding your endeavor are not at the root of your problem—your personal insecurities are. You hide in the shadows and then wonder why no one notices you. Ask yourself: "What talents do I possess that I'm unwilling to use? What insights have I had recently that I've totally ignored? What keeps me from communicating my ideas?" Your hopes and dreams have little chance of materializing if you don't express them.

The stage is set; the spotlight's on. To achieve your desire, you must take a chance and step into it. By openly accepting praise for your unique talents and abilities, you'll begin to overcome your insecurities. People are most likely to see you in the same light you see yourself. Therefore, acknowledge your accomplishments to begin to receive the support and recognition you deserve.

There's no one in the world that possesses your unique talents and resources. Taking care of you is the first step toward healthy self-esteem. Give yourself the same understanding and acceptance that you extend to other people and watch your attitudes change. Act like a "star" and soon you'll receive "star" billing!

· XVIII ·
The Moon

The Moon card indicates that—like the moon itself—our lives pass through many different phases. As we move between the darkness of night and the light of day, our feelings can cycle through anxiety, joy, satisfaction, frustration, or optimism.

You're experiencing the darkest part of night, a time in which you may be confronted by deepest fears and insecurities. Regarding this particular project or situation, what are you most afraid of?

Be mindful that your circumstances are unstable at this time; don't give credence to what you think you see. A blanket of confusion covers the situation itself, so stay alert to the chance that there may be a hidden agenda. In the moonlight your eyes can deceive you and your imagination can play tricks on you.

Postpone decisions until you understand completely what has come to pass. Sometimes the best thing that you can do, or say, is nothing. Act impulsively and you can easily make a mistake that will cause you a setback.

Keep in mind that this is not a permanent state of affairs; the night will soon give way to the dawn and then you'll be able to go forward once again with your plans.

To not have all the answers—indeed, to have to surrender to ambiguity and uncertainty—can be very healing at this time.

As bad as you feel at the moment, remember that your lightheartedness, confidence and optimism will return. Like all cycles, this too shall pass!

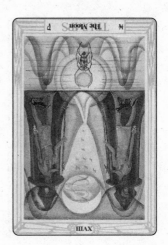

· XVIII ·
The Moon

Inverted

The most significant battles we will ever fight are the ones that rage within ourselves.

Drawing The Moon card inverted signifies that the darkness of night has passed and the sun is on the horizon. *One of the most difficult phases of your life is over.* Under the circumstances you did everything that you could do and everything that was necessary to do. Therefore, ask yourself: "Why am I still struggling? Why am I finding it so hard to let go?" Open your eyes and take a realistic look at what's happening. By not letting go of the situation you continue to swing through wide ranges of feelings: anger to remorse to incrimination and back again. Can you see how you've kept yourself in a constant state of turmoil? You need to realize that your circumstances have changed for the better and that in reality your life is improving daily.

Acknowledge the battle going on within you, if only to begin to let go of it. Grieving for the past and wishing the situation could have been different will leave you feeling disoriented and confused.

With that said, be aware that a person from the past (or some unresolved issue) may make a brief appearance in your life once again. This will give you a perfect opportunity to resolve any unfinished business and help you tie up loose ends. Meanwhile, relax, and be thankful that the worst is over.

· XIX ·
The Sun

When you select The Sun card, take the time to celebrate the fact that each moment of your life is a new beginning. Each moment brings a chance for growth and expansion. It's imperative to realize the confusion surrounding your situation has lifted and you'll soon be experiencing a resurgence of your optimism and vitality.

Expect your enthusiasm for this project to increase as you begin to see the potential for success within your current venture. Through previous achievements, you learned to trust yourself and your ability to accomplish whatever you put your mind to. It hasn't been easy for you. However, at the moment your inner critic is at rest and you need to "toot your own horn."

Your warmth and charisma will attract people to you who immediately want to help. Look for opportunities that open before you. Act on them, and you'll soon notice that your life will be more and more fun.

How do you feel about having help with this project or situation? If you desire companionship, this is the perfect time to draw someone into your life who's willing to work with you: a partner with whom you can share your hopes and dreams as well as express your concerns.

When The Sun card appears on the horizon, remember to acknowledge the success you've had and prepare to reap the rewards of new endeavors. Celebrate your good fortune and enjoy the happiness and contentment that come along with it.

· XIX ·
The Sun
Inverted

The Sun card inverted illustrates just how difficult it will be to accomplish the goals you've set for yourself if you insist on embracing unrealistic expectations.

At this moment, you expect too much from yourself and your situation. When you continually seek perfection from yourself it becomes virtually impossible to feel good about where you are and what you've accomplished up to this point. Why do you want to measure yourself or your situation against the so-called ideal? The ideal exists only in theory. Ask yourself: "Am I setting realistic goals? Do I expect the impossible from myself?"

You wouldn't let anyone treat you as badly as you've been treating yourself. Berating yourself for imperfections is not doing you or your situation any good. If you don't believe in yourself, who will?

It will help to jump into your situation wholeheartedly. At the moment, you're bored with life, yet you continually refuse to get involved. If you never commit to anything—how could you help but be bored?

Of course there are difficulties to overcome, but success will eventually be yours. Haven't you noticed that the circumstances surrounding the situation in question have been improving daily? Seize this opportunity to look at the brighter side, you're doing better than you realize. Stop moping around. The sun is shining into your life—wash your windows and let it pour in!

• XX •
The Aeon

Consider your present actions carefully to avoid making a mistake. Drawing The Aeon card sends the message that you are being given a second chance. There's a possibility to learn something new within this situation. Remember, each of us is accountable for the knowledge and wisdom we have acquired; the more fully you understand what has occurred in the past, the less likely you are to repeat mistakes.

In reference to your present circumstances, you may feel as though history is repeating itself. We become so comfortable with familiar behavior that it's easy to stop thinking, close our minds, and act out of habit. Ask yourself: "What have I learned from my past experiences? What do I now know that I can apply to this situation? What can I do differently?" Doing things the old way will not be of benefit; it can only make matters worse.

To improve circumstances you must take full responsibility to follow through on your ideas and be willing to walk your talk. Keep your eyes wide open and your mouth shut. Weigh your words before speaking and you won't have to take them back later.

You are entering a new phase of this situation and will be given an opportunity to demonstrate just how much you've learned. Use it wisely.

· XX ·
The Aeon
Inverted

The Aeon card inverted paints a dismal picture of self-recrimination. Ask yourself: "Why am I judging myself so severely?" This useless behavior is paralyzing you.

Because you're afraid of making the wrong choice, you opt to make no choice at all. When you don't choose for yourself, you end up living with choices that other people make for you. Is that what you want?

Your life would be simpler if you would stop judging yourself by other people's standards. If you respect differences in people, you'll find it easier to embrace your own individuality.

You've entered a new phase of your life. This is a new game—take advantage of it by using what you have learnt to help yourself win. Align your behavior with *your* sense of knowing and integrity rather than someone else's. What do *you* want to do? What do *you* think is right?

Act now, based on the knowledge and wisdom you've gathered. Be bold enough to accept personal responsibility for your current situation, and it will improve dramatically. It's essential that you realize you can no longer avoid making choices for yourself.

Are you willing to wipe the slate clean and give it another try? If you are, you'll be pleased with the results.

· XXI ·
The Universe

The Universe card comes to light to remind you that every situation is like a seed that contains within it all possible outcomes.

You need to be patient with the situation in question, because it is one that will evolve and develop over time. Your progress may not always appear to unfold in a linear sequence. At times it will feel as though you're taking one step forward, then two back. Don't worry—in the long run everything is moving forward.

Keep your master plan in mind while you employ a trial-and-error system. Ask yourself, "Am I willing to use what works and discard the rest?" To move forward with this endeavor it's simply a matter of letting each new experience build on the one before it.

If you're flexible in your approach you won't interfere with the natural order of things. In the meantime it's necessary that you continue to expand what you believe is possible for this venture. Begin by expecting miracles, and soon you will see them everywhere.

Once you're on track toward manifesting your goals, the universe suddenly seems as if it were providing you with the opportunities you need. Take advantage of them by maintaining a high level of commitment and self discipline. Can you do that? If you can, you'll create a firm platform for your project and a firm springboard into the next level of the game.

The world is your "oyster" and you are the "pearl" within it.

· XXI ·
The Universe
Inverted

When The Universe card is drawn inverted, expect that the question at hand will not be resolved quickly. It will take a lot of hard work and patience on your part to realize your dream. No matter how difficult it seems at the moment, stay with it until you succeed, and succeed you will.

Be careful not to rush ahead without first establishing a step-by-step plan of action. Are you willing to take the time to create one? For this particular situation, you'll definitely need to have one in place. If not, even with all your effort, you'll go nowhere fast.

As "energy," we possess unlimited potential. Nevertheless, you're living your life and expressing yourself in a finite world. While it's true that all things are possible, you have to make choices based on how much time and vitality you have. Unless you're clear about your priorities, you'll become overwhelmed by your options. As a result, it's important that you set limits for yourself and carefully choose your actions.

In regard to your particular circumstances: if you want to realize your hopes and dreams, be willing to roll up your sleeves and get to work.

This world has its own game rules, and when you're out in the world you need to play by them. The rules call for self-discipline, structure and tenacity. At this time in your life you can walk with your head in the clouds but your feet had better be on the ground.

Ace of Wands

The Ace of Wands heralds a time in your life when you are about to embark on a new venture. This venture will lead you toward success and good fortune. In regard to this particular endeavor you're "on fire." Such creative fire not only provides new insights, but moves you to a greater level of self-awareness. For that reason alone, follow your own passion, trust your own instincts and value your own creativity.

This is an exciting time in your life: you can approach the situation in question with a renewed sense of ambition—or just as easily create a completely new frontier to investigate.

Like most creative endeavors, yours will need some adjustment, and modification before the job is complete. Ask yourself: "Am I willing to make the adjustment necessary as the need arises? Am I willing to temporarily suspend my critical judgment and focus energy on my creative expression instead?"

As you focus your energy on the project or situation, you'll become increasingly inspired. This growing enthusiasm will keep you motivated and moving toward your goals.

This is a point in time to take full advantage of the fact that your artistic juices are flowing. Do you realize that anything is possible for this project or situation, if you are willing to get into the game? Remember—life itself is a work in progress, not a finished product. As far as your life is concerned, the best is yet to come.

Ace of Wands
Inverted

The role of the Ace of Wands inverted is to caution: Unless you're willing to look at your situation honestly, you'll find it difficult to succeed.

Consider changing your tactics and stop pretending that you know what you want, where you're going and what you're doing The truth is, at this point in time, you don't have the slightest idea of what's going on.

You've committed yourself to the project or situation in question, but can't seem to get excited about it. You can succeed here, but only if you take the time to figure out what happened to your initial enthusiasm, ambition and motivation. Go back to the beginning and find out what attracted you to the endeavor to start with. Then, see if you can re-establish your commitment from that point.

Ask yourself: "Can I back away from this situation long enough to allow my creative energy to start flowing once again? Am I open-minded enough to dream new visions, entertain new insights, and follow new ambitions? Am I willing to accept that I don't have a clue about how this situation will turn out? Am I alright with that and am I willing to proceed from that point?"

The Ace of Wands inverted reminds you to slow down and re-think this situation. Don't rush things. It would be more to your advantage if you let your spirit of adventure lead you into a new endeavor or show you the possibilities for bringing new life into this one. Remember; you are only going to reap what you have taken the time to sow!

Two of Wands

(Dominion)

The Two of Wands counsels you that in this particular situation you need to act assertively if you are to succeed. There's no better time then the present to take charge of your life by letting the fire of personal ambition fuel your actions.

Don't look to other people for help. You're being advised to trust your own creativity and passion because at this particular moment everything depends on you. Before you proceed any further ask yourself: "Do I have the necessary ambition to take this situation as far as it can go?"

Be mindful that the extent of your boldness and daring may at times even surprise you. Closely monitor your drive and enthusiasm so that you don't get carried away. With this level of will power, you can become so involved that you turn out to be domineering and lose track of your initial intent.

When strong determination is necessary, don't force the river to flow in the direction you want—instead work with the natural flow toward the results you desire.

You must be assertive yet diplomatic. Most important, you must be patient. It may take a while for you to get to your final destination, but you will eventually get there.

When you put a lot of creative energy into a situation, as you seem willing to do with this one, it would be difficult not to succeed.

Two of Wands

Inverted

D rawing the Two of Wands inverted indicates that you may be having some trouble with your level of self esteem. Could this lack of self-confidence be the reason you're unwilling to assert yourself in this specific situation?

Upon closer examination, you may find that even though your ambitions are strong, your doubts about your ability to reach your goals will undermine your power to act. When you lose faith in yourself you proceed very cautiously. Such trepidation may inadvertently extinguish the fires of your creativity. If you continue to remain non-committal and take as few risks as possible, how can this timidity help you to succeed? It will not.

Ask yourself: "What can I do to improve my self-confidence? How can I concentrate effort in one direction so that I'm completely involved in this enterprise? What can I do to motivate myself?"

Until you're fully committed to this project or situation, the resources you need will elude you. If you're waiting for someone to do it for you—you're going to have a long wait. Instead of giving in and giving up, why not try harder? Remember: your ambition, enthusiasm and inspiration can push you toward your goal, but they will not carry you all the way. Hard work, determination, and single-minded focus will.

Three of Wands
(Virtue)

Choosing the Three of Wands indicates that it is time to set all systems on go! Broaden your horizons and don't restrict yourself to the present area of exploration. Always be on the lookout for opportunities that move you toward unknown paths and give you a chance to investigate new territory.

This is a perfect time for you to expand your venture to encompass the full scope of your talent and resources. Be optimistic. Think big; in doing so, you can expect to see further progress and improvement in other aspects of your life as well.

Be courageous and assertive. You are being encouraged to move out into the very situations you've felt insecure about in the past. This is a time for action. The measures you choose will not only affect the current project or situation, but will have a direct influence on your future.

Be mindful that the stage is set for your success. Ask yourself: "Am I willing to speak up and allow my ideas and opinions to be heard?" Figure out what needs to be done and then create a network of like-minded people willing to help you do it. When you're willing to be vocal about what you want, you'll receive as much cooperation as you need. People will be eager to support your project and help you lay the foundation for future accomplishment.

This is an extremely creative and fertile period for you, so take full advantage of your circumstances.

Three of Wands

Inverted

When the Three of Wands appears inverted you may find it difficult to start new projects or proceed further with the ones already in progress.

It is crucial that you back up and re-evaluate your situation before continuing. Remember that change is an essential ingredient of success. Sometimes we sabotage ourselves without realizing it by being unwilling to change. Ask yourself: "Will I be comfortable with the changes that occur if I succeed? Is it possible that I harbor a secret fear of success?"

At this time your energy is low; this makes it difficult for you to grasp opportunities when they present themselves. Do you have any idea why you're so tired?

When you feel ineffectual, you must take care of yourself before trying to do anything else. Unless you can get your vitality back, this is not a favorable time for you to begin a new venture, or expand the one in which you're presently involved.

At the moment, you're more likely to get what you want if you quietly negotiate a compromise. There's a lot you want to say, although the words seem to get stuck in your throat. Nonetheless, try to be a bit more vocal, and cooperation will follow.

Take a sabbatical; enjoy some rest and relaxation. Then when you feel up to it, take on the project again, and it will be a whole new set of Tinker Toys!

Four of Wands

(Completion)

Selecting the Four of Wands implies that your current difficulties will soon be overcome as you approach a successful completion to this task or situation.

You can rest easy knowing that you've built this project on a strong foundation; as a result, it will soon be much simpler for you to go forward than it has been to get to this point.

As your circumstances change for the better, acknowledge that you're doing exactly what you set out to do, and doing it well.

The favorable completion of this project will give you the confidence to further develop the undertaking in question, or even to begin a totally new venture. Ask yourself: "Where do I want to go from here? What do I want to do next? How can I use the momentum of this accomplishment to my best advantage?"

Acknowledge and celebrate your achievements because they will carry you to the next phase of your journey. With victory in your corner, you'll find motivation easy. Relax and enjoy yourself because you're on a roll.

Remember, however, that it's fundamental to your long-term success to use the impetus of this particular situation to keep yourself going. It's like walking—each step we take gains momentum from the preceding one.

Four of Wands

Inverted

The Four of Wands inverted reminds you that if you want to realize your dreams you must be willing to persevere. Your vision for this venture is sure to fall apart if you continue to sabotage yourself. If you want this to work, you're going to have to put some effort into it.

In regard to this particular situation, it is crucial that you finish what you start. Now is the time to force yourself to complete all the projects you have going, even the little ones. Unfinished business leaves your energy tied up elsewhere and not available for the current task. You have many loose ends that need attention so you can build this project or situation on a firm foundation. That is—if you still want to. Do you?

If you do, it's essential to take full responsibility for motivating yourself. You haven't contributed much to this situation for quite a while. If you're to succeed you must start giving this endeavor your all, and regain the momentum you lost when you became lethargic. Your assignment is to find a way to have fun with this again.

At the moment, you seem to be caught in a conflict—wanting to go ahead with your mission but feeling trapped at the same time. The way to stop dragging your feet is to take one little step at a time. Then you will see just how easily and quickly the wheels of progress turn in your favor.

Five of Wands

(Strife)

The Five of Wands proclaims that your present state of frustration is temporary; therefore, don't allow it to undo all the work you've done.

Just because things aren't going the way you want them to, you're ready to ditch the whole project. That doesn't make any sense, does it?

Because you've accomplished so much already, you may find it difficult to motivate yourself to go the last mile. Whatever you do, don't quit now—you're almost there.

It's wise to step back far enough to get some perspective on the situation. What's happening is more of a nuisance than anything else. Don't risk making the problem bigger than it is, but realize that it's only a temporary delay. Ask yourself: "If I let frustration control my behavior will I be able to get this job done any quicker?" (I doubt it.)

If you've been working on a new project, or for that matter a new life, it can become extremely frustrating if things don't go as planned. Sometimes it's hard to get the project to fit the creative image you had in mind. This is a normal response and part of the exercise of creativity. Relax and take some time in the dugout so you can return to the game with renewed vigor, step up to the plate again and hit a home run.

Five of Wands

Inverted

When the Five of Wands surfaces in an inverted position, it signifies that you've come a long way in handling your frustration over the situation in question. It is of the utmost importance for you to realize that you will experience many peaks and valleys in your search for artistic expression. Creative energy doesn't always flow in a straight line; consequently, you must be flexible enough to undergo frequent changes.

Ask yourself: "Now that my frustration has passed, am I prepared to get up and get the job done?" Keep in mind that from this point on, it will be easier for you to maintain a steady flow of creative ideas.

You're being reminded that frustration with this endeavor has been an integral part of the creative process itself. If you let it, your natural curiosity will help to keep you motivated. Follow your bliss (i.e., whatever your ultimate driving force is) and it will carry you to the top of the mountain, where you can look back at the hard times and savor your victory.

Have you noticed that you seem to automatically receive support from others when you trust the creative process and just keep dancing? Let the music play on as you continue to move with the rhythm of change.

Six of Wands

(Victory)

When the Six of Wands appears in all its glory, it signifies that you're well on your way to achieving your goals.

In regard to the project or situation in question, the internal conflicts and struggles that have plagued you will soon be coming to an end, and you'll receive the recognition you deserve.

When success is a result of your inner strength, it brings with it a profound satisfaction because the goals you attained are in alignment with your personal value system. It leaves you knowing that your life has a purpose and you're living that life with integrity

Personal power is your ability to think for yourself, to choose your actions, and to participate fully and courageously in your life. As time goes by, you'll feel more independent, better able to express yourself in other areas of life, as well as in the current situation. A clear sense of comfort and confidence in your present position will help you triumph over future challenges.

Ask yourself: "Am I willing to continue to exert the same level of honesty and fortitude that have gotten me to this point in time? How can I best stay focused and prevent anything that may compromise or inhibit my self-expression?".

If you rely on your integrity, your virtue and your principles, you'll experience both outer success and inner victory.

Six of Wands

Inverted

When you draw the Six of Wands inverted, you're being forewarned that victory may temporarily elude you.

At the moment, you seem to be entangled in circumstances that have you feeling powerless. Bear in mind, however, that regarding this particular situation you're far from powerless. Because things aren't going according to your plan doesn't mean you should look outside yourself for answers. Instead, look deeper inside to determine what stands in your way.

When your path is blocked and failure looms, consider that you're being challenged to discover just how truly creative you are—by reaching deeper into your reserves, which are as yet untapped. This isn't time to give up, but time to dig in and determine what you can learn here.

The Six of Wands inverted encourages you to realize that delay at this time offers an opportunity for self-discovery, a chance to see the project or situation from a broader perspective.

Ask yourself: "Why am I feeling powerless? What can I do to change that? What's impeding my ability to see this situation in a more productive way?"

If you feel that your progress isn't fast enough, look deeper inside.

Keep in mind that you possess the internal power required to be victorious in this situation.

Seven of Wands

(Valor)

The Seven of Wands suggests that if you want to make the best of your situation, don't compromise, but rather hold steadfast to your current position.

Standing up for your beliefs is going to take all the courage and audacity you have. At this time, you certainly have your work cut out for you.

With your strength of conviction, you have unbelievable energy at your disposal. This inner resource will come to your aid as your dreams and aspirations are seriously tested.

For the moment, you might as well abandon any plan to maintain a neutral position; it's essential that you stand up and fight for what you want. When the going gets rough, ask yourself: "Am I willing to take a stand? Am I ready to stick my neck out?"

To win this battle you'll have to look your fears in the eye until they back down. Can you do that? Remember that every bit of self-confidence you've developed will be tested to its limit.

Since this project or situation has value and significance to you, let the present challenges inspire you rather than be overcome by them. Be tenacious; nothing short of total commitment will do. Go ahead—you're up to it.

In this situation you may have to fight long and hard to win, but win you will!

Seven of Wands

Inverted

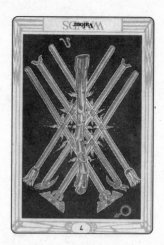

The Seven of Wands inverted calls attention to how much you're allowing fears and anxieties to control your life.

Why are you so quick to abandon your dreams? Is it because you're afraid to put yourself on the line? Can it be that your ego is getting in the way? If you insist on holding on to a false sense of pride, you'll seal your fate and remain unable to bring this endeavor to a successful conclusion.

Take the time now and decide just how far you're willing to extend yourself and your resources. Ask yourself: "Why am I so afraid to take a chance? Am I afraid to appear foolish if my project or situation doesn't work out? Do I need a guarantee of success before I will invest myself?"

Before you back down from this challenge, re-evaluate your commitment to the project or situation. Does this mean enough to you that you're willing to take a leap of faith? Can you live with yourself if you don't? How will you find out just how far you can go if you back down now?

Have the courage of your convictions and settle for nothing less than the fulfillment of your personal vision. Don't be afraid to take a risk—you have so much more to gain than to lose if you hold fast to your dreams.

Eight of Wands

(Swiftness)

The Eight of Wands illustrates just how quickly the circumstances of your life can change.

You must be poised, now more than ever, to articulate your needs and desires immediately. Don't waste precious time beating around the bush. Say what you need to say, to whom it needs to be said, when you need to say it. And, most importantly, say it with the intensity of your feelings!

When you speak out about the current situation, your words will be met with acceptance, understanding and appreciation. Be sure you've prepared to respond swiftly to any challenge or opportunity that presents itself.

The Eight of Wands suggests that this is the right time to trust your instincts, take the initiative, and proceed. Ask yourself: "What's my initial impression of this situation? What do my instincts tell me to do? Do I listen to them and am I willing to act on them?"

There won't be time for studied reflection in the present circumstances. You have to be able to think on your feet. Can you do that? It's essential to this endeavor that you're willing to move swiftly in the direction of your first impulse.

Act spontaneously and you will not go wrong. On the other hand, ignore your instincts and try to second-guess yourself and you will confuse the issue and yourself as well.

Eight of Wands

Inverted

The Eight of Wands inverted asks you to slow down and consider all aspects of the situation before you proceed.

Unless your actions are more carefully considered, you'll continue to miss the mark; in the end, you'll create only superficial changes.

You've said and done so much, that at this point, no one involved understands what you want or where you stand—least of all you. Ask yourself: "What's really going on with me? Why the excessive activity? What's the hurry?"

Underneath it all, you know exactly what you think and feel about this situation. However, your feelings seem to get lost in a sea of unnecessary words. Are you counting on this confusion? Is the superfluous chatter an attempt to hide your true opinions?

If you make a point of speaking slowly, softly, and deliberately, people are more apt to hear you. Remember that you need to proceed cautiously and avoid haste in this situation.

Do what your instincts tell you to, and say only what you intuitively know is important for you to say. If you do so, your communication will be right on point. Being direct will move you toward the success you desire and help you to avoid any further misunderstanding.

Nine of Wands

(Strength)

The Nine of Wands represents the strength and power you acquire when you learn to maintain a sense of balance, when confronted with the ups and downs of life.

You've demonstrated valor in dealing with a very difficult situation, and are now in an excellent position to achieve your goals. To maintain this position, you must continue to transcend the day-to-day fluctuations of the present circumstances. To do this, remain in a neutral place while keeping your eyes fixed on your long-term goals. Finding balance in your life is the key at the moment.

It will be easier to preserve your equilibrium if you give voice to all aspects of your personality. But be observant to what the situation calls for: it's essential that you know when to speak and when to remain silent.

Ask yourself: "Can I keep my eye on the goals ahead while everything around is in the process of change? Can I stay in a neutral place yet still hold firm to my dreams and aspirations?"

If you remain balanced and centered and follow the path of moderation, you won't be blown away. As your circumstances change, you'll be able to find your equilibrium and serenity even in the eye of the storm.

Nine of Wands

Inverted

The Nine of Wands inverted symbolizes your surrender to the present circumstances, allowing them to throw you off balance and subsequently overpower you. At the moment, you've lost your sense of equilibrium by identifying with an extreme position in the situation, and therefore find it difficult to defend yourself.

Your ability to see beyond the current state of affairs will determine the actions you should take. Do you know how to recognize what's pertinent to your long-term goals? Can you keep your eye on these goals rather than reacting to every little thing that happens?

When you lose the ability to transcend day-to-day difficulties, you begin to see yourself as part of the problem instead of part of the solution. Ask yourself: "How did I lose track of my goals and get bogged down in the present circumstances? How did I get so far off course?"

Whenever you feel like a ship tossed at sea, remember that it may be because you've identified with one extreme or the other. In the process, you've not only lost your course, your inflexibility has pitched you overboard.

By being more flexible you'll discover your own inner strength. The task at hand is to adapt to the everyday ups and downs by staying neutral. It won't always be easy, but you can do it if this situation's outcome is important enough to you.

Ten of Wands

(Oppression)

Y ou seem to be taking on way too much responsibility for the project or situation at hand. Choosing the Ten of Wands signifies that in the name of everyday duty and obligation, you've allowed yourself to lose track of your vision.

When that happens, the situation becomes oppressive and you end up feeling as though you'll suffocate from lack of freedom and spontaneity.

It seems that what was once a source of pleasure in your life may now be a cause for resentment. At the present time, it's necessary for your well being, as well as for the success of your project, that you delegate some responsibility to others. What are you trying to prove by doing it all yourself? Are you trying to be a martyr without a cause?

At this very moment, your life is supplying an opportunity to stop being your own worst enemy. Ask yourself: "How can I take advantage of this opportunity? What was so intriguing about this venture to begin with? Am I willing to try and recreate that kind of excitement again?"

Regarding your overzealous sense of responsibility—give it a rest! Maintain a comfortable level of activity, and you'll have the freedom to enjoy the creative process. If not, you'll find that the situation will get old quickly.

Ten of Wands

Inverted

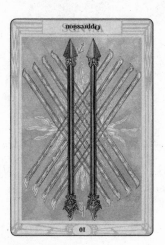

When you pull the Ten of Wands from the deck in an inverted position you're declaring enough is enough! You're tired of feeling responsible for everything and everybody involved in this endeavor.

Before you continue, you may wish to stand up and take a bow—because for you, this realization is a major breakthrough.

If you want to revitalize your situation, first be willing to take better care of yourself. What you need most at this time in your life is to relax and have fun with this project. As long as you're enjoying the creative process, you won't feel burdened by the tests and challenges that present themselves to you. In fact, you'll feel more and more energized by them and as a result ready to take on whatever the project or situation requires of you.

Remember that everything will get done in the due course of time, without you having to have your hands on every single thing. If other people are involved in your present endeavor, insist that they do their fair share. Ask yourself: "What needs to get done and who can I get to do it?"

Make it a point to stay away from negative people and oppressive situations; they will only impose themselves on your good nature. Align yourself with people who care about you and are willing to pull their own weight. Then, when success comes your way, you won't be too tired to enjoy it.

Ace of Cups

The Ace of Cups suggests that you take the opportunity to express exactly how you feel about the endeavor in question. If you're willing to give voice to the full range of your emotions (the good, bad or otherwise), it will help to clarify the situation. It will free you to map out a clear-cut plan of action.

Don't waste your energy trying to analyze why everything seems to be working so well at this moment. Instead, open your heart to the project and you'll be empowered to put your best effort forward. If you follow your passion and trust your instincts, it will be easier to work up to your full potential. Ask yourself: "How do I feel about this situation? Am I expressing the full range of my emotions?"

It is essential to the success of this project or situation to use every opportunity that comes your way to communicate your individuality. When you reveal your true feelings to the people involved, you'll be admired for your honesty; they in turn will get behind your enterprise. At the moment you have so much to offer this endeavor that you can readily express yourself with power and eloquence and move ahead.

To reach your goals you must continue to take risks, be innovative, have confidence in your convictions, but most of all let your own feelings guide you.

There has never been a better time to promote yourself, your ideas, or your situation. You love being number one, so why fight it? Enjoy it. It suits you.

Ace of Cups

Inverted

The Ace of Cups cautions that your inability to connect with your emotions will leave you feeling isolated, not only from others, but from yourself as well. At the moment, the very core of your being feels unloved or unlovable.

Know that feelings are neither right nor wrong—feelings are feelings. Keep in mind however that your emotions do follow your thoughts. Change your thoughts and you automatically change how you feel.

How you feel influences your actions. Thus, when you think of yourself as unworthy, you tend to avoid the demands of circumstances that lead to achieving your goals.

This is important: accept yourself as you are right now. Take responsibility for your present thoughts, attitudes, and feelings. You need to learn to love yourself unconditionally—it's time to recognize that you are a worthwhile human being .

Make a list of the things in your life that are positive and productive; you'll soon discover there's a lot more to be grateful for than you've imagined.

The more you think about and appreciate what you do have at this rich time in your life, optimism will fill your being. The more optimistic you feel, the more open you'll be to success; the more open you are to success, the more opportunities will come your way. Get the picture?

Two of Cups

(Love)

The Two of Cups describes a union based on mutual support, attraction, and respect. This card can represent a specific friendship, a love relationship, or a business partnership.

In regard to your specific question: If you're not involved in a mutually supportive relationship right now, you can expect to be very soon. If you don't know the person already, you'll meet someone for whom the attraction is undeniable—a kindred spirit. When the two of you are together, you'll know exactly what the other is thinking and feeling without a word being spoken. This type of understanding and total acceptance of another human being will help you toward a better understanding and acceptance of yourself. If you give without expectation, you're likely to receive everything you need in return.

The joy you feel within will radiate into the outer world. You'll smile more and basically be a more contented person. Any endeavor you undertake in this frame of mind is surely destined to succeed.

Keep your present goal in mind as you gather information. The more informed you are the better. Ask yourself: "Am I willing to talk to people about my innermost dreams and desires, and get them to open up and talk to me about theirs?" If you're willing to do this, it will create the rapport you need to achieve your goals.

Two of Cups

Inverted

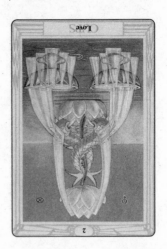

At the moment, you feel misunderstood and cut off from yourself as well as from others. The Two of Cups inverted indicates that you tend to retract emotionally when what you need to do most is open up.

When you feel disconnected, you feel defenseless. When you feel threatened, you're inclined to protect yourself and turn inward rather than reach out to others. Your inclination to withdraw will have a detrimental effect on your current venture. At this point in your life, if you attempt to protect yourself by concealing information, misunderstanding can easily occur.

More than anything else, you seem to fear appearing vulnerable. Ask yourself: "When and with whom do I feel the most vulnerable?"

Are you aware that within your vulnerability exists the very possibility for intimacy? And intimacy is the key to the relationship you seek.

Even though you have a heartfelt desire to interact with others, you seem to have trouble knowing where to begin. The best place to make a start is to acknowledge your own needs and desires. Your primary concern should be to get to know yourself. Once you establish a relationship with yourself you can move into relationships with other people.

Begin by becoming the type of person you want to attract. When you're open and receptive to a loving relationship, what you need will come to you.

Three of Cups

(Abundance)

The Three of Cups symbolizes the importance of getting your ideas into the marketplace. Because there is a profusion of optimism in the air at the present moment, this is a perfect time to let others know how strongly you feel about this project or situation.

At the moment the most significant thing you can do is to start networking. To achieve your goals, it's necessary that you seek groups of like-minded individuals; people who share the same interests and visions for life that you do. Networking will help further the growth and expansion of your venture.

Are you willing to take the time to talk about this endeavor with anyone who will listen? If you want people to support you they need to know what you have to offer. Be up front. This is not the time to be timid; ask for what you want. Can you do that?

Keep in mind that abundance and prosperity will flow into your life in direct proportion to how willing you are to ask for what you need.

It will help if you're prepared to socialize and enjoy the good times. A light-hearted sense of playfulness is one of the major ingredients to your imagination, your inspiration and your creativity. Celebrate victories openly no matter how small they seem.

Be advised that you are entering a very happy period in your life; delight in the camaraderie, success and good feelings that go along with it.

Three of Cups

Inverted

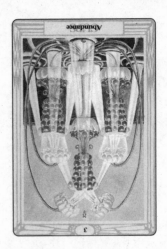

The Three of Cups inverted suggests that you give up trying to go it alone. At this time in your life you need all the help you can get.

Because it's important for you to communicate openly and honestly, ask yourself: "Why do I think it's safer to keep my ideas and desires to myself? Why am I unwilling to ask for help?" Friends are your greatest assets; nevertheless, it seems that you go out of your way to avoid the very people who are trying to help you.

Could it be that you feel vulnerable to the possibility of rejection? By not communicating, you succeed at keeping others in the dark, but remember that you keep yourself there as well. You can't lock other people out without locking yourself in!

For the current project or situation to succeed, it's crucial to express your feelings openly. Try a new strategy—take at least one emotional risk every single day.

Consider joining a group of people who have interests in common with yours. Socializing in an atmosphere of shared enthusiasms would certainly help you to come out of hiding and start expressing yourself.

Take this opportunity to rediscover the spirit of camaraderie and playfulness you've lost. Celebrate life in everything you do and the situation will benefit from your change in attitude.

Four of Cups

(Luxury)

The Four of Cups states that you may be losing your balance by becoming too self-absorbed. By being so self-centered, you've become oblivious to everything going on around you. Things may look all right on the surface, but you're headed for trouble unless you attend to the situation at hand.

Stop and examine where your feelings are taking you. When emotions are out of control, mental clarity goes out the window as well. Don't let emotions overpower your rational mind. Work to regain your focus. Ask yourself: "Am I still interested in achieving the goals I've set? Do I have realistic expectations? Have I built a firm foundation under this project or situation? Do I take other people's needs into consideration before acting? "

Something new will soon be offered to you if you can find a way to bring emotional stability back into your life and the situation at hand. Without this stability you won't recognize the opportunity when you see it.

Now is a perfect time to take a break from your project or situation and sort through the data you already have. The Four of Cups recommends that you behave in a way that serves you in the long run rather than act on momentary feelings.

Four of Cups

Inverted

When the Four of Cups appears in an inverted position, it indicates that you're not aware of your feelings. You're feeling cold, indifferent toward your circumstances—separated from the flow of life. This is because you've cut yourself off from your emotions.

Take time to uncover the feelings you may be hiding from yourself. These emotions want to be acknowledged, but you work overtime to keep them buried. This has left you mentally and emotionally exhausted.

Ask yourself: "How do I really feel about all of this? Am I bored, disillusioned, or just plain angry?"

Is it likely that anger is causing you to withdraw? If so, can you clarify the object of this anger? Repressed anger can affect your emotional stability and color your decisions. If anger is blocking you, talking things through will help you confront it so that you can set your anger aside.

When your emotions emerge in free and healthy expressions, your indifference will soon be replaced by exhilaration. By giving voice to buried feelings, you release vital energy and things will start moving once again. This energy helps to motivate you and get you back on track. Subsequently, you will be able to achieve any goal you choose to set for yourself.

Five of Cups

(Disappointment)

The Five of Cups indicates that your deepest fears have been realized because you've lost something you cared deeply about.

With your dreams shattered and the situation in disarray, you're left to grieve your unfulfilled expectations. If you're heavily invested in one particular outcome, it's failure can be devastating.

In reference to your present circumstances, you're angry with yourself because you feel you should have seen this coming and done something to prevent it. If you're feeling betrayed, either by yourself or someone else, it is essential that you take the time to regroup.

Before you can begin to accept the loss and get on with life, the balance of your inner world must be restored. Ask yourself: "Were my expectations realistic? Was I emotionally over-invested? Is there anything left of this situation that could be saved? Do I want to salvage it?"

When you start to pick up the pieces in a more composed state, you might be surprised at how much there is to work with. Remember that something new always grows from the ashes of the old. It is within these new circumstances that opportunities await you.

Five of Cups

Inverted

The Five of Cups inverted represents your disappointment, disillusionment, and grief about the project or situation in question.

You were emotionally left out in the cold when your expectations didn't materialize. No one could have forewarned you because this was a situation you needed to deal with firsthand.

It has taken time for you to pull it together. Nonetheless, you're well on your way to picking up the pieces and turning your life around. In retrospect, can you see what happened? You let unfounded expectations and wishful thinking cloud your better judgment. Even though it's a lesson learned the hard way, it brings with it the gift of wisdom. Sometimes we need difficult circumstances to disrupt our lives and "soften us up," so that we can go forward with an open heart.

Ask yourself: "Am I willing to detach from emotional turmoil and surrender this situation to the highest possible good? Am I willing to keep dreaming, to keep taking risks?" Herein lies the ultimate paradox of success—to be able to say: "I want what I want, but I'm all right if I don't receive it."

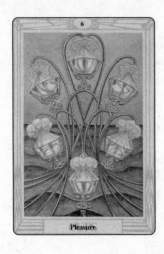

Six of Cups

(Pleasure)

D rawing the Six of Cups signifies that the project or situation in question is unfolding according to plan.

Things will happen quickly, so be flexible and alert to each new development. If you allow yourself to enjoy each step of the process, rather than just the goal itself, you'll find this a lot easier.

Each and every day, miracles are constantly occurring in your life: Have you taken the time to notice the pleasures of everyday life? They will not only help nurture you, but will also keep you motivated and intrigued by your present circumstances.

It is mandatory for the success of this endeavor that you surround yourself with loving and supportive people. Remember to stay connected to your feelings and communicate from your heart.

If you think you should put off enjoying yourself until your project is completed, *think again*! Enjoying yourself along the way regenerates the energy needed to complete the project successfully. If you don't stay in the present moment, you can easily get caught up in the relentless momentum of this venture—and forget to "stop and smell the roses." When you postpone taking pleasure from life, you run the risk of never enjoying your life at all. Remember that the future is not promised to you. All you have for certain is "now"— so learn to take full advantage of it. You're going to arrive at your destination whether you enjoy the process or not . . . and life itself is such a beautiful gift, it would be a shame if you didn't savor the journey.

Six of Cups

Inverted

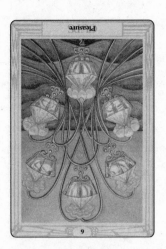

The Six of Cups inverted represents the emptiness we feel when we no longer find joy in the simple pleasures of life.

Have you noticed that your day-to-day life seems empty and devoid of fun? Nothing really pleases you anymore: What happened? Why do you approach your project or situation like a troublesome burden rather than the gratifying experience it once was?

To turn your circumstances around, you need to breathe new life into your situation. Begin by rediscovering the wonder of life itself: the magnificence of a sunset, a walk in the rain, or, most of all, the simple pleasures of friendship and good will.

It's no surprise that you sometimes get the feeling that life is passing you by. When you forget the simple gifts, you block your feelings and consequently find it difficult to sustain the very relationships that will support your goals.

You need to be open to the possibility of relishing life once again. Keep foremost in your mind that joy is a necessary ingredient to a soulful life. Accordingly, to bring pleasure back into your life, ask yourself: "With what or with whom would I like to re-establish a lost connection?"

Consider making a list of things you like to do just for the fun of it and dive into one of these each and every day. When you're able to find joy within each moment of the journey you will discover that your day-to-day life has a mystery and a magic all its own.

Seven of Cups
(Debauch)

I n selecting the Seven of Cups, you're being cautioned to examine
your options carefully before you commit yourself to any specific
direction.

Without meticulous examination of your motives, your fantasies
about this situation can color your sense of reason and negatively
influence your decision.

Ask yourself: "Of all the possible scenarios that intrigue me,
which ones are realistic? Which ones could I be using to divert my
attention from the real issue? Am I using food, work, drugs, or
relationships (the list of possibilities is endless) as distractions?"

Trying to escape emotional pain by obscuring it is not going to
solve your problem. Emotions are like water; a little quenches your
thirst—too much drowns you. At the moment you're drowning!

Bottled-up feelings are distorting your perception of reality. Be
aware that at times we can move so deeply into our emotions that
we get bogged down and need professional help to find our way
out—if you think you need help, don't be afraid to get it.

To be effective you must know your limitations. Be careful that
you're not being consumed by your feelings and letting your
fantasies run wild.

Come down to earth and take a look at the practical solutions
available to you. At the present time, it's necessary to put both feet
on the ground and get real.

Seven of Cups

Inverted

The Seven of Cups inverted indicates that your feelings about this particular project or situation are much deeper than they may appear on the surface, even to you.

The fear, anger, or guilt you feel is so difficult to express that you may choose to separate yourself from your emotions. This allows you to think you feel nothing, which is a far cry from the truth.

Consider asking yourself: "Do I feel as if I'm living on the periphery of my life, almost in slow motion? What feelings could I be repressing? Which parts of my personality do I reject?"

To begin expressing your emotions you need to put critical judgment aside. Bear in mind that your feelings are your feelings—they're not good or bad. The longer you deny them the vaguer they become. Soon they seem to disappear altogether and you think you're detached, but that isn't so.

You need to embrace your dreams and fantasies as well as your nightmares and fears in order to achieve your goals. You must acknowledge all of your feelings—not just the well-behaved ones you like.

The time has come to stretch yourself, put reason aside, and follow your heart. Your heart will lead you to your own truth, your own vitality, and your own path. When you're willing to express your feelings, you'll be able to spread your wings and soar like an eagle.

Eight of Cups

(Indolence)

When you draw the Eight of Cups, you're being asked to take better care of yourself by setting limits on your time, energy, and resources.

You have a vague feeling that something is missing, but you're not quite sure what that something is. Consider the possibility that you've spent an enormous amount of energy on the needs of others and run your own reserves into the red. Unless you get your priorities straight, you risk becoming physically and mentally exhausted. Your once attainable goals will appear out of reach.

Trying to please others at your own expense not only leaves you feeling angry and used; it also contributes to your feelings of failure. Ask yourself: "Am I living other people's lives instead of my own? If so, why do I do that? Am I run by what others think and feel? Can I say no?"

If you want to see your situation change, you need to take care of yourself the same way you take care of others. It's an illusion that you can be responsible for either the good or the bad things that happen to someone else. In reality, you can only be responsible for yourself. If you want to help other people, get out of their way by living your own life, not theirs.

Eight of Cups

Inverted

In choosing the Eight of Cups inverted, you acknowledge that you've been playing the role of martyr for a long time now and have finally decided that enough is enough. Good for you! At present you're free to devote yourself—your time and attention—to the project or situation at hand.

As you take full responsibility for your own life, everyone around you will benefit. It's been a difficult process to realize both the importance of self-nurturing and the necessity for maintaining good boundaries. Boundaries allow other people to know exactly what they can expect from you. Simply say *yes* when yes is what you mean and *no* when no is what you mean.

Ask yourself: "How can I be sure that I carry through with my own plans? How can I keep from getting side-tracked by what I think are others' needs?"

There was a day when you would work your fingers to the bone trying to please everyone else. Unquestionably times have changed for the better. This new attitude of yours transforms both you and your situation in a more positive way.

Whatever goals you set for yourself, you'll be able to achieve them if you continue to live your own life and allow other people to live theirs. It's great when you can help others, but remember: Never help anyone else when to do so means giving yourself away.

Nine of Cups

(Happiness)

The Nine of Cups represents the satisfaction, happiness, and contentment that are about to surface in your life.

As a long-cherished dream finally becomes a reality, you'll feel as if you're on top of the world, and nothing can stop you. At this time in your life, expect to feel as though you could successfully complete any project or situation you have your heart set on.

The personal fulfillment you experience will have you walking around with a big smile. You certainly have earned this period of peace and goodwill, so enjoy it. Take all the time you need to celebrate your good fortune and reap the benefits of your success.

Bear in mind that when you're blessed with emotional and material prosperity, it becomes even more important that you take every opportunity to give. Ask yourself: "What can I do to share my imminent good fortune with others?" Giving to others will not only help them, but it will also return a message of abundance and well being to your own mind.

Letting the inner wellspring of joy and contentment flow outward will enhance the current endeavor, and set the tone for your future success. Happiness and tranquility in turn give rise to feelings of kindness and compassion toward others. When you express these feelings openly people will see you as more approachable. As a result, you will attract more opportunities.

Nine of Cups

Inverted

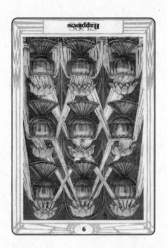

The Nine of Cups asks that you be mindful that your pessimistic attitude is causing you to lose interest in the current project or situation.

You've become a master of doom and gloom. If at the moment you're having difficulty reaching your goals, so what? It doesn't mean you'll never get there.

An illusion of hopelessness has detracted from your success and happiness. You seem to be saying "I want to be happy, but . . ." You're acting as if happiness is to be the last thing you want.

Ask yourself: "Is accepting defeat satisfying some old core belief in me? Am I expecting someone or something to make me happy, believing I can't do it myself?" Remember that happiness is an inside job that exists separate from the outer world. You already have it; you need only to rediscover the wellspring of grace and equilibrium within yourself. Happiness is your birthright.

The situation in question is full of possibilities, in spite of the fact that you don't see them at the present time. Even the smallest recognition of happiness in your life now will allow you to see the situation from a different perspective and break the stranglehold caused by negativity.

Do something that puts a smile on your face—you'll have a much better chance to create the success you desire. At the very least, it will be more becoming than the frown you've been wearing lately.

Ten of Cups
(Satiety)

The Ten of Cups signifies the sense of fulfillment that allows you to feel as if you could walk on water, so to speak. You've reached the last stage of the project or situation and have accomplished more than you ever dreamed possible. You're feeling so good about the pleasure and contentment your success has brought you. Now what?

Fulfillment cannot be the only result; every victory, conclusion or success forms to be the seed for the next cycle of growth as part of the natural ebb and flow of life. What is filled needs to be emptied so that it can fill itself again.

Be careful not to lose the sense of challenge that brought you to this point. Direct the passion and fulfillment of the moment into the vision of your next venture. Set new goals for yourself before you get carried away by the excitement and either become giddy or work against the gains you've made by resting too long on your laurels. Giddiness leaves you off balance to the point of distraction so that you lose your practicality and can stumble; savoring perfection becomes boring and counterproductive to future effort.

Before you proceed, ask yourself: "Where is my current success leading me? What challenge do I envision for myself?" Commit to moving past satiety to rebirth and boldly enter the next cycle of growth and fulfillment.

Ten of Cups

Inverted

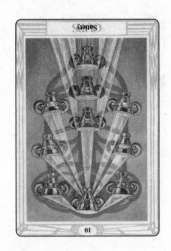

When you pull the Ten of Cups inverted, you're advising yourself to let go and move on. You've achieved a state of maximum fulfillment and pleasure but holding rather desperately to this state is going to become extremely uncomfortable. Relishing your accomplishments leads to a sense of being emotionally filled to capacity. However, satiety is just one step from gluttony.

Instead of enjoying a phase of contentment and moving on into a new venture, you're clinging to the present accomplishment as if it were all you will ever have. Did you expect this victory to fill every aspect of your life forevermore? It's just one step along the path that will take you to the next accomplishment.

Enough is enough! Use your present success and feelings of fulfillment to create the seeds for your next venture! Ask yourself: "Did I expect too much from success? Why am I afraid to do anything that may upset the apple cart? Am I willing to move forward and challenge myself with a new venture?"

When you're willing to see the potential for new accomplishments in your life, you will open the door to even greater possibilities. Don't let the comforts of satiety cloud your ability to recall—and act from—your original passion for this endeavor. Accept the challenge and get back in the game.

Ace of Swords

Ace of Swords

When the Ace of Swords is drawn it signifies that you're now in a good position to cut through the uncertainty that has surrounded your endeavor. As confusion evaporates, the next steps to take in this situation will become clear. As your mind becomes focused, you'll find it easier to cultivate new ideas to further your project or situation.

You have a clear shot at success if you're willing to learn the power of orchestrating your thoughts, attitudes, and beliefs into single-minded focus on your goals.

Help yourself achieve the results you want by following three simple steps. One: Write down the goal in as much detail as you can. Keep your attention on your objective. The more precise the goal, the more likely you are to realize it. Two: Ask yourself: "How will I know when I've arrived at my goal?" Practice visualizing the successful completion of your goal—it's essential to know exactly what the end results will look like. Three: Consciously choose to think in an innovative, creative, and independent manner.

The rich landscape of your inner world is always changing. With a certain knowledge of what you want, you can change your mind in a way that benefits you and your project. It's up to you to determine what you will think and believe. What you accept as true influences your behavior; for that reason, keep your thoughts in alignment with the direction you want to go and you're sure to get there.

Ace of Swords

Inverted

The Ace of Swords inverted suggests that your thinking is unclear at the moment; therefore, it's appropriate for you to wait until the "dust settles" before you continue.

Proceed only when you're clear about what you want and how to go about creating it. Ask yourself: "What is it I really want? What steps do I need to take to achieve my goals?" It's to your best advantage to stop and honestly work through the situation in your mind until you've set a clear purpose and direction.

This approach will require that you be precise in your thinking, organize your time carefully, and pay close attention to details. The mind is continuously active, teeming with thoughts—make sure you fill your mind with productive intent to promote goal-oriented behavior. Keep your own counsel about this process; for the time being watch what you say and how you say it.

At this particular time in your life, take care not to be distracted by other people. Don't let anyone intimidate you or pressure you into making a premature decision.

In any case, it's essential that you don't rush this project or situation. When the time is right you'll be able to act decisively. At the moment, however, do nothing. Remember that choosing *not* to act is a major decision.

Two of Swords

(Peace)

Selecting the Two of Swords illuminates the fact that you can no longer avoid making a decision. There will be no peace or tranquility within this situation until you're willing to make the choices for yourself.

It is mandatory that you take the time to discover what *you* want to do next. You can't leave the responsibility to resolve this project or situation to someone else. If you do, it will only complicate matters.

It's important that when making a decision, you take the time to listen to your rational mind as well as your intuition; each has its own special information to contribute.

Look at the alternatives available to you, then examine the possible outcome of each. Until you look ahead and decide exactly what you want to do next, you'll be preoccupied with the complexities of the situation as it is now. When you finally make a decision, the pressure will be off and you'll feel a renewed sense of purpose and gusto in life.

Once you've made up your mind, get going—don't second-guess your own wisdom. Indecisiveness will destroy the present moment and plunge you back into uncertainty. Ask yourself: "What decisions do I need to make? What are my options? What do I want to do?"

Let the decision you make be one you're willing to commit to and live with. Then you can truly relax and enjoy yourself.

Two of Swords

Inverted

The Two of Swords inverted depicts a mind that never shuts off. You reach a decision and immediately start second-guessing yourself.

If you look around, you'll see that everyone seems to have a different opinion about what you need to do. When are you going to stop listening to them and start trusting yourself?

Start by removing "should have" and "ought to" from your vocabulary. No one knows better than you what's best for you; it's time you start making your own decisions.

In regard to the situation at hand: When you receive advice from others it's usually well meant, but soon creates a swamp of confusion. Ask yourself: "Given my particular circumstances, what is best for me? What do I feel comfortable doing?"

You'll be able to think more clearly if you relax and stop taking yourself and the situation so seriously. Lighten up; this is not a life-or-death situation.

Give some thought to the possibility that you don't need to reach a decision at this exact moment. Why not wait a while and give yourself time to determine what you really want to do? Regarding this particular situation, do not let anybody pressure you into reaching a decision you are not ready to make. Sometimes, doing nothing is the most powerful decision of all.

Three of Swords

(Sorrow)

The Three of Swords speaks to the mental anguish we experience when we're unwilling to let go of our past sorrow.

At this time in your life you feel paralyzed, unable to move forward because you doubt your ability to make choices for yourself. You seem to be holding your breath, expecting the worst, and waiting for the past to repeat itself.

It's no wonder your life looks like a soap opera. Keep this up and the situation or project will be sabotaged before you even have a chance to get started. It's essential that you approach this venture with a "beginner's mind" unburdened by either past success or failure. Ask yourself: "What is the attraction I have to the pain and sorrow I've experienced? Am I finally ready to move on?"

If you continue looking back at the past, you'll live in fear of history repeating itself. If, beset by this apprehension, you look to the future, you'll only project your anxiety. Soon non-productive thoughts will overwhelm you. Only when you're thoroughly immersed in the present moment will you be able to tap into the limitless capacities of your mind. The data that is pertinent to the current situation is the only data you should take into account. Let everything else go.

Yes, you've made mistakes in the past—so what? Why not consider yourself lucky since you've learned what *not* to do. Remember that it's impossible to repeat an action or a situation in exactly the same way. This is a time of new beginnings, a time to confront your grief and move past it.

Three of Swords

Inverted

Selecting the Three of Swords inverted calls your attention to the fact that the "soap opera" you've called your life is in the process of becoming less intense.

You seem to be more and more exhausted lately by what's transpired: Does this mean that you're finally ready to let go of the past and live in the present?

Take into consideration that nothing you experience is ever wasted. Be grateful for the experiences you've had because they contribute not only to your unique talents and resources but also to the wisdom you possess. Your knowledge is unique. No one knows exactly what you know.

Nonetheless, the time has come to heal your wounds and create a successful outcome to your situation. Ask yourself: "Am I willing to integrate what has occurred and move on?"

Your life will become easier when you're able to put down the burdens of the past. Everything you need to go forward is contained within the present moment. Your experiences have given you the knowledge necessary to make wise choices for yourself. Remember that there's no need to relive the painful memories . . . wasn't once enough?

Memories belong to who you were. The present belongs to who you are. Enjoy your life while you create a new and more exciting history.

Four of Swords

(Truce)

When you draw the Four of Swords, you need to ask: "Why am I trying to push a square peg into a round hole?" Have you noticed lately that, pertaining to this situation, you've been speeding up, working harder—and getting nowhere fast?

It is essential for you to realize that—if you continue with the present approach—things are going to get messy.

It's in the best interest of your project or situation at this time that you're open to negotiating a compromise. Develop a more flexible approach and try being more cooperative. Other people also have their opinions (just as well-founded to them). When you take the feelings of others into consideration, you'll establish a productive flow in communications.

Take time out to rethink your situation. Ask yourself: "If I continue doing what I am doing, where am I going to end up?"

Until you're better able to determine what's truly going on, don't take action. Now is the time to withdraw temporarily and regroup. This way, everyone gets a break and you can come together later in a more cooperative atmosphere.

In the meantime, nourish yourself. Have fun, seek out enlivening activities that have nothing to do with the current situation. Give your mind the time it needs to return to its own peace and balance. You'll know when it's time to go back and try again because you will feel completely relaxed, energized and clear-minded.

Four of Swords

Inverted

When the Four of Swords appears inverted, consider the possibility that you've been making too many concessions. In an effort to keep peace at any cost, you've lost your anchor by compromising much of what you believe in. It's no wonder you feel like a ship tossed at sea.

This is not a time to negotiate your position, but rather a time to scrutinize the situation and determine what your position really is. What do you think about the project or situation? Can you see where keeping everything nice is not always the right approach?

Ask yourself: "Why am I afraid to speak my mind and stand up for myself? Why am I usually the one to give in? Am I afraid of looking stubborn, or losing my composure?" So what if you lose your composure? A little chaos and confusion won't hurt you; it may in fact help you to determine what you want and how to get it.

If you continue to appease instead of confront, conciliate instead of negotiate, the confusion in the present project or situation will hold you fast. In this particular case, create a plan of action shaped by your needs and desires, and then let others accommodate you. Stay steadfast with your goals and in a state of integrity with your own beliefs. If you don't sell yourself short, you'll get what you want.

Five of Swords
(Defeat)

If you continue to experience setbacks in this situation, the Five of Swords suggests that you stop to examine your core beliefs about winning and losing. If you think you can't—you can't!

Are you defeating yourself by entertaining pessimistic thoughts and attitudes? You are not your thoughts; you exist apart from them, and therefore you—the real you—can control, monitor, and manipulate the rich complexities of the mental process. You *choose* what you want to think.

So why sabotage yourself by letting doubt set your mental climate? Ask yourself whether you believe in your innate ability to succeed and whether you consider your wants valid.

Are you more invested in losing than winning? The desire to succeed must override your expectation of failure. If not, you may find yourself continually choosing to "romance" a no-win situation that fulfills the anticipation of defeat.

Ask yourself: "Do I continually set goals for myself that are impossible to attain and then beat myself up for failing? Do I have an investment in being a victim? Do I confirm the doubts about myself by losing?"

It is within the mind that we are our most fiendish saboteurs and assassins. When you expect defeat and then take pride in knowing you were right, you literally kill your life moment by moment: "I knew I couldn't do it and I didn't . . . ."

Five of Swords

Inverted

The Five of Swords inverted reminds you that the first step in turning a loss into a win is not accepting defeat.

Ask yourself: "Is there success for me within the existing situation? Am I willing to believe I can succeed?"

Never lose sight of the fact that *personal power* is your ability to decide how you want to think, how you want to feel, and how you want to interpret the circumstances.

You may not have control over these specific events, but you do have power over your thoughts, attitudes, and beliefs about them.

Remember that your thoughts don't have meaning in and of themselves; they have only the meanings you impart to them. How you choose to think and feel about your endeavor is your responsibility. Therefore, you decide how you wish to portray the existing situation. Consider representing it to yourself in a manner that helps move you into more productive behavior.

Don't accept defeat. Don't allow a false sense of pride to stand in the way of trying again. Use the opposition you have presently experienced to help strengthen your determination. You're a winner and when you fully expect to win, odds are you will.

Six of Swords

(Science)

The Six of Swords announces that you've left trouble behind you and moved into calmer waters. From here, you can open your mind to new possibilities, and see that your project or situation continues to improve.

This is a good time for you to investigate, research, and brainstorm new ideas. When you think objectively your mind is free to experience things as they really are, not just how you want them to be.

At this time in your life, your thinking process may be working to keep the status quo. But don't rule out new ideas just because they don't support your current set of beliefs. Ask yourself: "Can I suspend my beliefs long enough to consider new possibilities?"

Use your creative intelligence, combined with research and reflection. Before you commit to anything, get all the information you can. Include honest reflection on your mistakes (rather than denying them) so they reveal what to avoid. Take the time you need to get all the pieces of the puzzle in your possession before you attempt to put them together.

Be inquisitive and ask as many questions as you can. If you do not have an answer, do not worry, you just have not asked the right question yet but you will.

Six of Swords

Inverted

You've been able to put a Band-Aid on the situation, but it's not going to help for long.

The Six of Swords inverted cautions that when you become emotionally involved in your circumstances, you risk losing the objectivity needed for clear thinking. It's essential to your success that you see how your feelings are influencing your thoughts and behavior.

In regard to this situation, you seem to have developed a tendency to see or hear only what you want. Your myopic vision has limited you to only one point of view—yours! When you close your mind to new information, creative solutions are out of reach. True wisdom is being able to admit that you don't know everything, and then enjoying the adventure of discovery.

Keep an open mind. Try bearing witness to your own thoughts, feelings, and behavior: Stop yourself throughout the day and ask yourself: "Do I really know what is happening? Am I really listening to what's being said? Am I filtering what I hear so it suits my point of view?"

Be advised that you need to give others a chance to speak instead of assuming you know what they think or feel; in other words, shut up and listen!

Delay action until you have researched the situation and feel comfortable that you've restored a sense of objectivity.

Seven of Swords

(Futility)

The Seven of Swords represents your present state of mind. So much is happening within the project or situation that you're overwhelmed by its circumstances, leaving you with a sense of futility.

You need to snap out of it and get the facts straight before you proceed. The truth of the matter is that your current situation is progressing according to plan; it is neither hopeless nor out of control. Are you making the problem bigger than it needs to be?

In reality, the problems aren't insurmountable; consider taking one step at a time. Begin by clarifying your thoughts and realizing that you needn't do everything at once. When you try to be everything to everybody, it's no wonder your mind becomes exhausted and shuts itself off. Can you see how your current mental state will render your actions ineffectual?

Keep the project or situation manageable by creating short-term goals that focus your mind and actions on what needs to be done today. Stop perceiving yourself at the foot of a sheer cliff, staring up hopelessly. Look directly in front and you'll see the toeholds to support your climb—one step at a time.

To break the cycle of self-defeat, you need to separate yourself from your thoughts. Be more objective and you will be more productive. Remember, you are not your present state of mind; you are an intelligent, creative person with an abundance of talent and resources to produce the results you desire.

Seven of Swords

Inverted

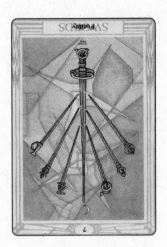

The Seven of Swords inverted portrays a situation riddled with tests and challenges.

This is a situation that will, in the long run, help you discover the source of your own inner security. By developing healthy self-reliance, you'll feel less vulnerable and more in charge of your life. As a result, you'll be able to act with control and direction, rather than react to the vagaries of the present circumstances.

This is a time for progress, so get ready to take the next step toward your goal. Ask yourself: "How would my circumstances change if I didn't have so much doubt about this situation? What would I do differently if I were more secure?"

Your present state of affairs has a lot to offer you: trust it. This endeavor allows you to experiment with different beliefs and ideas to determine which ones work best for you.

At this time, strive for competency rather than for perfection. If you get locked into the illusory demands of perfection, you'll soon doubt yourself again and find it difficult to get started. Remember that procrastination is nothing more than self-doubt canceling out your natural drive.

Success seldom follows negative thoughts. Don't let your mind defeat you. Anything is possible for this situation if you call on your innate resources. You have a choice: When self-doubt speaks, choose not to listen.

Eight of Swords

(Interference)

The Eight of Swords suggests a temporary delay to allow you to come to terms with the non-productive thoughts that are interfering with the situation at hand. You need to confront your doubts and deal with the mental confusion that's obscuring the path ahead. It's important to realize that the interference you're experiencing originates within your mental attitudes and beliefs and you can change these. Good fortune is most likely to come your way when you forge a belief system that supports your goals and allows you to win.

Ask yourself: "How do my beliefs affect my situation? Do I see myself as a capable person with the resources necessary to create what I want? Is the world a friendly place, or do I see a hostile world?"

Which of the damaging mental games do you play? To uncover some of your core beliefs, fill in the appropriate blanks: Life is _____. The world is _____. Money is _____. Love is _____. Relationships are _____. In regard to the present situation, which beliefs are deleterious and need to change so that you have a better chance at success? It is just as important to know how to think as it is to know how to act.

It will be to your great benefit to root out any non-productive thoughts, choose instead to see the possibilities for success in the current situation, and then act accordingly.

Eight of Swords

Inverted

The Eight of Swords inverted concerns itself with the fact that you, like many other people, are being held prisoner by your own thoughts.

To be free you must first realize that you've imprisoned yourself in a world of limiting beliefs. If these limiting beliefs go unexamined, if you're not even aware of them, they will work against the successful outcome for the situation in question.

Up until this point, how much have your restrictive beliefs cost you? Are you ready to consider changing them? The easiest way to change your beliefs is to change your mind.

The first step in creating a more productive mental state is to admit the need for change. The second step is to accept full responsibility for the changes you choose to make. The third step is to monitor your thoughts so that you can immediately counter self-defeating thoughts with productive ones. The fourth step is to keep your thoughts goal-oriented. Make choices based on your priorities, and create behaviors that enable you to reach your goals.

The interference you've experienced in the past has vanished, and nothing stops you from having what you want—unless you choose to stop yourself.

When you're willing to believe in yourself and your situation, you'll experience little or no opposition in your journey toward success. You don't have to think positively to succeed, but it certainly will make the journey a lot easier for you.

Nine of Swords

(Cruelty)

C hoosing the Nine of Swords means that beyond a doubt, you have been caught in a cycle of hopelessness and despair. Your mind has become your worst enemy because you've identified your sense of self-worth with your feeling of desperation, rather than acknowledge your existence separate from them. These non-productive thoughts are now running your life. You're drowning in tears of self-recrimination, guilt and anxiety.

Degrading and demoralizing thoughts about yourself can severely wound your spirit. Caving in to inner voices of condemnation creates more problems in your world. You need to regain your sense of reason and objectivity if you want to get your life back on track.

As an adult, it's important that you acknowledge a need not only to heal past wounds but also to end self-destructive behavior.

Ask yourself: "Has self-condemnation ever brought me the acceptance and love I desire? Has it helped or hindered my present circumstances?"

Be careful that you don't mistake your current state of mind for your fundamental character. You may be feeling powerless at the moment, but you're much more than this feeling.

Remember that how you choose to think and feel about yourself will affect every aspect of your life. To begin the healing process you must realize that you don't have to do anything to be loved. Unconditional love of self is our natural birthright!

Nine of Swords

Inverted

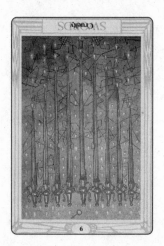

The Nine of Swords inverted encourages you to stop seeing yourself as a victim. At this time in your life it is essential that you take full responsibility for altering the course of your circumstances. You can begin by changing the way you think.

Thoughts are like clouds, they come and they go. Keep sight of the ones that support you and let the other ones just drift on by!

Of course you have had problems in the past: Who hasn't? Why not use these experiences as a source of additional understanding and compassion for yourself. No one can, or will, do for you what you are unwilling to do for yourself.

Ask yourself: "Am I ready to break this cycle of self-destruction? Am I willing to treat myself with the same respect and kindness I give to others?" When you come to terms with your mental demons, you will be able to turn this situation around in your favor.

Question any voice that says there is something wrong with you! Pay attention to internal dialogue so that you can stop using such self-abusive language. Change your mind and you will begin to change your life.

Everything will fall into place when you accept that your value as a person is within your own being, not within the outer trappings of your life. Also, remember that success in this world is basically a matter of getting up more times than you fall down.

Ten of Swords

(Ruin)

Selecting the Ten of Swords indicates that your thoughts, with regard to the circumstances in question, are totally "off the wall."

What's happening is that your imagination is getting the best of you and allowing you to see problems where none exist. Ask yourself: "What sense does it make to look for trouble around each and every corner?"

You're advised to stop running long enough to see that you've been chasing your own shadow. Excess anxiety has you defending yourself against imaginary foes. Your uneasiness not only colors your judgment, but if ignored can make you physically ill.

Continue this type of thinking and you're likely to create adversity within the project or situation. When you obsess over all the things that could go wrong, you find yourself overcompensating to avoid these imaginary pitfalls. In reality, your project or situation is doing just fine: Why insist on making everything more complicated than it needs to be?

Until you're able to come to your senses and feel more secure about this venture, monitor your thoughts and emotional responses closely. Take every precaution to stay out of your own way and avoid projecting problems. Make sure you know what is in actuality going on—not what you imagine is happening.

Ten of Swords

Inverted

Drawing the Ten of Swords inverted signifies that congratulations are finally in order. The vague fear and anxiety that has haunted you has now all but disappeared.

Within the near future, you'll not only heal emotionally, but also be able to act in a more positive and more opportunistic way.

In reference to the current circumstances, remember to keep your mind focused on the present moment. Make a list of all the things that are going well for you so that you can reinforce just why you have good reasons to be optimistic.

At this very special time in your life, condition yourself to see more rainbows than rain clouds. Don't waste precious time or energy worrying about all the things that could possibly go wrong; in this specific situation, the chances are remote that they will.

Because the conflicts surrounding your endeavor seem to be coming to an end, you'll soon be able to relax and appreciate the changes that occur. Are you willing to allow yourself to do that?

A positive state of mind, one that encourages you to trust your abilities, will give you the self-assurance you need to take more risks than you normally would. Consequently, the more you're willing to risk, the more likely you are to succeed.

Ace of Disks

Ace of Disks

When you select the Ace of Disks, you're being advised of the necessity to create a firm foundation for this project or situation before attempting to move ahead. When an endeavor such as yours has a reliable basis from which to operate, it will enable you to weather the winds of change and turn obstacles into opportunities.

Take into account that your feelings about your relationships, career, finances, etc., will be in direct alliance with your inner sense of security and the confidence you have in your own abilities.

Yet, because each of us defines security in a different way, you need to ask yourself: "What exactly does it take for *me* to feel secure? What makes *me* feel prosperous? Am I confident enough with myself to allow abundance in my life?"

You also create a foundation for prosperity when you value your earthly experiences. Being alive on a physical plane is an opportunity to demonstrate, in material form, the creative force within you. When you have respect for the physical world, you're respecting the energy of life itself. The more grounded you are in your everyday life, the more prosperous you'll feel.

In regard to this particular situation, plant your feet firmly on the ground so you'll be ready to have your spirit soar as you bring your dreams to life.

Ace of Disks

Inverted

The Ace of Disks inverted reminds you that it's difficult to fly from the nest until you develop the essential resources needed to maintain flight—your "adult feathers."

Each of us has access to the latent potential of abundance and prosperity that life itself possesses. Nevertheless, we must grow into prosperity in the same way nature grows into its seasons . . . from the inside out.

To successfully complete the enterprise at hand, it's necessary for you to cultivate a sense of trust in yourself as well as in the inherent abundance within your life at the present time.

You have the potential to create deep inner security about your situation or project if you're willing to invest some time in learning the "confidence game." Start by making a list of all the things in your life that you're grateful for. If you take the time to put everything you appreciate on this list, you'll see there's more—much more—to be thankful for than you thought.

Ask yourself: "Am I willing to let go of a belief in scarcity and a cynical attitude so that I can fully recognize what I have right now? What resources do I have at this moment that can help me to achieve my goals?"

Are you willing to fully submerge yourself in the concepts of abundance and prosperity until they're not just ideas you entertain, but an integral part of your belief system? When you can do that, you'll be ready to fly!

Two of Disks

(Change)

Y ou've chosen the Two of Disks as a reminder that you may have to juggle your time, energy, and money to achieve the goals you've set for yourself. Let go of any resistance to doing this because these particular shifts and changes will end with the good fortune you deserve.

If you're willing to maintain a relaxed attitude, you'll find it easier to handle the present situation. You don't have to take big, bold steps to achieve your goals; instead you can take small but consistent ones. Ask yourself: "What small steps can I take to move closer to my goals?"

From time to time, you may be asked to do a little maneuvering; a minor adjustment here and another there. Just when you think you have this enterprise nailed down, it may change again. Instead of being discouraged, celebrate these shifts, because each will further the growth and expansion your venture needs to succeed.

Be mindful that all life is in constant motion, always evolving from one form to another. In fact, remember that change itself is the very foundation on which stability is built. You must be willing to shift gears when you see the circumstances surrounding your project or situation changing.

At this moment in your life, don't try to hold on to anything; be generous with your time, talents, and finances—the more you're willing to give, the more will come back to you.

Two of Disks

Inverted

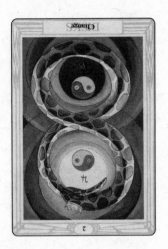

When the Two of Disks is selected in an inverted position, it advises that you'll be able to cope with the present situation a lot better if you loosen up.

You've become attached to the way you think your project or situation should progress and therefore have made judgments limiting your possibilities. It's time to be a little more flexible.

You must take into account the subtle and not-so-subtle shifts that are occurring. If you lose your sense of humor and succumb to discouragement, these changes can throw you off balance. Lighten up or you'll create unnecessary problems for yourself.

This project or situation will improve the minute you perceive these changes as opportunities for expansion rather than as growing problems to be dealt with.

Life itself is subject to change without notification. In fact, if your life were to stay the same, it would be the worst thing that could happen to you.

Ask yourself: "Why am I so locked into one particular way of doing things? Why do I hold on so tight? What is more important to me at this point, my ego or the end results?"

Your daily life, at this particular moment, is like a juggling act. You might as well have fun with it. If you loosen up and remain flexible, it's less likely that you'll drop the ball.

Three of Disks

(Work)

The Three of Disks symbolizes the success you encounter when you're willing to apply all of your talents, skills, and resources to the situation at hand.

This particular venture requires not only commitment and determination on your part, but hard work as well. Are you up to it?

Ask yourself: "Because this endeavor seems so important to me, am I motivated to give it all I have? Am I willing to devote the time, effort, even the finances necessary to reach my goals? Am I prepared to pursue this undertaking, no matter how long it takes, until I get the results I desire?"

When you're ready to totally commit yourself to the project or situation at hand, the world seems to open up and send you the opportunities and support you need.

Be aware that people are attracted to your strong sense of propriety, and as a result they have faith in your ability to do what you say you will. This makes them want to help you in any way they can.

If you want to see this venture through to a successful conclusion, use your common sense, develop a down-to-earth approach to any obstacles you encounter, and attend to your day-to-day business. Before long, good things will start materializing for you.

Three of Disks

Inverted

Selecting the Three of Disks inverted advises you to step back enough to determine why you're having so much difficulty committing yourself to this particular project or situation.

At the present time you're tired and therefore unwilling to put more energy into this venture. Do you think you're temporarily discouraged because you've lost sight of your original motivation and become sidetracked?

At the beginning you may have been overzealous and underestimated the time, energy, and resources that were necessary to carry this project through. Your total commitment is now demanded for success in this situation. Unless you're motivated to put everything on the line for this enterprise, things won't work out in your favor.

Ask yourself: "Is this endeavor still important to me? How strongly do I feel about it? How much time, effort, or money, am I willing to devote to this venture to have it succeed? If I can't make such a commitment, am I willing to accept defeat?"

If you want to move ahead with this project or situation remember that growth and expansion will be found not by trying to stay in a safe comfortable space, but by taking the bull by the horns and doing whatever is necessary to succeed.

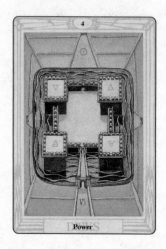

Four of Disks

(Power)

When you pull the Four of Disks from the deck, it emphasizes the value that structure, planning, and organization will have on your particular circumstances.

Before you proceed, it's important for you to recognize just how much you've accomplished up till now in the project or situation in question. Your achievements will provide a strong foundation for the current endeavor. Once you have acknowledged what you've already completed, prepare yourself to move out into the world once again and finish what you started.

Ask yourself: "Am I willing to create an updated plan and stick to it?" It's essential that you don't let yourself get thrown off course. At the moment you've got all the pieces for what you're building; however, you still need to draft a blueprint to help you put the pieces together.

The first thing is to determine exactly what you want the end results to look like. The second is to list the resources you have to work with. The third is to get organized. Draft a step-by-step plan for achieving your goals. It's helpful to start by describing in detail the outcome you desire, and then work backward until you've uncovered the very first thing that needs to be done.

Do this and before long, when it's time for you to act, you'll be able to take the initiative, knowing that you have covered all your bases.

Four of Disks

Inverted

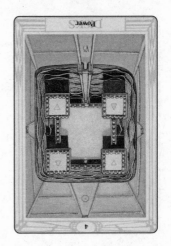

You seem to have started out with a big bang, but did not have a well-structured plan of how to continue.

Picking the Four of Disks inverted implies that the task at hand requires discrimination on your part. You need to decide what your priorities are and what you wish to achieve in the long run.

Ask yourself: "What are my goals? What practical skills do I need to develop in order to accomplish these goals?" If you value this project or situation, you must be willing to take a stand to ensure that your venture is not compromised.

Know what is important to you and then be willing to defend your boundaries. Learn to say "no" when it's appropriate. Realize that when you say *no* to something that benefits neither you nor your situation, you're virtually saying *yes* to success.

Creating a secure foundation for your endeavor lets you act from strength, rather than from weakness. Before you get ahead of yourself be sure that you have the resources necessary to guarantee your victory. If not, go and get what you need first. Through proper planning, discipline and hard work, you'll get what you want.

Five of Disks

(Worry)

The time has come for you to attempt something new and different in regard to the situation in question. You're being asked to leave the security of the familiar behind and break down the very structure and routine to which you've become accustomed.

The Five of Disks cautions you to keep the faith as you move through the uncertainty and anxiety that usually accompanies a new endeavor. The process itself is unsettling, to say the least, without your being overly concerned about every little thing that could possibly go wrong. The anxiety you're experiencing is only a temporary state of affairs. Worry is often a stage in the realization of one's dreams; don't let it get the best of you.

Ask yourself: "How can I cultivate a less stressful and therefore a more positive attitude? Am I willing to put some effort into monitoring my non-productive thoughts?" If left unattended, worry causes undue stress to your body and may lead to physical problems. How about making a game out of it? If you see a problem, consider it not only a challenge, but also an opportunity to demonstrate just how resourceful you are.

Rest assured that when all is said and done, either the very foundation of your situation will be successfully restructured or you will develop a totally different approach to your circumstances. Either way, you will win.

Five of Disks

Inverted

When you draw the Five of Disks inverted, it's telling you that success is on the horizon even if you don't see its light yet. You're being asked to recognize that all the worrying you've done hasn't helped your situation, but has in fact hindered your progress and consumed precious time, energy, and resources.

You need to ask: "Am I willing to admit that things aren't as bad as I think? Have I underestimated my resources? What talents do I have that I've been unwilling to use? How can I apply these skills to this situation?"

How many times, in the past, have you allowed unnecessary concerns to get the best of you? Do you want to do that now? To be successful, you must direct your time, energy, and resources with a positive attitude, turning away from doubt.

If you still find it difficult not to worry, why not consider this simple exercise: Set aside ten minutes out of each and every day just to worry; worry as hard as you can for a full ten minutes—be sure you give it all you've got! Then when you're finished, give it up and go do something more constructive—something that will contribute to your success.

Six of Disks

(Success)

You've drawn the Six of Disks to underscore the effort you've put into this project or situation. It advises you that you're well on your way to success. With patience and determination you're giving structure and form to your dreams, and will experience the gratification of seeing them slowly manifest in your life.

This particular endeavor is one that you hold near and dear to your heart. Nonetheless, it hasn't always been easy to stay committed to your goals. It's required a lot of "elbow grease" on your part. Because you've felt so deeply about this project or situation, when success comes, it will be sweet indeed.

Keep in mind that success takes courage because it will truly change life as you know it. This change will not only affect your life but the lives of those around you. Be prepared to accommodate the changes success will bring. Now is a good time to ask yourself: "How will success change my life? Can I handle it? Am I willing to put myself out there on the world's playing field, even if my loved ones do not always understand or approve?"

It's important that you also bear in mind that success is fleeting. There's a lot of truth in the statement that you are only as good as your last performance. For that reason, acknowledge your worth separately from your outer success, and you'll be able to better deal with the situation as you move ahead.

Six of Disks

Inverted

The Six of Disks inverted warns you of the possibility of becoming overwhelmed by the enormity of your present circumstances. In regard to this project or situation, ask yourself: "What can I do to make this endeavor more manageable for myself?"

For a start, don't be so impulsive; take it slow and steady. You've put a lot of time and effort into this project. Therefore, don't permit feelings of discouragement to undermine your confidence. Be mindful that in this situation, there's no such thing as failure, only results. Every time you fall short, you learn how *not* to do it!

Maintain a conventional approach to this endeavor and you'll create an environment in which both you and your circumstances will flourish. It will take unwavering tenacity on your part, but the end results will be extremely rewarding. Hard work hasn't stopped you in the past, so why should it now?

You're being asked to hold firmly to your path and continue to believe in your venture, no matter how difficult laboring toward success may seem. This steadfastness will help you see many different solutions to the problems that confront you, and enable you to power through the obstacles in your path.

Seven of Disks

(Failure)

Y ou've selected the Seven of Disks to remind yourself that success is not a goal in itself. It's nothing more than a state of mind. What you have, or have not, does not make you successful; instead, what you feel about your situation and about yourself does.

It seems you've convinced yourself that you can't possibly achieve this goal. Examine the reasons you believe your endeavor will not prosper. Which of these beliefs comes from your ideas of what constitutes success or failure, as opposed to objective reality?

Do you see how you're dooming yourself to fail? Can you suspend your beliefs long enough to allow yourself half a chance to succeed? If not, you might as well throw in the towel right now and give up.

Instead of telling yourself all the reasons for failure, why not list all the reasons your endeavor will succeed? While positive thinking will not actually guarantee success, your state of mind can influence your behavior and therefore make the path to success more fulfilling every day, instead of only for a few moments of keen satisfaction.

Ask yourself: "Am I willing to orchestrate my thinking into a steady flow of productive self-talk? Am I willing to change my beliefs about success and failure?"

When you create a belief system that includes your eventual success, you'll have a better journey to your ultimate destination. Isn't this what you want?

Seven of Disks

Inverted

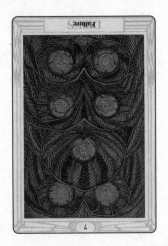

The Seven of Disks inverted points to the fact that your attitudes about success and failure are slowly changing. You've begun to take a serious look at your project or situation and have concluded that failure is not an option.

Therefore, it's time for you to further take control of your life, determine what you wish to create, and then go ahead and do it. The Seven of Pentacles addresses the seven steps that will help you to materialize your goals:

Step one: Envision your goal. Let your dream take shape in your mind.

Step two: Imagine yourself living your dream. Picture as much detail as you can. Hear what others will be saying to you and about you. Most importantly, what will you be saying to yourself?

Step three: Measure this project or situation against your values and priorities. If the goal is not in alignment with your integrity, it will be an empty victory.

Step four: Let your passion and desire for this goal empower you and motivate you.

Step five: Chisel the project down to a size you can work with. Structure, plan and organize what needs to be done.

Step six: Develop a network of support. Delegate authority and let other people help.

Step seven: Do it. Don't worry about whether you succeed or fail. If you plunge in for the sheer pleasure of doing it, you've already succeeded.

Eight of Disks

(Prudence)

The Eight of Disks underscores the patience you'll need to cultivate if you want to complete the project or situation at hand. There's an old saying that applies directly to the present venture: Anything worth doing is worth doing well.

It's imperative that you allow this enterprise to develop at its own pace. What's your hurry? Slow down and remember that time itself has the power to nurture your situation.

On the other hand, there is also the opposite side of the coin: Being overly cautious and not taking any chances can undermine your progress. Before you proceed, be sure that you have found the middle of the road. If you attempt to move too fast or too slow, you'll sabotage your venture.

Do what needs to be done on a day-to-day basis, being mindful to pay special attention to details. Don't get too far ahead of yourself, but be willing to patiently "chop wood and carry water" so your project matures naturally.

Even though your situation may seem a bit tedious from time to time, be aware that even a small step forward will eventually bring you to the goal. Ask yourself: "How can I develop a moderate approach to this situation so that I'm not moving too fast or too slow? What small adjustments do I need to make to regain a state of balance?"

Everything will work out to your benefit, but only when the time is right. With a patient spirit, you'll know the time.

Eight of Disks
Inverted

When the Eight of Disks is selected in an inverted position, the time has come for you to sit down and take stock of the situation. You're being impatient, and therefore want to abandon this project or situation way too soon. What are you thinking?

Ask yourself: "Do I really want to give up on this, or am I just plain frustrated by it? Am I acting from a well-thought plan or just reacting haphazardly?"

At this moment, you seem to be hypercritical of both yourself and the circumstances in which you're involved. Because you have a critical eye for detail, you're able to act quickly when necessary. However, now you should be using your keen sense of judgment to get the job done rather than to pull it apart.

Take everything that has occurred into account, and then act; just waiting for things to happen will not accomplish anything. At this time in your life you cannot put the burden of success on anyone else's shoulders. You must be the one to put consistent effort into this venture; if you don't, it will not see the light of day.

Be mindful that each time you delay action you undermine the completion of this enterprise. If you want your endeavor to reach its full potential, do not procrastinate; do what needs to be done today and every day after that. And do it consistently.

Move ahead one step at a time so that you do not become overwhelmed. With hard work, foresight and discipline you will be successful.

Nine of Disks

(Gain)

When you draw the Nine of Disks, you're being told that if you want to see your dreams materialize, keep your priorities straight.

You've taken the time to plant the seeds and nurture this endeavor. Soon you'll be able to realize the full bounty of your harvest. But first, it's essential that you tie up loose ends. Unfinished business in the present situation, however insignificant, needs to be resolved or completed to insure a full harvest of your efforts.

You've made a lot of sacrifices to get to this point and before long you will be able to relax and put the whole affair on automatic pilot. But before you do, ask yourself: "Where are the loose ends and how do I go about tying them together?"

Because of your impending success, you can expect a blossoming in your relationships, career, and general well-being. Remember that when good fortune comes to you, you should take the time to appreciate the good feelings of abundance and prosperity that come with it. Nothing compares to the emotional fulfillment of a job well done. This sense of satisfaction will affect all areas of your life, and will be more complete if you've done the "housekeeping" called for in the current circumstances.

Your feelings of complete contentment will allow you to begin to envision new dreams and build on the blueprint you've established with care and attention.

Nine of Disks

Inverted

S omething or someone is blocking your progress. The Nine of Disks inverted forewarns that unless you're able to find a satisfactory solution to problems specific to the present circumstances, it will be difficult to complete the project or situation in question.

At this junction, the lack of real progress is slowly wearing you down and leaving your enterprise in disarray. Before you do anything else, consider reevaluating your priorities and long-term goals.

Ask yourself: "Am I tired of putting my life on hold for this project or situation? Is someone else contributing to my lack of progress? Do I really want to go on with this? If I want to continue, how do I get things moving again?"

Remember: You are under no obligation at this point to do anything that you don't want to. In fact, you'll find it extremely difficult to persevere if your heart isn't in it. If you don't want to commit yourself completely to this venture, you might as well cut your losses and get out while you can.

However, if you want this venture to succeed, make a strong commitment now to getting it completed.

You need to realize that it will take enormous amounts of hard work, sacrifice, and discipline on your part to achieve your goals . . . but there will be a substantial reward at the end of this journey if you choose to take it.

Ten of Disks
(Wealth)

The Ten of Disks alludes to the sense of wealth and prosperity that's possible for you to experience at this time in your life.

Bear in mind, however, that no other person or material thing can bring you feelings of abundance and prosperity except yourself. You're being given an opportunity to realize that it's never the money, love, or acclaim present in your life, but how you *feel* about these things that makes you a wealthy person. When you're willing to fully enjoy the abundance already present, more prosperity is likely to follow.

Ask yourself: "What can I do to create a feeling of abundance no matter what occurs in my outer world? To find a permanent place of prosperity within myself, am I willing to change the way I view personal wealth?"

In regard to your present situation, allow yourself a period of time to enjoy the feelings of material and emotional security that are based on what you've already accomplished.

If you share your good fortune willingly with others, your own riches will increase. It's as real as any law of physics: The more you give the more you receive.

Be forever mindful that success without fulfillment is nothing more than an empty show. If you concentrate on doing the things that have value, purpose, and meaning *to you*, you have the potential to fill your soul with joy and your pockets with money.

Ten of Disks

Inverted

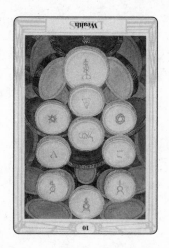

Scarcity seems to be the major issue in your life at the moment. Drawing the Ten of Disks inverted signifies that you're caught in a no-win situation: You desire prosperity, but you fight with it at the same time.

In reference to the current question, you need a major breakthrough in your thinking process if you're to proceed toward your goal.

To begin with, ask yourself: "Do I feel that my wants are valid? Do I feel that success and prosperity are possible in the situation at hand? If not, why?"

We all learned to stop wanting very early in life because wanting seemed to get us in trouble. But to manifest your goals, you must want them badly enough to motivate and empower yourself to achieve them.

Each of us lives within a world of abundance. It is only your illusion of being separate from this abundance that makes you feel impoverished. Prosperity requires a belief in the bounty of life itself. Choose to live in a state of affluence by acknowledging the creative force that flows through you.

You're not a victim of life, but a co-creator of your life and, in turn, of all life. Abundance will manifest itself in your situation in direct proportion to your willingness to believe in yourself and your ability to succeed.

Knight of Wands

Knight of Wands

The Knight of Wands encourages you to persevere no matter how intense the situation appears. Be forewarned, however, that if you give in to your fears, the unpredictable nature of your circumstances will take its toll on you. Keep in mind that change isn't just inevitable—it's one of the basic laws of nature.

It's normal to become apprehensive when you're in the vortex of rapid change. Accept your anxiety as part of the path to future expansion—you'll be able to survive the present circumstances and prosper and grow in the process.

For the time being, trust your impulse to take charge. Put all the energy you have into revolutionizing the situation. Personal power, at this time in your life, is the ability to take action.

Ask yourself: "Am I listening to my instincts? In which direction do they draw me? Am I willing to be honest and straightforward in acting on my instincts?" Remember to say what you think, even at the risk of sounding too blunt; let people know exactly what's going on in your mind.

Have faith in the bigger picture, do what your instincts tell you to do, and everything will work out well for you.

Knight of Wands

Inverted

The Knight of Wands inverted underscores the necessity for you to adapt to the changes that are occurring. Pertaining to the question at hand, the situation may not turn out exactly as you expected.

When the bigger picture unfolds differently than expected, you need to take time and reevaluate your position. Keep in mind that fate will favor those who remain adaptable, and will literally drag those who do not. Do you want to be dragged through these changes or would you prefer to go along with some semblance of dignity and decorum? The choice is always yours to make.

A major revolution in your circumstances is underway. Are you willing to accept these transformations as a vehicle of growth? In working through the obstacles in your path, you'll expand your self-confidence, increase self-esteem, and create the possibility to turn circumstances around to your best interests.

Proceed by accepting your situation as it is, and do what you can with what you have to work with. Learn to work with existing resources by adjusting to changes that occur. It will benefit you to cultivate a respect for the wisdom of life itself. On some level this is unfolding according to plan. Trust it.

Everything changes; some changes you'll understand, and some you won't. Nothing stays the same: Even these hard times will end, and good fortune will follow.

Queen of Wands

Queen of Wands

The Queen of Wands illustrates how important it is that you acquire a complete understanding of the situation in question. When you're able to do this, you'll know when to take the lead, and when to assume a subordinate role.

Because you're able to see the far-reaching potential of these circumstances, you may at times become impatient with any opposition. Your impatience will not help you; it will only work against you.

You'll find yourself having trouble with this project or situation until you accept the fact that everyone has something useful to contribute, if you will only give them a hearing.

To be successful, you don't always have to play "first fiddle." Be willing to share your vast knowledge and insight with others; then relax and give them the opportunity to do the same. Ask yourself: "What does this person have to contribute to my understanding of this situation?" With this extra knowledge, use your unique talent to see more possibilities for success within the endeavor.

You can also learn a lot by listening to your own inner voice. You'll be amazed by what your "antennae" pick-up and your instincts tell you.

Be advised that intuitively you know what to do; so go ahead and empower other people to assist you in doing it. There's nothing wrong with recruiting help to get the job done. If you're diplomatic, you may even get it done entirely on your own terms.

Queen of Wands

Inverted

When you draw the Queen of Wands inverted, you're being put on notice that unless you're less argumentative and a little more flexible, your project or situation is sure to fail.

You talk a good story, but underneath it all you're not that secure about your position. In reality, indecisiveness will keep you floundering, and making one unproductive decision after another.

When confronted with opposition, you need to relax and open your mind to new possibilities, rather than become defensive and even more rigid. If not, people who want to approach you and offer their help will become intimidated.

If you continue to be obstinate, it will be your undoing. Put your pride aside and begin to develop a new strategy that will allow you to listen to the expertise of others as well as to your own.

Times are changing and you must change with them. Ask yourself: "Am I willing to adapt my needs and desires to the changes that are occurring? How can I work within the situation rather than swim against the current? Am I willing to listen honestly and be receptive when others respond to changes?"

Set aside the "queen bee" attitude; adjust with a willing spirit to new situations that emerge and you will have a good chance for success in the near future.

Prince of Wands

Prince of Wands

A symbol of bravery, adventure, and freedom, the Prince of Wands states that you are eager to accept the tests and challenges inherent in the goals you have set for yourself.

In reference to the situation in question, you must trust yourself completely, speak up boldly, and move full speed ahead. Don't let anything sidetrack you. You know what needs to be done, so go ahead and do it! When you make a decision, stick to it and keep the momentum—if you second-guess yourself, you'll lose ground.

This enterprise is full of mystery, intrigue and new experiences. It will give you an opportunity to do what you've wanted to do . . . and that is to stop planning and start doing.

Watch for the unexpected. After all, where would the challenge and adventure be without it? Even though the circumstances surrounding your project or situation are unpredictable, take heart, for you possess the courage, charisma and stamina necessary to navigate the storm and see this venture through to a conclusion you'll cherish.

Ask yourself: "What new heights will the flames of creativity inspire me to? How can I best deal with the unexpected?" When challenges appear in your path, use them as opportunities to demonstrate just what you can accomplish. Go ahead—get out there and knock their socks off!

Prince of Wands

Inverted

S electing the Prince of Wands inverted represents your feelings of indecisiveness, confusion and stagnation.

At the moment, you seem to be having difficulty focusing on your goals. The fact that you listen to others more than yourself feeds your self-doubt and exacerbates the confusion surrounding your situation.

Take the time to re-energize your convictions by asking yourself: "What would I want to be doing right now if I could do anything I wanted to? What do I think is stopping me from doing what I want?" If you can determine what's stopping you, you're halfway to breaking through the barriers.

Are you sure about what you really want? Without focus and a clear destination, you'll continue to go in circles. Without passion for the situation you won't be sufficiently motivated. If you're not motivated, you won't have enough energy to complete what you start; it will be difficult for you to accomplish anything at this time.

This project or situation affords you the opportunity to become your own person by learning to focus on goals, and continuously motivate yourself. The ability to succeed is present now—go ahead and prove to yourself and to the world just how capable you are!

Princess of Wands

Princess of Wands

Drawing the Princess of Wands reminds you that, in this situation, there's no such thing as a sure thing. There's going to be risk in anything you attempt. Still, the time has come to move forward with this project or situation, despite the concerns you have.

Because this venture is an endeavor of love, you'll be empowered to act with the enthusiasm, inspiration and vitality needed to achieve you goals. Because you will be asked to put in a lot of long hours and hard work, the reality that you care as much as you do will aid in your quest for success.

In this specific situation, it doesn't hurt to be a bit pushy. If things don't go your way, don't hesitate to exert a little pressure. You'll be rewarded for the way you take control of the circumstances. In fact, people will envy your courage as much as your ability to grab the ball and run with it.

Ask yourself: "Am I willing to be bold and daring in my approach to this situation? Am I willing to be totally up front in my actions and communication?"

Of course it's necessary to go through the proper channels, but at the same time don't be afraid to question authority. Your circumstances are unique and call for innovative ideas and inspirations. Trust your insights, because at the moment they're right on.

Princess of Wands

Inverted

When you receive the Princess of Wands inverted, it's critical to the success of this endeavor that you're willing to work much harder than you have in the past.

At the moment, you avoid doing what you know you need to do. Why? This type of behavior can only demoralize you and leave you feeling depressed and discouraged. Have you been wondering what happened to the enthusiasm and vitality you once had?

Your present state of mind is not only unproductive, but is also sabotaging any further progress you may try to make. The time has come for you to abandon the false comfort of retreat and procrastination, and start being more assertive.

When you started thinking more about risks than reaching your heart's desire, the project or situation began to unravel. Ask yourself: "What am I so afraid of? Why not take the tiger by the tail, and get on with the adventure?"

If you want a guarantee of certainty in this life, you're out of luck. There's no such thing. There will always be dark alleys to walk down. Maybe it's time for you to learn to walk in the dark—to move forward in spite of your doubts and fears.

If this project or situation is as important to you as you say it is, redirect your energy from avoiding what needs to be done, to doing what needs to be done.

Knight of Cups

Knight of Cups

D rawing the Knight of Cups indicates the necessity to give voice to your innermost feelings. We all have emotional needs that must be met if we're to feel successful in life. You must be emotionally assertive to achieve the results you desire; playing the role of a wallflower now will not help you to succeed.

At this point in your situation, be aware of both your positive and negative emotions. If you don't communicate your negative feelings, at least by acknowledging them to yourself, they are sure to undermine your venture. Remember that beneath anger always lie hurt and disappointment.

You can uncover positive emotions by being more conscious when negativity tries to take over. Ask yourself, "Do I accept the responsibility of appropriately expressing the total range of my emotions? Am I openly demonstrative when I can rightly be so?" If you're willing to be explicit and forthright in conveying feelings, you'll have the ability to present your ideas, fantasies, and dreams in ways that creatively influence the success of the project or situation.

Your enthusiasm for this venture will infuse it with spontaneous expression; therefore, let your emotions guide you. Listen to your intuition; trust your feelings about the right things to say and do, and success will be yours.

Knight of Cups

Inverted

When the Knight of Cups appears inverted, he's implying that you're having difficulties expressing your feelings about the situation in question. Why?

If you insist on keeping your feelings to yourself, you risk becoming emotionally frustrated and then will no longer know what you feel.

You may think that you're protecting yourself, but the truth of the matter is that you're suppressing the very energy you need to succeed.

In regard to this situation, don't get involved any further until you acknowledge your real feelings to those concerned; in fact, you won't see the project or situation in its true light until you're able to do this. Stop pretending you don't feel the way you do. The armor of false pride that you've been wearing will only prevent you from getting what you want. Whatever you may be feeling, this is the time to express it.

Ask yourself: "What emotional risks do I need to take to realize the full potential of my circumstances?" Let yourself be vulnerable in expressing your needs and desires. Be willing to display your feelings like a badge of honor—be proud of them! That way, when you do succeed, it will be a success based on what's truly important to you.

Queen of Cups

Queen of Cups

When the Queen of Cups appears, she states that your success depends on maintaining warm relationships with others. When you exercise understanding and kindness, you'll attract people who (a) understand you and (b) are willing to help your dreams become reality. For that reason, be sure that you take into account everyone involved before you proceed.

The forces affecting the situation in question may be elusive and fluid, so don't rely on outside circumstances to guide you. To know how to proceed, you must be receptive to the information your unconscious mind is seeking to communicate to you.

Ask yourself: "Hidden beneath my relationship to the world around me, what do my inner dreams and fantasies tell me?" The message may be veiled and subtle, but nevertheless it's there.

In reference to these particular circumstances, your intuition is crucial to your success. Allow your feelings to surface so that they may guide you in making correct choices for yourself. Therefore, listen with a quiet mind and an open heart. With this receptivity, look for signals that tell you when to move and when to stay still . . . and you'll see the right way to proceed.

When you're acting with intuitive wisdom, you can expect things to work out for you with little or no effort on your part.

Queen of Cups

Inverted

The Queen of Cups inverted alludes to the fact that this is not a time to chase rainbows, but a time for practical, no nonsense behavior. You need to better understand your circumstances before you proceed; if not, the endeavor will culminate in less than desirable results.

For some reason, this particular situation seems to lack substance. At the moment your endeavor is a more accurate reflection of your conflicted inner state than of the outside world. Therefore, take the time to look within yourself and see if you're sabotaging your own progress.

Many people are trying to help you, but because you're frustrated with yourself, you've become overly sensitive and are distorting much of what is being said to you. Why are you personalizing this situation? It's not *all* about you. However, what goes on inside of your mind *is* about you.

Before you proceed, ask yourself some pertinent questions: "Do I know what I need from this situation? What must I do to bring about order and clarity?" When you know more about yourself, you'll be able to see through the veil of illusion that has draped itself over this project or situation. Then and only then will you be able to progress toward your goals.

Prince of Cups

Prince of Cups

The Prince of Cups asks that you listen to your passions and then let those feelings guide you. With regard to your present circumstances, even though your emotions run deep, you don't always choose to express them. Are you afraid of having strong feelings about this endeavor?

Powerful feelings, when tempered with self-discipline, are great assets in achieving your goals. Wanting, wishing, and desiring are necessary ingredients of creative activity. Without them nothing would ever happen. It's desire that animates your thoughts and directs your intentions so that you can manifest what you need. Desire will help you sort through the many ideas and thoughts that pass through your mind; it empowers you to instantly discern what will help and what will hinder your endeavor.

With respect to the situation in question, it's vital that you acknowledge your overwhelming passion to succeed. How could you best do that? Consider developing a state of equilibrium that will let your feelings guide you but at the same time tempers them with cool-headedness and self-discipline.

If you permit your feelings to supply the fuel of ambition while you use your head to keep your eyes on the road, you can go anywhere and succeed.

Prince of Cups

Inverted

Selecting the Prince of Cups inverted suggests that you've been on an emotional roller coaster, and that you need to calm down before acting.

Because you've been somewhat self-absorbed, you haven't always seen what's going on around you. Therefore, you need to realize that the surface appearances of your circumstances are unreliable and shouldn't be trusted at this moment.

Even though you have very strong feelings about this situation, you don't always express them as easily as you would like too. Consequently, when you finally do assert yourself your communication can be too intense.

It's time to examine your underlying feelings about the current situation to determine what you need to do next. Sometimes we're more attached to the fantasy than we are to the actuality of the circumstances. Begin by being more objective about what's happening. Are your expectations realistic? What seemed like a good idea when you were daydreaming may not be a good idea now.

Because you have an overwhelming desire to succeed, you seem to be living each day as though it were your last. Be careful not to spread yourself too thin. Ask yourself: "Have I been doing a little too much running around lately? Do I want to do this, or am I just trying to prove I can?" Remember that this card is calling you to put your heart into it!

Princess of Cups

Princess of Cups

Selecting the Princess of Cups indicates that to achieve your goals, you must be willing to remain in the background and work from behind the scenes. Keep in mind that when all is said and done, you may receive very little appreciation or recognition for your accomplishments.

The situation at hand will demand considerable self-sacrifice and hard work. Even so, if you choose to move forward with this project, it will be a perfect opportunity to use the many talents and resources you've developed.

At this time in your life, it would be to your advantage to learn how to support others without diminishing yourself. One way to do this is to give with an open hand. In the long run, anything not given willingly is a burden to everyone involved.

Before you proceed any further, decide whether you are content being the unrecognized power behind the throne. Ask yourself: "Can I do without being center stage? Am I willing to commit to this project or situation even though I may not receive adequate recognition and appreciation?"

Remember that even though you may not be given the credit due to you, it's your commitment, your idealism and your perseverance that will bring good fortune to the situation at hand. Without you, this endeavor may not have the resources to succeed.

Princess of Cups

Inverted

When the Princess of Cups is chosen in an inverted position it indicates that you're no longer content working behind the scenes.

At this particular time in your life, you want the full appreciation and recognition you deserve. However, you're still apprehensive about taking a chance on standing up, asking for what you need, and claiming your accomplishment. Being one's self without pretense is always a risk. When you're out there on your own, there really is nowhere to hide.

Until now, you've been willing to do more for others than for yourself. Therefore, you need to ask yourself: "Do I tend to do more for others because I want to, or is it because I feel vulnerable being out there on my own? In this situation, am I willing to take a chance on stepping forward to achieve my goals? Do I have the courage to act even though I'm afraid?"

If you step up to the plate with discipline and determination, you will find the success you have been seeking. You know that when you want something badly enough, you're an immovable force; do you want this badly enough? If the answer is yes, then act with the courage of your convictions.

Knight of Swords

Knight of Swords

The Knight of Swords suggests that you spend some time gathering new information. You need to know a lot more about your project or situation before you proceed.

It will take less effort to accomplish the goals you set for yourself if you keep an open mind. It's a lot easier to categorize information and see your options when your mind isn't so busy with conjecture and guesswork.

Because you're able to analyze information quickly, you must make an effort to be patient with others who think more slowly. It's possible to hurt someone with your words as easily as with your actions; therefore, think before you speak to avoid unintentionally offending or intimidating people.

Ask yourself: "Have I done the research this project calls for? Have I looked at the situation from every angle? Am I receptive to new information no matter how it's presented to me?"

We process information through our minds and emotions as well as our physical bodies. At this particular moment, so much is going on in your head that you're often deaf to important outside information. For that reason, you need to gain an inner quiet, and listen more so that you don't miss pertinent details.

If you suspend judgment until you've gathered enough data and looked at all the facts, you'll know exactly what to do when the time comes to proceed.

Knight of Swords
Inverted

Selecting the Knight of Swords inverted argues that until you're sure of what you want, it will be difficult for you to proceed. Take the time to stop and evaluate the ultimate purpose of your endeavor so that you don't risk "chasing your tail" indefinitely.

Indecision creates conflict; as internal conflict increases, it becomes harder for you to act. When you experience the frustration of internal confusion, it's all too easy to indiscriminately strike out at someone who is trying to help you. To have your opinions about this situation questioned can be very threatening. If you're insecure about what you're doing, it will be difficult for you to even see—let alone accept—another person's point of view.

With that in mind, it is mandatory that you put yourself on track before you continue. To do that, you need a lot more information than you have at the moment. Ask yourself: "How can I acquire the information I need? Can I stop talking long enough to hear the sound advice I'm being offered?"

Keep an open mind so that you can accommodate new information.

At this time in your life, if you are willing to use the information others give you to make new choices, you'll begin to see your indecision end, and the progress you long for resume.

Queen of Swords

Queen of Swords

W hen you select the Queen of Swords, you're being asked to put your feelings aside for the time being and think with your head, not your heart.

Take a more objective view of your circumstances. The last thing you want is to let your emotional attachment to this enterprise, and the people involved in it, color your judgment. No matter how difficult it may be, you must examine any ties with the past that may be negatively influencing your current venture.

This project or situation demands astute perception, independent thinking and a strong commitment to see through your own defenses. Take time now to look behind the façade of this situation or project, to see what's really going on. If you can set your feelings aside, your discerning mind will go to work for you.

Ask yourself: "How can I use my intellect to cut this situation down to size? Am I thinking independently? Am I willing to respect my own point of view and give it as much validity as I do anyone else's?"

Because of your compassion and understanding, people have always looked up to you and sought your advice. This is a perfect time to "cut to the chase" by thinking for yourself, trusting your own ideas and seeking your own counsel.

Queen of Swords

Inverted

The Queen of Swords appears in an inverted position to warn you that the time has come for you to set aside anger and resentment that has collected from previous experiences. You need to approach the situation in question with kindness and consideration.

When you hold on to the past, you become locked in a time warp where nothing ever changes; everyone else moves on and you're left alone with your pain. Because you feel so strongly about the situation, you're afraid to open your heart to the dreams and desires hidden deep within you.

To gain a clear picture of your circumstances, seek a state of objectivity and detachment. Before things get out of hand, ask yourself: "Does my defensiveness protect me or does it cause me to feel lonely and resentful? How can I be more objective about my situation?"

What happened in the past is no longer occurring, unless you personally work overtime to keep these negative thoughts and images alive. Wise up! Can't you see that you're hurting no one but yourself? Being able to transcend your anger and resentment would make it a lot easier for you, at this time, to achieve your goals.

A little compassion and some understanding for yourself, as well as for others, will help you to realize your dreams. To succeed, drop your defensiveness and the situation will present itself more clearly.

Prince of Swords

Prince of Swords

D rawing the Prince of Swords indicates just how determined you are to succeed. Be forewarned, however, that an abundance of ideas may block your path before you ultimately reach your final goal.

When a person has as many good ideas as you do, it can be difficult to decide which ones to pursue. Realize that you need to choose one specific idea and focus all of your attention on it. It's difficult to go in four directions at the same time and get anywhere— admit it, you've already tried!

Ask yourself: "Of all these appealing ideas, which one do I really want to pursue? Am I willing to put other ideas or projects on hold while I concentrate on this particular one?"

Keep in mind that someone who enjoys mental gymnastics as much as you do needs to be careful not to get lost in the planning stage of a project. Decide what you want to do and then do it. Without a concrete agenda, you can easily become bored and do nothing—or complicate matters by generating chaos so you can flex your mental muscles and alleviate your boredom.

Decide what you want to do, focus your energy in that direction, and you'll be able to move down a path toward success.

Prince of Swords

Inverted

Misconceptions have clouded your thinking and confused the issue. When you select the Prince of Swords inverted, you're being asked not only to broaden your perspective, but also to deepen your understanding of the situation.

You've assumed too much and now you're paying the consequences. Inflexibility has allowed you to take yourself and your opinions too seriously. You need to loosen up. Sometimes you give the impression that you're walking around with a chip on your shoulder just hoping that someone will try to knock it off.

The task at hand is to be reasonable—even humble—and use your energy in constructive ways rather than in empty confrontation. Ask yourself: "Why do I react so intensely when my opinions are questioned? Am I so insecure that I need to prove I know it all? Am I as sure of myself as I thought, or underneath it all do I question my own beliefs?"

You'll be more inclined to get what you want if you pursue this situation with tact. Don't forget how clever, quick-witted, and resourceful you are. Use your talents to accomplish your goals instead of letting these very same talents make you arrogant.

Stop and think before you jump to conclusions. Better yet, assume you don't know anything about the situation and proceed from there.

Princess of Swords

Princess of Swords

Choosing the Princess of Swords signifies that the time has come to stop talking about your ideas and to start acting on them.

You can trust your capacity to handle practical problems in a direct, outspoken way if you can continue to act spontaneously and don't over-analyze your situation.

In reference to the circumstances at hand, it's your very naiveté that gives you the freedom to venture into uncharted waters. It's to your benefit now that you are unaware of the situation's full significance, because you're less likely to panic and give up.

Because you're taking on a complex task, realize that periodically the vagaries of the process may get the best of you. Be forewarned: When you try to put your ideas into physical form, there's bound to be some discrepancy between what you imagine and what is created in reality. You can agonize indefinitely over the divergence between your vision and the way it materializes—or you can expect that this will frustrate you at times, and move ahead in spite of it.

To achieve the results you desire, you must behave like a true warrior. It takes a great amount of courage to put yourself on the line by doing what others only dare to dream of.

To achieve your goals, keep in mind that you must be bold in your approach, fearless in your actions, and daring in your quest to succeed.

Princess of Swords
Inverted

Selecting the Princess of Swords inverted directs your attention to the fact that you can't win if you don't try. If you want recognition for your ideas, you're going to have to take a chance on yourself. Sometimes a fear of failure can stand in the way of our trying something new.

Regarding the situation in question, you seem to be reacting to your circumstances by becoming cynical and then allowing this attitude to justify your inertia. A pessimistic attitude will only distort your thinking and subsequently the results of your actions. It is important that you function from a more relaxed and adventurous frame of mind.

Ask yourself: "Am I trying to cover up my insecurities by burying them under a layer of cynicism? Underneath it all, am I afraid to put my dreams on the line? Do I realize that when I don't at least try I end up feeling angry at myself?"

No matter what else you do, if you want to achieve your goals, you must take an active role in doing so. You must even risk exposing yourself to criticism in order to realize your dreams.

You'll be able to handle your practical affairs easily if you're willing to adopt a different attitude. Why not speak out, say what is on your mind and get it over with? This isn't a good time to be reticent. It's a time to speak from your heart. Are you willing to give it a try?

Knight of Disks

Knight of Disks

The Knight of Disks draws your attention to the fact that a time of harvest is at hand—you'll soon be able to relax and reap the profits of your labor.

In the meantime, however, realize that you must continue to maintain a practical approach to the situation. The present circumstances ask that you behave in a conventional manner and use good, old-fashioned common sense.

It's not enough for you to have great ideas; you also need to have a well-structured plan in place to implement them. Ask yourself: "How do I go about creating a solid foundation for this endeavor so that the harvest will be assured?"

Be aware that this is not a good time for innovative maneuvers; you're being advised to follow a well-worn path rather than construct a new road. Pay attention to details. If you see something out of place, stop and fix it before you go on. When in doubt, be sure to keep things simple.

Ask yourself: "How can I get the job done with an economy of effort?" There's no use running around unnecessarily when all you need to do is relax and wait for the right time to act. When it is the right time you will see that everything falls into place.

Knight of Disks

Inverted

Drawing the Knight of Disks inverted tells you that all the worry in the world is not going to alleviate the problem, but using a practical approach will.

Lately, you've been spreading yourself too thin. If you want the situation to change, consider digging in and focusing all your effort in one direction. It's time you came down to earth and planted your feet firmly on the ground to achieve this focus. To acquire a more structured approach, begin by developing the roots that will sustain you throughout this project or situation.

Ask yourself: "Am I willing to get back to basics before going forward with this effort? How do I go about building a firm foundation beneath this endeavor?"

You're being advised to retrench, reconsider and take things one step at a time. Get a feel for the next part of the process before you rush into it. Be cautious. Pay attention to details that need resolving. If you ignore them, they will come back to haunt you.

Avoid untested waters; go with a proven approach—this is not a time to be bold and daring. You'll do your best when you slow down and take things as they come.

Bear in mind that no matter how bad things look at the moment, your sober regard and perseverance will pay off. Acting conservatively, practically and conscientiously will bring success.

Queen of Disks

Queen of Disks

Selecting the Queen of Disks implies that you've been experiencing a dry spell lately; but take heart—you're about to arrive at a fertile green oasis.

In reference to the present circumstances, this is a time to be calm, cool and collected. You're not going to have to work as hard as you've been working. Even though you possess a strong desire to contribute your diverse talents to this enterprise, very little effort on your part will be needed to realize success.

You've completed all the assigned homework. All that's needed now is to allow this endeavor to evolve in its own way, at its own pace. Nurture it with your keen understanding, emotional sensitivity and practical ideas, and it will bloom to its full potential.

Remember not to rely solely on your intellect, but to continue to follow your instincts, your intuition and your imagination. When you fully accept that this situation is one of unlimited possibilities, both you and the situation will prosper.

Ask yourself: "How can I best nurture this endeavor without being too actively involved? How can I remain passive, yet willing to help when I'm needed?"

It's important that you act only when you can influence the circumstances. It will help if you consider the following: Don't stand if you can sit, and don't sit if you can lie down!

Queen of Disks

Inverted

The Queen of Disks inverted alludes to the fact that you started your project or situation with enthusiasm, but when the results didn't materialize as quickly as you wanted, you gave up hope and threatened to quit.

By quitting too soon, you'll be unable to relish the results of your labors. It's as though you planted a tree and now plan to cut it down before it has a chance to bear fruit.

Regarding the present circumstances, don't make things more difficult than they need to be. This doesn't have to be an uphill climb! If you stopped long enough to take a deep breath, you would realize that the hills are behind you and you're now on level ground.

Ask yourself: "Am I so used to struggling with this situation that I'm unaware things have changed, that I'm now surrounded by peace and prosperity?"

Sometimes we work so hard that we begin to think life is only about struggle and hardship; remember that there is also abundant joy and pleasure to be had. Therefore, before you decide to quit consider taking it easy for a while and letting the dust settle.

You may be looking out at a barren desert now, but with a little patience and perseverance, this desert landscape transforms into a lush green environment for you and your situation.

Prince of Disks

The Prince of Disks advises that you need to be more objective regarding the circumstances in question. Leave your emotions out of it so that you can be cool-headed and think clearly.

Before rushing into action, take the time to investigate the situation; gather all the information you can and make sure that you have the facts straight.

This specific endeavor will benefit from a conservative approach. Don't play the odds. It is mandatory that you operate from a well-thought-out, well-structured plan with clear-cut goals. At this particular time, a prudent approach may seem unchallenging; however, ask yourself: "Do I want a challenge or do I want success?"

You know that when it comes to the art of making a deal you're an excellent negotiator. When you put your energy into practical matters, time, patience and skill move you through the obstacles in your path. You're bright enough to let people think you've made concessions, but when the dust clears you always seem to get what you want. Are you ready to do a little negotiating to turn this project or situation around for yourself?

If you want to bring new visions and new ideas into your present enterprise, be prepared to do it through conventional avenues.

Prince of Disks

Inverted

The Prince of Disks inverted acknowledges your concern over the lack of progress with this particular project or situation. When you draw this card, don't expect quick results. This venture will take some time to unfold and materialize.

At the moment, you seem to be at loose ends, fluctuating from manic activity to complete lethargy. You're becoming more emotional and more physically exhausted as time goes by. This constant internal struggle will continue to deplete your vitality. Take an objective stance and determine what's really going on with you.

Ask yourself: "What am I trying to prove? What do I realistically expect to gain? Am I willing to allow the situation to develop naturally?" In the meantime, learn everything you can about your situation and you'll gain a renewed sense of purpose tempered with objectivity and patience.

Of the many ways to accomplish your goals, with this particular situation you'll advance more surely through tried-and-true methods. They will help you to simplify your life and conserve precious time and energy. Be flexible not only with this enterprise, but with yourself as well.

The situation will evolve slowly at its own pace; meanwhile, be cool-headed and patient.

Princess of Disks

Princess of Disks

The Princess of Disks represents the courage and daring it takes to live your dreams, take a chance on yourself and claim your place in the world. You've been through hard times, but times are changing. Your decision to openly pursue and nurture this situation will soon pay off.

Your ideas in regard to this endeavor are imaginative, but need to be practical as well. At this time, don't allow your native energy to be dampened by the dull, routine work that you're being asked to do. Things will be exciting soon enough.

It's important that you take your time and not hurry. Be sure to dot all the i's and cross all the t's. If you start off slowly and methodically, you'll be able to develop a solid foundation for this project or situation.

Your experiences have given you the basis of your wisdom and knowledge. How can you bring these experiences to a new level of understanding that will assist you in your present circumstances?

Ask yourself: "What do I need for my imaginative ideas to take practical form? What do I need to get organized? How can I best draw on my past experiences?"

Stand tall, because the world is looking at you, and is unquestionably impressed by what it sees. In the meantime, pay attention to details, be patient and hang in there. This may take a little doing, but rest assured that with your talents and perseverance, you will succeed.

Princess of Disks

Inverted

D rawing the Princess of Disks inverted reveals that your present circumstances have left you emotionally drained and lethargic. It seems as though all the vitality and fun has gone out of your life. What happened?

Regarding this specific project or situation, it seems as though you're afraid to take a chance . . . afraid to take the hopes and dreams you have for this endeavor into the marketplace. Unacknowledged fears can sap energy and enthusiasm.

Ask yourself: "Why am I so tired lately? Have I become so depressed and discouraged that I don't see the new possibilities open to me?"

A change of scenery will jumpstart the shift in attitude you need to get yourself going again. Relax, sleep, meditate, go on a retreat—do whatever you need to restore your energy and well-being. Without physical vitality, it will be difficult to meet the demands of getting your show on the road.

You've spent a lot of time dreaming about this venture—it's about time you started living those dreams! Decide what you want to do, and then get out there and do it!

It's not easy to take a chance on yourself. However, if you don't take a chance on yourself, how will you ever know whether you could have succeeded?

Section II

SYMBOLS
of the
THOTH TAROT

Symbols of the Thoth Tarot

The Symbolic Language of the Tarot

This section explains the symbols you see on each of the 78 cards. These powerful images allow the cards to speak directly to your intuition. As you broaden your vocabulary of symbols, you'll be able to form a story about the images and personalize the information you receive. In this way, you not only grasp the arcane meaning of the card but are able to interact with its message. By relating the symbols to your own knowledge and wisdom, you create a living image that changes as you change. This image plays a dynamic role in your own growth by being a catalyst for and reflection of your thoughts, feelings and actions. The tarot, through symbols, visually depicts the workings of each stage of your personal transformation.

The symbols of Aleister Crowley's Thoth Tarot are universal and rooted in his expansive knowledge of the occult arts. The Thoth Tarot encompasses visual representations from the Qabalah, astrology, numerology, Eastern and Western mythology, alchemy, yoga, and Magick. Crowley wrote *The Book of Thoth* to explain these symbols, but it's a difficult read. Crowley's vast understanding of metaphysical systems is equaled by few readers—every other sentence seems to send you back to the research library. Yet, if you study *The Book of Thoth*, you'll eventually understand more of it and come to appreciate its underlying structure. Eventually is the key word, because it can take the commitment of a lifetime. Until then, I hope that this section will help you to begin the journey.

The best way to use this section is to read it through as an overview, and then go back and work with each card, taking the time to relate the symbols to your own life. Contemplating the image and the message of the symbols, ask yourself: How has this message expressed itself in my life? For example, reflect on the Death card and ask: How easily do I adapt to change? Am I willing to let go and move on? Or the Princess of Cups: Can I love without condition? Can I work in the background? Take the time to make these cards your own.

The Thoth Tarot is a storehouse of wisdom just waiting for you to uncover its jewels. There are many facets to it that just as soon as you think you have captured its brilliance, there appears another level for you to explore.

Blessings on your journey; may you find the treasure you seek.

Symbols of the Major Arcana

Crowley viewed the 22 Major Arcana cards as the "Atu" or "Keys" of the Egyptian God Tahuti (Thoth)—each card an initiation into a different phase of our personal as well as collective awakening. As we move through each level of initiation, we become more aware of the multiple dimensions of our existence. Each Key or Trump of the Major Arcana is part of a visual description of how life manifests here on earth.

As you look at the Major Arcana cards, you'll see that they have an astrological sun sign, planetary or elemental symbol on the lower right of the card, as well as a letter of the Hebrew alphabet on the lower left. Crowley used these symbols on the Thoth Tarot to enrich the cards and help us to achieve a deeper understanding of the tarot.

Along with others before him, Crowley saw a direct connection between the 22 Major Arcana Trumps and the 22 letters of the Hebrew alphabet and assigned a letter to each card. The 22 Major Arcana cards are also allotted a particular path between the Sephiroth (spheres of consciousness) on the Qabahla's Tree of Life. Each path is attributed to a specific Zodiac sign, Planet or Element. In this section I've listed the symbols of each card and their interpretations giving special mention to the letter of the Hebrew alphabet, Astrological sign or Planet as well as the card's elemental significance. Further study of the Qabahla, alchemy and astrology will benefit your exploration of the Thoth Tarot, therefore I've included in the Appendix a basic explanation of these subjects as they pertain to the Thoth Tarot. If you desire more information, the Bibliography includes representative books that will assist you in delving into astrology and alchemy as well as the mysteries of the Qabahla.

The Major Arcana Trumps also represent the universal human characteristics that we all share. They are the archetypes of human behavior and together portray the three major phases of our life. The Fool card as number 0 embodies the world of No-thing and therefore the potential of all things. The Fool Trump represents the spark and subsequent journey of *creative intent*. If you take The Fool card out of the equation (remember he stands alone and has all of the other cards within him), the 21 cards that are left can be divided into three levels of seven cards each.

Cards 1-7 (The Magus through The Chariot) deal with *finding a personal identity* in the outer world. The Magus becomes the messenger of creative intent (spirit) while The Priestess gives meaning (soul) to his message. Both spirit and soul exist within our consciousness as we begin our journey toward self awareness. The Empress gives direction to our journey. The Emperor gives it form and The Hierophant gives it structure. In The Lovers card, the Masculine and Feminine energy join forces within our psyche and represent the birth of our ego. It is in The Chariot that we move into the outer world a separate entity with a personality of our own.

Cards 8-15 (Adjustment through The Devil) have to do with *withdrawing into ourselves* and *connecting deeply with our inner world*. In the Adjustment card, we develop the ability to self regulate, in The Hermit we adopt a state of introspection, and in Fortune subsequently break through into our inner world. We gather the strength within ourselves in Lust, learn the importance of surrender in The Hanged Man and the necessity for change in the Death card. The Art card asks that we synthesize all aspects of ourselves, and acknowledge even our deepest shadow in The Devil.

Cards 16-21 (The Tower through The Universe) relate to the *re-integration* of our spiritual essence, which culminates in *our collective unity with all that exists*. When our ego gets too full of itself, The Tower card tosses us back to earth and, as we hit the ground, releases the insights we have gained. In The Star card we have access to the insights we acquired in The Tower card and find ways to share this understanding with others. In The Moon, we come face to face with our illusions and delusions. The Sun brings the light of day and new beginnings, The Aeon ushers in judgment day and with it a second chance to demonstrate what we have learned— *that the essence of human experience lies within our power of choice.* With The Universe card comes our final journey home—unity with all things (The Fool)—and recognition of the true self.

Take time to learn the symbols on each card because they are the language used to communicate the card's meaning. Keep in mind that the card's message is not static—it will speak to you at the level of your awareness; as you change, your relationship with the card changes. Use the interpretations provided as a guideline—a place from which to develop personal rapport with the image on the card.

Spend time with each of the Major Arcana cards and ask yourself questions about the card. For example: What is the general atmosphere of this particular card? What does the body language of the main character tell you? What emotional response is the card illustrating to you? What emotional reaction do you have to the card? Weave your own narrative regarding the action portrayed on the card. Considering that all 22 cards are in play at any given moment in your life, realize that these cards are all about you. Keep in mind that your level of awareness determines how you relate to each card, how you receive its message, and the action you take.

• 0 •
The Fool

The Fool is ruled by Uranus and is given the number 0. Contained within the zero is infinite potential. The Fool is the beginning and the end and everything in between. We are The Fool moving through the different stages of our life here on earth. We come, we create and we return to wherever we came from. The Fool is the force of springtime energy, the hope and renewal of the spirit. He floats with his feet off the ground, marches to his own drummer, dances through life on a new adventure and lives in a world we can only aspire to. With a devilish smile, he enjoys life to the fullest, and sees the funny side of the human predicament.

The card has many symbols of transformation and metamorphosis. You think you have him figured out—then he's off in another direction, on another adventure. He's living in his own world of joy and bliss; even though the Tiger is chewing on his leg he doesn't give it power over him. In fact he seems to be oblivious to it. He understands that there is more to life than we even begin to imagine. He lives an eternal life in the world of potential. He belongs everywhere and nowhere.

CARD SYMBOLS	INTERPRETATIONS
Number 0	formless, potential
Element	Aethyr
Astrology: Universe	universal
Hebrew letter	א *Aleph* (ox)
Green man	springtime energy, renewal
Horns	evolving awareness
Facial expression	divine madness, wonder of it all
Spiral wings	spiral energy of creation
Butterfly	metamorphosis
Fire in hand	purification
Crystal in hand	visionary
Dove	unconditional love
Boots/golden path	walk the path to enlightenment
Tiger	sharp instincts, fearlessness
Crocodile	ultimate creativity
Four circles	creativity and regeneration on all levels
Rainbow	integration
Caduceus	healing energy
Arrow	straight forward
Sack full of coins	material abundance
Grapes	ecstasy
Sun disk	power of creativity, vital life force
Breast/muscles	androgynous
Three flowers	different stages of growth, culminating in the union of body, mind and soul
Colors	gold: malleability, transformation, reward; aqua: intuition; blue: mental wisdom; orange: life force; violet: spirit; white: clarity

The Magus

· I ·
The Magus

The Magus is ruled by Mercury and symbolizes the archetypal magician found within each of us. He represents the will to create and is influenced by Mercury which governs our ability to transmute energy. He understands that Space and Time are not absolute and that all things are relative. Matter is not solid and space is not empty. The Magus is aware of the "illusion" we live within—the Maya of the physical plane. He is able to perform the sleight of hand necessary to keep our personal as well as collective illusions intact. He is able to manipulate his mind, emotions, intent and physical resources to create the world he chooses to live in.

Every breath we take, every action we initiate is magic. Magic begins as divine imagination and is culminated in the world of form. The Magus uses "tools of the trade" (his will, intuition, intellect and physical resources) to create change. He orchestrates resources available and is conscious of the life he is creating for himself. He can think on his feet and communicate his thoughts clearly and effectively. He is willing to acknowledge his natural talents and ability, is fascinated with the creation process, and enjoys the full scope of his imagination.

CARD SYMBOLS	INTERPRETATIONS
Number 1	initiate, primal masculine principle
Astrology: Mercury	swiftness of communication, quick wit and razor-sharp intellect
Element	Air
Hebrew letter	ב *Beth* (house)
Staff of Horus	seer, psychic perception, ESP
Monkey	instinct, illusionist, adroit
Sword	intellect, mental differentiation, analysis
Cup	emotions, feelings, intuition
Wand	intent, inspiration, creativity, insight
Coin	worldly affairs, materialization
Smiling face	humor and optimism
Lines in background	primal energy source (æther)
Fan above his head	ever-expanding awareness
Snake/Caduceus	life and death, heals oneself
Phoenix wand	perfection through regeneration
Scroll	written word
Arrow	communication is to the point
Winged egg, orphic egg	ability to transmute energy
Genii lamp	recognizes the genius of others
Lion's paw	creative energy, strength
Position of hands	willing to listen as well as to speak
Nakedness	defenses lowered, totally open
Colors	blue: mental energy; gold: flexibility, malleability; purple: spirit, divinity

• II •
The Priestess

The Priestess is ruled by the Moon and represents all that is passive and receptive in human nature. She embodies the primal feminine principle. Veiled as if she is guarding some hidden mystery, she sits between two pillars—the pillar of Mercy and the pillar of Judgment. She is our connection to the unconscious mind. If we want to partake of her knowledge, we must sit quietly and wait patiently. She will speak only when we have released our illusion of control.

To begin the process of creation, we need both The Magus and The Priestess. The Priestess influences our intuition, imagination, fantasies and dreams. She provides the raw material The Magus needs to work his magic. She has no agenda for the wisdom she has access to. The secrets of the feminine remain hidden from the logical aspect of our mind, but without her our life would be void of meaning. She dreams the dream that creates the vision for The Magus. The Priestess is sensitive to her surroundings and has direct knowledge of what is going beneath the surface of our lives. Through The Priestess, we come to understand the power and strength of passivity.

CARD SYMBOLS	INTERPRETATIONS
Number 2	duality, primal feminine principle
Element	Water
Astrology: Moon	receptive, passive, reflective nature
Hebrew letter	ג *Gimel* (camel)
Two pillars	she sits between the pillars of Mercy and Judgment
Luminous veils	keeps the feminine mysteries hidden
Crystals	clarity of her perception on all four levels: will, understanding, mind and physicality
Crown	the world of vision and intuition that she has access to
Bow and arrow	her information is direct from the source (she is the truth behind the illusion)
Sea goggles	she comes from the depths of the oceans (feminine mysteries)
Camel	self sufficient, able to cross the abyss between the archetypal world and the formative world
Fruit/seedpods	beginning of life, primal "seed" vision
Nakedness/bare chest	deep sensitivity
Colors	white: purity, clarity; aqua blue: softness, feminine nature, peace; yellow/purple: spirit; green: creativity; pink: unconditional love

· III ·
The Empress

The Empress represents the fulfillment of the tension between The Magus and The Priestess that results in creative ideas. Through the Empress, the Magus and Priestess are united. Since she is ruled by Venus, she epitomizes the nurturing mother that gives life to the dreams of The Priestess and content to the vision of The Magus. She brings creative ideas into the world. To give them structure and form she looks toward her consort, The Emperor (logical mind). It is his rational mind that will help her to maintain the balance between her head and her heart.

The position of her arms and hands represents the ability to give and to receive. The Empress will allow herself to be loved as well as to nurture and love those in her care. She has an artistic nature and an appreciation of beautiful things. She is an inspiration to those in her life and always has an entourage of admirers. She inspires you to listen to your dreams and visions, to protect and nurture them. Like mother earth, she is extremely creative; because of the magnetism of the moon/earth relationship The Empress is able to attract what she needs to get the job done.

CARD SYMBOLS	INTERPRETATIONS
Number 3	synthesis, creativity
Astrology: Venus	beauty, harmony and love
Element	Water
Hebrew letter	ד *Daleth* (door)
Facing to her left	looks toward the Emperor—toward the rational mind
Position of hands	receives love as well as gives it
Moon/Earth	power of attraction
Twisted blue flames	Venus's birth from water (unconscious)
Lotus in right hand	passive power of love
Girdle/Zodiac	blends diverse groups of people
Pelican	nurturing mother
Birds	spirit, sacred thoughts
Bees	she is the queen bee
Red blouse	personal integrity
Green pants	manifesting on this earth
Crown	the world of imagination, dreams and fantasies that she has access to
Fleur de Lys	union of all levels of being
Shield	divine rule
Phoenix	transformation, rebirth
Colors	blue: mental wisdom; aqua blue: feminine nature; green: creativity, healing, regeneration; red: integrity; grey metallic color: magnetism, attraction; pink: unconditional love

• IV •
The Emperor

The Emperor is ruled by Mars and refers to Aries. He takes us from the nonverbal world of The Priestess and The Empress into the world of logic and reason. He looks toward his consort, The Empress, to receive his creative ideas. He takes the ideas she gives him and initiates their materialization. The Empress and The Emperor are opposite sides of the same coin. They need each other if our imagination and subsequent ideas are to be expressed in the physical world. He is the active male principle, the father, the protector and the leader.

The fires of Mars give The Emperor his decisiveness and single-minded focus. With legs crossed, his body takes on the position of the number four, which represents solidity, stability, power and authority. The Emperor holds the world in his hand; he feels as if there's nothing he can't accomplish and behaves accordingly. He has an optimistic warm energetic demeanor yet remains truly committed to the situation at hand and lives his life totally in the present moment. He is willing to take up the cause and lead the charge. His actions embody courage and determination as he plants the seeds of the new world.

CARD SYMBOLS	INTERPRETATIONS
Number 4	form, manifestation
Element	Fire
Astrology: Mars/Aries	assertive, forceful
Hebrew letter	צ Tzaddi (fishhook)
Seated in "4" position	form, power and stability
Ram	forerunner always charging ahead
Lamb	willing to sacrifice for a cause
Crown	ability to rule/lead
Sun	new beginnings
Coin	successful in physical world
Globe in his hand	builder, participator, activist, global awareness
Bees	active, hard worker
Fleur de Lys	union of all levels of being
Facing to his right	looks toward the Empress to access the intuitive mind
Shield/Phoenix	divine rule, transformation, rebirth from ashes of the old
Flag	carries the banner of his cause
Colors	gold/orange: energy, optimism, vitality; red: integrity

The Hierophant

· V ·
The Hierophant

The Hierophant is ruled by Venus and refers to Taurus. He seeks to unite heaven and earth and through this union give meaning to our lives. He represents our innate need to make sense of our experiences by aligning them with a higher purpose. In other decks he has been called the Pope. The word pope or pontiff means "bridge." The Hierophant is essential to magic because as our "internal guru" he spans the gap between our humanness and our divinity. As a spiritual master, this philosopher and teacher shares his wisdom directly with the world.

It is through The Hierophant that we can reconnect to our spiritual core. Humankind has an innate predisposition toward structure and design in life. The Hierophant makes accessible to us the world of our spiritual nature, yet at the same time he is grounded in the materiality of structure and form. He appreciates the value of life itself and respects the sacredness of the physical world. He follows tradition and preaches a gospel of transcendence.

CARD SYMBOLS	INTERPRETATIONS
Number 5	union of spirit and earth
Element	Earth
Astrology: Venus/Taurus	stable, loyal, conservative
Hebrew letter	ו *Vau* (nail)
Elephant	keeper of history, tradition
Taurus "Bull"	the divine in physical form, tenacity, loyalty, commitment
Wand with three rings	Aeons of Isis, Osiris, and Horus—union of body, mind, soul
The Priestess inside	listens to the inner voice of intuition
Four fixed Zodiac signs	Taurus, Leo, Scorpio, Aquarius represent wholeness
Man, woman and child	integration of all aspects of psyche
Open hand	willing to share information
Finger extended	intuition and creativity
Nine thorns	tests and challenges of life (disruption)
Dove	love, spirit
Snake	shed the old—forever young
Flower	always learning, growing, evolving
Smiling face	understands "bigger picture," can see the humor in a situation
Color	earth colors: warmth, kindness, compassion; blue: wisdom; white: purity

• VI •
The Lovers

The Lovers card is ruled by Mercury and refers to Gemini. It represents wholeness and is symbolized by the union of the King and Queen as our masculine and feminine energy. The Hermit appears as the "wise old man," giving his blessing to this marriage. Mercury gives The Lovers their strong mental capacity and Gemini gives them the ability to appreciate opposites. All the dualities pictured in the card illustrate the capacity to embrace conflicting information and form a composite world view. It can represent all types of relationships, from friends and lovers to acquaintances or lifelong partnerships.

To be a whole person, we need to be able to relate to others and offer our love (feminine) and at the same time be able to protect and defend our personal boundaries (masculine). The Lovers is a card of perfect balance and equilibrium. To be complete, we need to integrate the dualities within. We need to be both active and passive, assertive and yielding, introverted and extroverted—in short, we need to be all things to ourselves. If we rely on the different aspects of our own being for support, we will be able to move into a healthy and balanced relationship with another, based on strength rather than weakness.

CARD SYMBOLS	INTERPRETATIONS
Number 6	harmony and equilibrium restored
Element	Air
Astrology: Mercury/Gemini	integration of opposites
Hebrew letter	ז *Zain* (sword)
Orphic egg/snake	transformation through relationship
Duality Symbols	anima and animus, feminine and masculine
Sword/Holy Grail	the mind and the intuition
Hermit	hidden knowledge
Scroll around arms	Wisdom he posseses
Cupid	Eros love
Bars in background	freedom within commitment
Marriage	union of opposites
Eve/Lillith	primal feminine energy
Children's tools	club: physical union; flowers: spiritual union; cup: emotional union; sword: mental union
Leo/Scorpio	fire and water; masculine and feminine
Hermit's pink robe	unconditional love and understanding

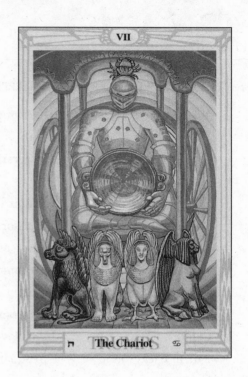

• VII •
The Chariot

The Chariot is ruled by the Moon and refers to Cancer. Sitting as he does, the Charioteer seems to have no visible means of controlling the movement of the Chariot. In front of him sit four strange animals that symbolize his four basic instincts. They represent his physical sensations, feelings, intuition and mental capacities. To move along on his journey, he must respect the intelligence of his body, mind, heart and spirit. He holds the Holy Grail which represents the totality of his essence. He wears a suit of armor to illustrate that he is on a hero's journey, ready to do battle if necessary.

The card is called The Chariot, not the Charioteer, which puts the emphasis on the process itself. He must yield to the strategy of adventure and exploration so that he maximizes his interaction with the outer world. Thus he becomes more secure and feels more at home wherever his life takes him. The Charioteer is seated above his instincts and must be careful that by exalting his mental capacities he does not lose his natural connection to instincts. It is only through that connection that he is able to move in the direction he desires.

CARD SYMBOLS	INTERPRETATIONS
Number 7	challenge, expansions, experimentation, and desire
Element	Water
Astrology: Moon, Jupiter/Cancer	the deeper he's willing to go, the greater the expansion
Hebrew letter	ח *Cheth* (fence)
The Chariot	process by which we move out into the world
Yellow Brick Road	path toward developing his own identity
Holding the Holy Grail	holds the potential totality of his essence, seeks knowledge of his Higher Self
Ball of fire	"chi," personal power, motivation
Four animals	thinking, feeling, sensing and intuitive sense
Crab at his head	tendency to zigzag as he travels
Crystals on his breastplate	needs to open his heart to the clarity of his inner voice
Abracadabra on canopy	both he and the journey are magical
Armor	great warrior when necessary
Meditative position	in touch with inner calm
Colors	red: integrity; gold: malleability; blue: mental wisdom; aqua blue: emotions, intuition; purple: spirit

· VIII ·
Adjustment

The Adjustment card is ruled by Venus and refers to Libra. She is the Egyptian Goddess Maat who weighs the souls of the newly departed against a feather to determine the balance between their humanness and their divinity. The two pans of her scale hold the Alpha and Omega, the beginning and the end. Equilibrium occurs in our lives when these two aspects are in balance. To keep this balance we must listen to our own conscience and follow our own truth and intuition.

She represents the feminine principle, yet holds the masculine sword of logic in her hand. This sword of logic will help you separate fantasy from reality. The Adjustment card represents the time in your life when you need to act consciously rather than react to what occurs. She is blindfolded to illustrate her ability to rely on her inner wisdom to keep a sense of balance. She listens to her own conscience, develops her own equilibrium, determines her own truth (she realizes that all things are equally true) and weighs all sides of a situation before she acts. She understands that there is no absolute answer to a situation and that the scales of justice need constant adjustment.

CARDS SYMBOLS	INTERPRETATIONS
Number 8	adaptation, reason, stability through change
Element	Air
Astrology: Venus/Libra	balance harmony equilibrium
Hebrew letter	ל *Lamed* (ox goad)
Scales	ability to produce a state of equilibrium
Alpha and Omega	able to see the pros and cons of a situation
Blindfolded	no preconceived ideas, intuitive
Tiptoes	alert to the compensation that needs to be made moment to moment
Feathered cape	Maat the Goddess of Justice
Cross made by her body and the sword	balance between our human nature and our divine nature
Pyramids/spheres	law of exactness in nature—nature is not always just but it is exact
Harlequin design	connects her to The Fool, marches to her own inner voice
Colors	green: creativity; blue: mental wisdom, peace, harmony; white: purity, clarity

· IX ·
The Hermit

The Hermit card is ruled by Mercury and refers to Virgo. His cloak is blood red because he represents the flesh and blood of human existence and the potential for transcendence in this lifetime. The Hermit moves away from the outer world and goes deep within himself to sort out his life and to integrate his personal belief system. Like Virgo, he has an unwavering sense of honesty in his evaluation of himself and his situation. He has no particular sermon to deliver, since his life is his message.

He represents inner wisdom within each of us. His body is turned away from the outer world and toward a world of seclusion. In solitude, he comes to know what is important to him. The Hermit, by spending time alone, is able to define himself as separate from the collective. Through a process of discrimination, he evaluates what's working in his life and what is not. He sees things clearly and—no matter how painful it may be—he is able to let go when necessary. He carries the lamp of wisdom and guidance in his hand and illuminates the path to self knowledge for each of us. What he knows as truth deep within determines his behavior in the outer world.

CARD SYMBOLS	INTERPRETATIONS
Number 9	ending of cycle, completion
Element	Earth
Astrology: Mercury/Virgo	discriminating communication
Hebrew letter	' *Yod* (hand)
Hermit	solitude, introverted
Cloistered position	he actively seeks solitude
Turned away	he has turned his back on the external world
Light in his hand	his life is his message and it serves to illuminate the world
Red cloak	honesty and integrity
Wheat	fertility of his mind, harvest
Spermatozoa	procreative
Egg/snake	regeneration brought about by solitude
White hands	heals whatever he touches
Cerberus (three-headed dog)	to move forward we must integrate the past, keeping what works and discarding the rest
Colors	red: honesty, integrity; green: creativity, healing, regeneration; white: purity, clarity; gold: malleability

· X ·
Fortune

The Fortune card is ruled by Jupiter and represents the transforming events in our lives. Jupiter will move us out of our comfort zone and encourages us to take chances we would not normally take. Nothing is static in life. Everything is either becoming or dying. The wheel is constantly turning and therefore life is always changing. The hub of the wheel represents universal law and the rim of the wheel symbolizes how one works within this law and personalizes it. The wheel is being turned by the three Hindhu *Gunas—Sattvas*, *Rajas* and *Tamas*. On this card they are pictured as the Sphinx, Hermanubis and Typhon.

We cannot seem to escape the wheel of fate, but with a little luck and the proper attitude we can use it to our advantage. The Fortune card generates tremendous energy and can motivate us to move out into the world and participate consciously in our lives. Notice that all spokes of the wheel are equidistant from the center hub. This signifies that all paths are equally true. They all end up in the same place. In life there really is nothing to win or lose. It's more about how you play the game.

CARD SYMBOLS	INTERPRETATIONS
Number 10	culmination, transition period, new beginning
Element	Fire
Astrology: Jupiter	expansion luck
Hebrew letter	כ *Kaph* (open hand)
Wheel	fate, the wheel of life keeps spinning, change
Lightning bolts	powerful energy created by the ever-turning wheel, life is dymanic and ever-evolving
Ape, Crocodile, Sphinx (*Gunas*)	catalysts that keep the wheel of life turning
Triangle	stability in center of motion
Circle at top	self in its wholeness
Colors	purple: universal law, divine presence; gold: reward, flexibility, malleability; yellow: spirit

· XI ·
Lust

Lust is ruled by the Sun and refers to Leo. The Primal life force energy of the Sun is being expressed within the confines of our human nature. The woman (feminine principle) has the courage to straddle the lion (animal nature) which represents her passion and love of physical life. Our animal nature is our need for food, love, sex, touching and all sensual and sexual experience. She is living her life to its fullest in spite of her fears and inner demons, which are pushed to the background and under her control.

With her hand on the Holy Grail she applies her feminine instincts to gently tame and harmonize her animal nature. She awakens her connection with spirit through her physical experience. In this way she empowers not only her physical passion but experiences the divine ecstasy of her spiritual essence. Her strength lies in her ability to relate to and express each part of herself consciously. She is able to integrate each aspect of her mental, emotional, spiritual and physical life.

CARD SYMBOLS	INTERPRETATIONS
Number 11	primal force, inspired, illuminated
Element	Fire
Astrology: Sun/Leo	inspiration, creativity, passion
Hebrew letter	ט _Teth_ (serpent)
Lion	power and strength of our human animal instincts, needs and desires
Woman (state of ecstasy)	feminine principle, energy is primitive and creative independent of logic and reason
Dark figures	dark mysterious aspects of her inner demons
Holy Grail	she can embody the totality of her essence and communicate with her Higher Self
Right hand touching Holy Grail	connection to primal fire through the feminine
Light rays	dawn of a new aeon
Ten serpents	destruction of the old, emergence of the new
Multiple faces of the lion	keeps a rein on her human instincts, reins in all aspects of her being
Lion/serpent	creative change that brings about an upsurge of power
Colors	orange/gold/red: vitality, life force, integrity; green: creative force

The Hanged Man ▽

• XII •
The Hanged Man

The Hanged Man is ruled by Neptune and influenced by the element Water. A man hangs upside down over a somber pool of water in which the serpent of change lies dormant. The pool of water is dark and therefore symbolizes the unknown depths of the mind. Behind the figure is a grid representing the structure of nature that supports his physical world. The man is crucified to this grid, unable to move or exert his own will. His legs cross in the form of an inverted number four, characterizing his inability to manifest a stable world for himself. Yet a serpent wraps around his foot—signifying the potential for change and regeneration.

Every symbol on this card is upside down as well. The inverted Ankh and the Sun at the top of the card denote that his life is overturned and in this position he has no choice but to yield. It is the moment of hopelessness before transition occurs . . . the moment when we feel that time has stopped and we are outside our lives, looking in. This is a time of initiation, when trust is needed, and surrender called for.

CARD SYMBOLS	INTERPRETATIONS
Number 12	surrender of ego
Element	Water
Astrology: Neptune	depth of the unconscious
Hebrew letter	ם *Mem* (water)
Hung upside down	we must surrender our illusion of control, seeing life from a different angle
Four position	the beginning of a new reality
Ankh upside down	his life feels upside down
Crucified	carrying the burden, feeling victimized
Cross	descent of spirit into matter in order to redeem it
Serpents	life as one knows it is "on hold," no motion, no action
Sun on the horizon	a new day is coming
Gridwork	his back is against the wall of outworn patterns, ideas, attitudes and behaviors
Head in water	moving deep into the unconscious to redeem oneself
Colors	green: hope (creativity) that comes with surrender; blue: wisdom (new ideas); black: depth of the unconscious

• XIII •
Death

The Death card is ruled by Mars and Pluto and refers to Scorpio. It is symbolized by a moving skeleton that represents the dance of death. This Saturnian figure is experiencing his final death throes as his outworn beliefs and concepts fall away. Everything he has believed in has failed him and he has nothing left to hold onto. However, the motion of the dance causes new figures to emerge in the background of the card. These denote the potential new forms of life being created by this dance of death.

The card is influenced by Scorpio, the master of transition. Pluto, the Lord of the Underworld, is at work in this card. The deep cutting away of the old offers us the promise of the new and the resurrection of our spirit. Like decaying flesh we are left only with the bones of our being and will soon have the opportunity to rebuild our lives upon a new structure. Life and death are connected—they are one and the same; death is a phase of life. Without death, life is not possible.

CARD SYMBOLS	INTERPRETATIONS
Number 13	back to basics
Element	Water
Astrology: Mars/Scorpio	ever-changing, transforming
Hebrew letter	נ *Nun* (fish)
Skeleton	down to the basic bones of things
Position of skeletal figure	Saturn, dance of continual transformation
Scorpion	change can be painful
Snake	shedding the old
Fish	resurrection
Scythe	cutting through, with force, what we refuse to release
Eagle	soaring to new heights through transformation
Lily	death, transformation
Phoenix	something new is born from the ashes of the old
Onion	peeling away layer after layer
Emerging figures	aspects of oneself that have been waiting for expression
Colors	black/brown: material world, physical matter; aqua blue: intuition, emotions

· XIV ·
Art

The Art card is ruled by Jupiter and refers to Sagittarius. The main figure symbolizes the marriage of the King and Queen (masculine and feminine principles). She holds fire in one hand and water in the other, and is placing them in a cauldron where the magic of assimilation will take place. Fire and water are by nature incompatible—yet when handled properly (the cauldron) produce something new and original (steam). Transformation comes from the fires of purification. We burn the old . . . from the ashes of the old the new arises.

This process can be painful but we need to be aware of its value. Art is like an angel telling us that all the things that have happened in our lives have a purpose. Our experiences change us. Even when we do not know what is in our best interest, we need to recognize that she's looking out for us. In fact, we are the "work of art" she is helping to create. She magically blends the essence of one's humanness with that of one's divine nature. She helps us develop a new philosophy, a new belief system and a new reality map based on this assimilation.

CARD SYMBOLS	INTERPRETATIONS
Number 14	new opportunities, reorganizing
Element	Fire
Astrology:	
Jupiter/Sagittarius	growth, expansion
Hebrew letter	ס *Samekh* (tent)
Androgynous figure of Art	King and Queen (the feminine and masculine principles)
Green gown	creativity released through union
Cauldron	something new is brewing
Raven/skull	death that supports new life
Many-breasted	nurturing the new creation
Lion–Eagle; Water–Fire King–Queen; Sun–Moon	blending of opposites forces in the creative process
Bows and arrow	communication from subconscious
Rainbow	faith
Bees	industrious
Serpent	change, rebirth, transformation
Alchemy	process through which incompatible elements are combined; precursor to chemistry
Message on disk behind Art	"Visit the interior parts of the earth; by rectification [setting things right] thou shalt find the hidden stone [real self]."
Colors	green: creativity, regeneration; orange: vitality, energy; blue: wisdom, peace, harmony; aqua blue: intuition; white: clarity

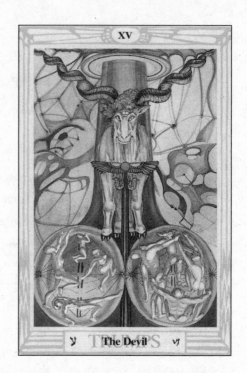

· XV ·
The Devil

The Devil is ruled by Saturn and refers to Capricorn. He is symbolized by the God Pan. In front of him is the Uraeus Staff, the symbol of life and death, of light and dark, of the good and evil within each of us. Good and evil do not exist separate from each other. The Devil is of god in the same respect that everything that exists is of god. In this card the god of the old religion has become the devil of the new. What we do not understand, we fear; what we fear we call evil. Pan is smiling because he sees how foolish this is and is asking us to lighten up, so to speak. Everything that exists in the material world has its purpose. His horns spiral toward the heavens to tell us that we need to experience all aspects of human life to grow and to evolve. Not that evil doesn't exist in our world— it certainly does. However, the capacity for evil exists within us, not outside of us. Because we have been taught to devalue the material world we inadvertently devalue life. The Devil depicts life in its most material form.

On this card we see people trying to break out of the testes or roots of the Tree of Life, asking to be heard. They represent aspects of our humanness that have not been given expression. If we do not acknowledge, at least to ourselves, all attributes of our being, we diminish our power and squander our vitality. To be fully alive we need to come out of the shadow into the light, and experience the full pleasure and pain of life.

CARD SYMBOLS	INTERPRETATIONS
Number 15	giving expression to the shadow
Element	Earth
Astrology: Saturn/Capricorn	steadfast, persistent
Hebrew letter	ע *Ayin* (eye)
Goat	Pan, the god of the old religion
Spiraling horns	growth and evolution
Smile	the need for humor in life
Grapes	partake of the pleasures of the senses
Third eye	intuition
Tree and its roots	spirit penetrating the earth, appreciation of all that exists, the Tree of Life
Penis	sexuality, sensuality
People in the testicles	many diverse aspects of personality that want expression
Rings of Saturn	focus of intent
Staff of Horus/Wand	protection, creative energy
Colors	pink/violet: compassion, understanding; purple: spirit; blue: wisdom and harmony; aqua blue: emotion, intuition; white: clarity; earth tones: physical world

· XVI ·
The Tower

The Tower card is ruled by Mars and exemplified by a tower being consumed in fire. The Eye of Shiva ignites the fire; before it the dove carries an olive branch, symbol of the protection of love. While the structure is crumbling its occupants are being tossed out and plummet headfirst to the ground. This is exactly what happens when we get too rigid in our thinking. Through selective seeing and hearing we create a tower (consciousness) that is impervious to new ideas, therefore becoming brittle—susceptible to being the fuel of its own destruction. We become static and do not want to disturb the status quo. Even when we know change is imminent, we reinforce our mental structure and resist the natural flow of transition.

When we close ourselves off from the world and think we are above it all, we lose touch with our instincts and become imprisoned within the dogma of our own mind. Our world becomes smaller and smaller until we self-destruct, or an unexpected turn of events tosses us to the ground. As you lie there in the dirt, you may curse fate for what has happened—but in retrospect you'll see that this is a blessing of love in disguise.

CARD SYMBOLS	INTERPRETATIONS
Number 16	tests, challenges, initiation
Element	Fire
Astrology: Mars	aggressive battle
Hebrew letter	פ *Pé* (mouth)
Tower	self
Disintegrating tower	sudden, unexpected, devastating change
Four figures falling from tower	four aspects of one's being (mind, emotions, desires, physical) that are being thrown to the ground
Fire	purification; burning away the false self
Dove	love, peace, a gift of grace
Eye of Shiva	creative destruction
Snake/lion head	will to live and will to die, to shed old skin and begin anew
Fire-breathing dragon	ultimate creative energy
Colors	red/orange: life force, strength, vitality; brown/black: material world, the earth

· XVII ·
The Star

The Star card is ruled by Uranus and refers to Aquarius. She is symbolized by the Goddess Nuith, "Our Lady of the Stars," and represents the continuation of life. After the destruction of The Tower, The Star brings hope, optimism and renewal into our lives. As Aquarius, the water bearer, she is able to irrigate the barren earth with her insights and illuminations in a way that serves humanity. The cup in her right hand pours the water of celestial wisdom through her to the cup in her left. She then pours this into the earth beneath her feet. This signifies that our experiences are different, and therefore each of us puts a personal imprint on the information we share.

She is a dreamer and is committed to sharing her rich inner life with those around her, and manifesting her visions. She represents the journey from the infinite to the finite and back again. Ideas flow to her from out of nowhere. Like the stars, her insights may flicker on and off. She is able, however, to assimilate this information. The message she delivers is that each of us is "a star" in our own universe. We have an obligation to participate in the collective process of humankind by expressing our natural abilities openly so that we live in harmony with our true will.

CARD SYMBOLS	INTERPRETATIONS
Number 17	stability through change, continuation
Element	Air
Astrology: Uranus Aquarius	innovative, humanitarian
Hebrew letter	ה *Hé* (window)
Lady	feminine principle in action
Pouring water	water goes from above to below while passing through the earth
Crystallization of water	insight and illumination
Celestial orb	concept of infinite space, unlimited possibilities, hope
Nakedness	totally vulnerable and open to the unknown
Dry barren ground	she nourishes the rational mind (air) with the waters of the unconscious
Feet on ground	serves humanity by manifesting her insights
Cups shaped like breasts	the feminine serves as a container for the unconscious
Stars	progressive, innovative, star-quality
Seven-pointed Star of Venus	love, caring, beauty
Arm positions	all-encompassing
Colors	blue: wisdom; pink/violet: love, caring; green: creativity

• XVIII •
The Moon

The Moon card is ruled by the Moon and refers to Pisces. The black towers represent the entrance into the darkest recesses of our being. In the bottom half of the card, we see a Scarab Beetle holding the Sun in its jaws through the long dark night in readiness for a new day. Twin figures of the Egyptian God Anubis, holding the keys of Mercury, watch over the threshold into the Underworld. As we proceed across the threshold, we need to confront our fear of the unknown—particularly the fear of our own physical mortality. The small jackals represent our animal instincts. If we accept their help they will be our anchors to the physical world and our greatest ally in our search for immortality; if we panic they will consume us. It is our physical life—our family, relationships, work, and our bodies in particular—that will call us back.

Once we start this stage of our journey, there will be no turning back. We must walk into the unknown with complete trust in our spirit for the deeper we go, the more we lose our orientation to the physical world. Because there are psychological dangers in this process, we need a strong support system to bring us back to earth.

CARD SYMBOLS	INTERPRETATIONS
Number 18	completion
Element	Water
Astrology: Moon/Pisces	reflection, illusive, sensitive
Hebrew letter	ק Qoph (back of the head)
Anubis figures	guides of the underworld (the unconscious)
Jackals	feed off those that fail in their attempt; animal instincts; clean up the past
Moon	unconscious
Teardrops	healing tears
Scarab holding the Midnight Sun	the ability to survive "the dark night of the soul;" a new day will come and this too shall pass
Keys of Mercury	communication from the unconscious
Waves	continual ebb and flow of the life force
Ankh	symbol of life
Colors	light and dark: the dark shadows cast by bright light

· XIX ·
The Sun

The Sun card is ruled by the Sun. With the sunrise comes a new day. Direct sunlight eliminates the shadows and allows us to see clearly. When the sun shines, we have more confidence and self reliance. We feel vital, healed and protected by the sun. The Fire element represents our will to be. It illustrates a strong desire for life. It symbolizes that a new day is on the horizon and a new world is beginning to unfold for us.

The two dancing children celebrate the potential creativity within physical life—the possibility of living spontaneously, transformed in each new moment. These children are children of the New Aeon (the new order). Like children, they are in awe of life itself. The two roses beneath their feet symbolize the Old Aeon (the passing of the old ways). These children have been transformed, and no longer fear the earth plane but rejoice in their bodies and fully express the pleasures of physical life. They have come to understand the immortality of consciousness and realize that their spirit is alive and well in the physical world. They begin to understand that life is not a challenge to be dealt with—but a joy to be experienced.

CARD SYMBOLS	INTERPRETATIONS
Number 19	individuality, leadership
Element	Fire
Astrology: Sun	primal energy
Hebrew letter	ר *Resh* (head)
Green mountain	fertile earth; physical plane aspires toward heaven
Wall girdling top of mountain	boundaries, discipline within the confines of the physical plane
Zodiac signs	understands the true union of humanity, gets along with everyone
Dancing figures	playfully involved in the game of life, dancing in the light of a new day
Butterfly wings	transformed energy, enthusiasm, divine ecstasy
Rays emanating from Sun	we emanate from the source
Rainbow	the sun is shining through and creating possibilities
Colors	red/yellow/orange: optimism, vitality, life force; green: creativity, regeneration and hope

· XX ·
The Aeon

The Aeon card is ruled by infinite space. This card symbolizes a time of resurrection and rebirth. It represents the end of the old order and the beginning of a new era. We have come through the purification of fire and have entered the New Aeon. The body of the Goddess Nuith arches around the top of the card. The God Hadit is depicted by the winged solar disk. The twin forms of Horus are seated, as Ra-Hoor-Khuit, the elder form of Horus, and standing, as Hoor-pa-kraat—the child form of the God Horus. Those wonderful eyes characterize the wide-eyed, innocent look of a child seeing everything for the first time. He is shown with his finger to his lips, giving counsel to us to be silent and listen to our intuition. The elder form of Horus is seated within the younger, representing the inner knowledge and wisdom necessary to navigate one's life consciously.

We are being given a chance to live our lives with awareness, a chance to demonstrate what we have learned, and to experience the full potential of who we are and what we are a part of. We cannot claim ignorance as an excuse any longer. The time has come to walk our talk and take full responsibility for our actions.

CARD SYMBOLS	INTERPRETATIONS
Number 20	choice
Element	Fire
Astrology: Infinite Space	blank slate ready for the next chapter to be written
Hebrew letter	𝐖 *Shin* (tooth)
Nuith	star goddess, unlimited possibility
Large transparent youth	Child God Horus, Hoor-pa-kraat
Ra-hoor-khuit in background	elder form of the dual God Horus
Androgynous	merging of feminine and masculine principle
Wide-eyed expression	beginner's mind, childlike wonder
Large eyes	looking at life through new eyes
Finger to mouth	silence; think before you speak
Transparency of the Child God	being in the world but not of it
Eye of Horus	sees everything, intuition
Birds	new ideas
Fetus	new life, rebirth, regeneration
Straight hair	rational mind
Wavy hair	intuitive, imaginative, holistic vision
Letter *Shin* with three human figures	signifies the body, mind and soul of the human being
Winged serpent	open mind; without preconceived ideas
Colors	blue: mental wisdom; orange: optimism; red: life force; gold: flexibility; white: clarity; green: creativity

• XXI •
The Universe

The Universe card is ruled by Saturn and influenced by the earth. It represents the infinite world of possibilities within the confines of earth's limitations. The four fixed zodiac signs symbolize the process of creation. Anything we choose to create begins with will and intent. We have an intuitive response to our desire and this triggers an emotion that moves us into the next phase, where we begin to think about what we need to do to create what we want. We realize that the world is not somewhere out there but somewhere deep within us. We co-create the world we live in by our perceptions, attitudes and beliefs.

The Eye of Shiva brings its creative/destructive life force energy into play as the raw material of earth is formed into new creation. This life force radiates and expresses itself through us. The beauty of life is captured in the movement of the universal dance; the dance between invisible energy and manifested form. In the blink of eye we exist in and out of time. The headdress like a chambered nautilus characterizes the evolution of our consciousness. I become aware of the fact that I am everything and everything is me. No-thing exists separate from me. All is one, one is all and all is nothing.

CARD SYMBOLS	INTERPRETATIONS
Number 21	creativity, possibility
Element	Earth
Astrology: Saturn	time of harvest
Hebrew letter	ת *Tau* (cross)
Circle within the square	freedom through discipline
Dancing figure	life is an eternal dance
Leg in number four shape	time to build something new
Snake	cycle of change; regeneration
Gridwork	using one's limitations to grow from
Headdress	evolution of consciousness
Diamond	many-faceted awareness
Pelvic	ultimate creative act: giving birth to one's self
Building	ability to work from within existing structure and convention
Four fixed zodiac signs	elements of the creative process
Eye of Shiva	creative destruction
Wheel	completion with a new beginning
Scythe	ability to cut away the old; the time to let go
Colors:	green: regeneration, creativity; gold: flexibility; brown/black: material world; blue: mental wisdom

Symbols of the Minor Arcana

In the Small Cards of the Minor Arcana, each Suit reveals a cycle of phases (Ace through Ten) regarding your life in general or the specific situation in question.

Aces are symbolic of the primordial element of their specific suit.

Twos represent the first expression of the energy.

Threes give birth in form to the energy.

Fours solidify the energy.

Fives express the natural disruption of energy as it evolves.

Sixes represent the energy at its most balanced.

Sevens correspond to a struggle as energy approaches the physical.

Eights symbolize a response to the above struggle.

Nines return balance to the situation.

Tens epitomize the culmination of energy in the physical state.

When the energy is expressed in the physical, it eventually deteriorates and returns to an unmanifested state—then begins the cycle once again. You can view the cards in your readings in relation to the overall cycle of the specific Suit, and gain additional insight into the Thoth Tarot's revelations. In the descriptions below, you will see an example of the Ace through Ten of each Suit as a progressive path. Note how the process swings back and forth on the way to a culmination of that Suit's physical manifestation.

Symbols of the Wands Suit

The element Fire is associated with the Wands Suit. Fire symbolizes our will to live; it represents the primal life force that ignites our human form. At its best it invigorates, supplying physical vitality, passion, inspiration, and motivation. At its worst it will create a manic state followed by complete exhaustion and total burnout. A fire can bring warmth into your home, but if it's out of control it can burn your house down to the ground.

In the form of a fever, fire can purify your life by burning physical toxins from your body. It can cleanse your emotions by destroying the debris of past emotional trauma. Fire can clear your thinking process by purging your mind of old data and putting the past to rest. We can use our inner fire as charisma to attract people to us, or we use it as rage and hostility to push people away.

Through the process of creativity we try to harness this energy and direct it. This in itself is difficult to do. Fire can create and it can destroy. To handle something as hot as the creative potential within us is no easy trick. As we move from the Ace through the Ten of Wands, we experience the play of primal life force from raw, undifferentiated energy to manifested form.

For example: Ace of Wands—You recognize the stirring of primordial energy, and feel drawn to create something. Two of Wands (Dominion)—Thinking of what you desire, the *will* to create it rises. You begin to focus your intent. Three of Wands (Virtue)—Now your endeavor starts to take shape in your mind. You feel very optimistic, and seek out like-minded individuals to share your passion with. By doing something you love, you're able to stay with it until successful. Four of Wands (Completion)—Finishing this endeavor, you free up energy to move into other projects. If you go with the flow, everything seems to be driven by a force of its own. If, however, you try to control the direction of the energy, you run into obstacles such as intense aggravation because what you envision is not appearing. Five of Wands (Strife)—Your creative energy is high, but countered by frustration. Six of Wands (Victory)—If you can keep working with the energy, you can push through the hindrance of frustration and experience an inner victory that restores your sense of balance. Seven of Wands (Valour)—Inner victory gives you the courage to go out on a limb, though you risk that it will be cut off behind you, resulting in complete failure. Eight of Wands (Swiftness)—Now you're really fired up and the energy of your original passion drives you to act quickly and accomplish your object. You must act spontaneously and hope that your actions help rather than hinder. Nine of Wands (Strength)—If you can find a balance of spontaneity and continuity, you can act productively. You need to find a way to ground the passion driving you so you don't burn out. Ten of Wands (Oppression)—If you can't ground your energy, you're faced with defeat. Everything is just too hot to handle and you're totally exhausted.

Ace of Wands

This card represents the primordial energy of the Archetypal World. The fiery torch is shown in the shape of the Tree of Life and symbolizes a dynamic explosion of energy going in all directions. Primal life force moves this potential energy into all levels of our lives. It denotes the thrust of spirit as it begins its journey into matter. The green lightning bolts symbolize the raw power of this energy and how it is able to renew itself.

Two of Wands (Dominion)

Mars is in Aries. Two red Tibetan Dorjes are crossed and represent the power of will—the initial destruction that clears the way for the creative process. This is the initiation of action in its most primal form. Six flames come from the center of the image field and contribute to the balance of this card. The blue color in the background represents the air (ideas) in which this explosion of Mars energy has taken place. The destruction has its purpose in the cycle of creativity—it allows new ideas to form.

Three of Wands (Virtue)

The Sun is in Aries. Three golden wands with lotuses that are beginning to open are crossed through the rays of the sun's fire. This symbolizes springtime, generative energy that gets things going. A blossoming of one's energy inspires and motivates one to create something new. The white star signifies that each of us is unique. The stars themselves are made of fire, and if we are to be a radiant star in our own right, we need to be active and willing to shine.

Four of Wands (Completion)

Venus is in Aries. The four wands have the head of the Aries ram on one side and the dove of Venus on the other. They are crossed through the fire and appear as spokes on a wheel. The wheel represents the fact that life moves on. The circle denotes completion. The dove symbolizes the finishing of something we have cared deeply about and now our energy is free to move into the next adventure (ram).

Five of Wands (Strife)

Saturn is in Leo. The large green center staff appears cumbersome. Green being the color of new life, the card symbolizes that our creative energy is blocked. Two wands, each with the head of a Phoenix, and two other green wands with lotuses on them point away from each other. They illustrate that the possibility for renewal and creative manifestation is also being thwarted. The yellow symbolizes the intellect trying to break through the resistance. We are frustrated and irritable because our creative energy (Leo) is running at full force, but Saturn weighs it down and makes it hard to fly. Creative energy will eventually break through . . . but in the meantime it is disturbing.

Six of Wands (Victory)

Jupiter is in Leo. There are two wands with the Eye of Horus, two Phoenix-headed wands and two wands with lotuses. These six golden wands are now facing each other and placed in perfect balance. There are nine contained flames burning brightly like candles. These will light your way to inner victory. You fought the good fight and are victorious (the light purple background is the color of victory). Jupiter makes this a glorious triumph—one that is expansive and moves you on to even greater success.

Seven of Wands (Valour)

Mars is in Leo. A large club appears in front of the Six of Wands, signifying a loss of balance. The flames seem disordered; the energy, which is weakening, is chaotic and difficult to work with. Getting a handle on this situation requires a struggle to the finish. The dark purple color denotes the courage you will need to move forward, the strong convictions you need to have. To be victorious, you must take a chance—go out on a limb and risk having it cut off behind you.

Eight of Wands (Swiftness)

Mercury is in Sagittarius. Eight fiery arrows pierce geometric forms. We are looking at the speed of fire. The arrows are moving very fast. Communication is swift. Everything is occurring quickly. The rainbow at the top of the card shows light broken into the whole spectrum of color. It illustrates energy expressing itself in all areas of your life. The blue background of the card is trying to soften a high energy situation and cool it before it burns out.

Nine of Wands (Strength)

The Moon is in Sagittarius. The center wand has the moon on one side and the sun on the other. This signifies the necessity for balance. This card has nine arrows, all pointed toward the ground. This represents the fact that the energy is growing stronger; in fact, in its material form it is stronger than in any of the other wand cards. If you are to use it properly, you need to keep your balance and live in the moment so that you act spontaneously.

Ten of Wands (Oppression)

Saturn is in Sagittarius. Two large Dorjes are in front of eight crossed wands that seem to have flames coming from both ends. The Dorjes are elongated rods that look menacing and we are made aware that if things continue this way, destruction may be inevitable. The deep orange color in the card, and the flames in the background, also illustrate that the situation is out of control.

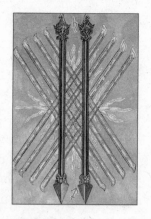

Symbols of the Cups Suit

The element Water is associated with the Cups Suit. It symbolizes emotions, understanding and intuition. At its best, it adds a sense of meaning and purpose to one's life. At its worst, it overwhelms you in a flood of emotions and you drown in your own feelings. Water is a universal solvent. It can break down and absorb many things, transmuting them in the process.

As there are vast depths to the sea, so there are different levels to the constantly changing ocean of our feelings. The deeper part of the ocean would represent the subconscious, holding feelings that influence our lives even though we are unaware of them. A sudden intense reaction surprises us—we had no idea we felt that strongly and wonder where those feelings came from. The full range of emotions gives depth to our personality as well as substance and food to our souls.

The element of Water is very powerful. It can drive energy-producing plants, smooth the surface of rock, and eventually erode the tallest of mountains.

When we move from the Ace through the Ten of Cups, we progress from being immersed in a formless ocean of emotions and intuitions, to a state of focused response to the immediate currents of life.

For example: The Ace of Cups provides you with a desire to help others. The Two of Cups (Dominion) begins the process of determining what form this help will take. You follow your intuition and decide to work at your local youth center and create an after school program for neighborhood children. Three of Cups (Abundance)—Everything goes according to plan and you experience joy in seeing the project do so well. As you savor your achievement, your feelings rise to an all time high—Four of Cups (Luxury). Soon the Five of Cups (Disappointment) suggests that progress does not always occur in a straight line. As times goes by, the status quo is disrupted. You're feeling disillusioned as the project starts to unravel. Then the Six of Cups (Pleasure) brings new growth and balance returns, renewing not only the initial satisfaction, but an exalted happiness. The Seven of Cups (Debauch) reveals that you're mired in the quicksand of your feelings. Now you're in danger of ignoring your intuition. Eight of Cups (Indolence)—If you become addicted to the status quo, and refuse to move forward, you'll sabotage the project. The Nine of Cups (Happiness)—As the pendulum swings back to balance the cycle, you've returned to a state of equipoise. The Ten of Cups (Satiety) will put you in a place that if you got any happier you couldn't stand it! Be attentive as you float in this bliss, for the pendulum will swing again.

Ace of Cups

The blue cup is filled with the primordial energy of the Creative World. The waters of understanding and compassion pour through the cup into the earth. This is sensitivity and receptiveness in its purest form. The two blue-green serpents on the handles speak to the renewal of the soul. A double white lotus at the base of the cup illustrates the abundance of this energy. The red color represents the life force that pulses through the physical body and expresses itself as emotion. The brown-colored waves are a reminder that this energy can be experienced right here on earth. It permeates everything.

Two of Cups (Love)

Venus is in Cancer. A large pink lotus serves as part of a fountain that pours love—shown as a translucent liquid—down around two entwined Dolphins that characterize the exchange of feelings. The love continues its journey as two separate streams into two cups. Love unites us but does not enmesh us. The background of the card is divided into three colors: blue to represent our emotions, yellow-green to illustrate the joy we are feeling, and spring green to symbolize the healing that is taking place.

Three of Cups (Abundance)

Mercury is in Cancer. The three cups are overflowing with the waters of our feelings, our love and our joy. The pomegranate represents the abundance of physical life. They are prominently placed in this card, and carry a warning: Emotional pleasure can be seductive. We may be so addicted to it that we resist transformation and subsequent growth. The cups are above the water which again reminds us that we exist separate from our minds and our emotional life.

Four of Cups (Luxury)

Moon is in Cancer. Four large gold cups flowing with water are sitting just above the water. The water beneath it is beginning to look slightly agitated. This card symbolizes the fine line we may cross when our emotions pour forth so profusely that we begin to lose our sense of balance. The pink lotus from which our feelings flow is looking a little the worse for the wear. The water flows into the second set of cups as small pointed arrows, as if it were losing its natural form and fluidity.

Five of Cups (Disappointment)

Mars is in Scorpio. A pentagram is inverted and on each point is an empty, fragile-looking cup. Our feelings have dried up. The lotus leaves at the top of the card are reaching toward each other but are unable to make a connection. The lotuses are dying and their petals are falling off. What may have started out well is coming apart. The background of the card is a fiery orange-red and seems angry and hostile. Did action occur too quickly? The color of the water at the bottom of the card is a murky green. The situation is decaying. The cups are fragile but still there, the lotuses have a little life left. Can the situation be rescued? Who knows?

Six of Cups (Pleasure)

The Sun is in Scorpio. Six golden copper cups are perched on long copper stems that seem to be brimming with the energy of pure pleasure. Copper has a healing effect on our emotional body. The water is flowing into the cups but not overflowing. There is a sense of containment. The card itself looks warm and inviting and signifies a general sense of well being. As a six card, there is balance and harmony present. We're comfortable with our feelings and are enjoying the pleasures of life.

Seven of Cups (Debauch)

Venus is in Scorpio. Everything looks stagnant and decaying. The blue cups are oozing drops of green slime. The water beneath is a rotten bubbling pool of toxic matter. The bottom cup has slipped beneath the surface. The lotuses are upside down. Everything is out of balance. You are drowning in your emotions. All sense of propriety has been lost. There has been too much of a good thing, and overindulgence has taken its toll.

Eight of Cups (Indolence)

Saturn is in Pisces. The living sea of water has died and cannot support life. Only two of the lotuses were able to bloom. The top three cups are empty as well as the one on the bottom. The flow of emotions is weak and cannot sustain their clarity. The water is dark and dismal. The handles of the cups are broken symbolizing that it is hard for us to get a handle on this situation. We need to look at our lives and see where our energy is being focused. We seem to be giving more than we are receiving. If we do not feed our own emotional bodies we dry up emotionally and will eventually have little left to give.

Nine of Cups (Happiness)

Jupiter is in Pisces. Nine cups are returned to a position of strength and balance. The water is once again flowing. The lotuses are healthy and fill each of the cups. There is emotional wisdom and a sense of structure to this card. The roots of this card go deep into the water. This is not a superficial sense of pleasure—it is a sense that radiates from within the depth of the psyche. You're not happy because of something. You're happy just because you're happy.

Ten of Cups (Satiety)

Mars is in Pisces. The cups are in the shape of a ram's head and seem to be a little tilted. The water flows in a rigid way; as if it were not a natural flow but a forced one. The background is fiery orange. The Tree of Life is red-orange. These are strong emotions bordering on compulsion. This is as happy as you dare to get. Anything more than this will be counterproductive and work against you. This is as emotionally filled as you can be and still function in a human body.

Symbols of the Swords Suit

The element Air is associated with the Swords Suit. At its best, air is crystal clear, and at its worst it is dense and polluted. Like the air, our thoughts can go from crystal clear to dark and chaotic, and all points in between. When the mind is clear, it reflects our thoughts with precision. We perceive things accurately. The Sword (intellect) helps us cut through the chaos, separate our thoughts, organize them, and manage them. It helps us gather and analyze information, make decisions, and even learn to compromise.

The mind can be our greatest asset or deadliest saboteur. When we move from the Ace through the Ten of Swords, we're moving from thoughts in a complex whirl of abstractions to thoughts that generate outcomes: manifestation in the world of matter.

For example: Ace of Swords—You have a clear thought in mind about what you would like to accomplish. Two of Swords (Peace)—You're able to see your vision clearly. Three of Swords (Sorrow)—As you think about the idea, past memories and experiences are activated, casting a dark shadow on your mind; your original thought is clouded. You're no longer confident about your own ability. Four of Swords (Truce)—If you're to accomplish your objective, you must negotiate a temporary truce with past sorrow and disappointments. Shut off the tape of failure, and, realizing that this is a new situation, replace non-productive thoughts with optimism. Five of Swords (Defeat)—Though you've renewed your vision, your mind doesn't give up its negativity easily. It anxiously lists all the reasons for failure. Six of Swords (Science)—You get a grip on your thinking process, firmly deciding which thoughts to foster and which to negate. You resolve to be more objective about the project, to research the situation, and to cut through the obstacles. Seven of Swords (Futility)—You may become overwhelmed by thinking of all that needs to be done; you even consider giving up the whole idea. Eight of Swords (Interference)— The harpies of doubt are again interfering with your progress. Nine of Swords (Cruelty)—You start undermining yourself with a litany of criticism; your soul suffers the onslaught. Ten of Swords (Ruin)—The welter of mental conflict is about to sabotage the whole idea, so that you end up doing nothing.

Ace of Swords

The green sword represents the primordial energy of the Formative World as it parts the dark clouds and allows light to penetrate the confusion of the mind so that we can think clearly. The word *Thelema* (Will) is on the blade. The philosophy of *Thelema* states that each of us has a unique place in creation and it is our duty to exercise our Will and stay in harmony with the forces of the universe. This is the sword of the Magician and pierces a crown of 22 rays of light representing the manifestation of wisdom. The snake on the handle symbolizes transformation. The three solar disks and two crescent moons represent the unconscious brought into conscious awareness.

Two of Swords (Peace)

The Moon is in Libra. Two swords are crossed through a blue rose. The position of the swords prevents them from creating chaos of the mind. We have made a decision and have temporarily found some peace of mind. The green color represents regeneration of the mind and the yellow characterizes intellectual development taking place. The four pinwheels (stylized angels) signify that the mind gives form and structure to all four aspects of life. What transpires in the mind affects the mental state as well as emotional, physical and spiritual well being. The praying figures on the handles pray for peace.

Three of Swords (Sorrow)

Saturn is in Libra. Three swords destroy the center rose (harmony) as the sorrow we carry within devastates our minds. The rose petals fall like tears from the heart of humankind. Human struggle creates pain and a profound state of sorrow. However, it is important that we do not let our minds be totally consumed by this sorrow. The crescent moons and solar disks tell us to allow this deep sorrow to surface so that we can acknowledge it, begin to process it. The snake represents the need to shed the old, release the sorrow and move back into a state of balance.

Four of Swords (Truce)

Jupiter is in Libra. Four swords are arrayed in the shape of St. Andrews Cross, symbolizing rigidity, as they cross through a large rose (harmony). The Four of Swords represents an impasse in the chaos of the mind. It indicates that you must declare a temporary truce if mental harmony is to be restored. Since at this point we would rather give in than fight for ourselves, the necessity for compromise becomes evident. The light blue color represents the calmness of the moment, but the yellow lines in the background illustrate that nothing has really changed.

Five of Swords (Defeat)

Venus is in Aquarius. The inverted pentagram, representing the self, indicates that my life is upside down. The mind is bent and broken and at this point is of no help. One's defeat is due to pacifism. You've allowed nonproductive ideas to overcome you and didn't even put up a fight. The rose (harmony) is gone and only the petals remain. All the handles of the swords are different—there is no continuity among them. Balance and harmony are lost. The blue border characterizes the need for mental clarity. The yellow and green colors suggest that, with time and objectivity, healing will come.

Six of Swords (Science)

Mercury is in Aquarius. The six similar swords pass through the Rose Cross. They represent all the powers of mind focused in a single direction. The scientific mind is able to analyze, synthesize and discriminate. It is able to maintain a state of objectivity, to observe research and gather information. The lines in the background show that there is abundant activity. However, the circle tells us that the mind is whole, integrated, organized and focused on understanding the situation.

Seven of Swords (Futility)

The Moon is in Aquarius. The card is called Futility, but in spite of its title structure and balance are present. Each sword has an astrological sign on its handle: Neptune, Venus, Mars, Jupiter, Mercury and Saturn. The center sword has the Moon and the Sun. Their message: decide what you want, communicate that desire to yourself, be sure it is something you love, be ready to do battle for it if necessary, don't be afraid to think big, have a well-thought-out plan of action, and listen to your intuition. The background shapes and color represent the fragility of our minds—the overwhelming sense of frustration that exists.

Eight of Swords (Interference)

Jupiter is in Gemini. Everything seems to be happening to you. Six small swords are behind and cross two larger ones that point down toward the earth. The position of the large swords is beneficial because at least there's a possibility of getting out ahead of the problem. The wings in the background illustrate the frustration which in itself may be interfering. The crossed swords represent the roadblocks the mind is setting up. The patterns in the background represent a mind working overtime.

Nine of Swords (Cruelty)

Mars is in Gemini. Nine swords of different lengths, each dripping blood, have been given center stage in this card. The red drops are life force slowly slipping away. The swords look battle scarred and have obviously done the mind great damage. The different lengths signify the many ways mind can slay creative potential. Red signifies the power and force these swords possess. Your self esteem has been wounded. The white tears represent the pain and suffering of your soul. The background color is heavy, dull and lifeless. There is no clarity left. Reason has abandoned you.

Ten of Swords (Ruin)

The Sun is in Gemini. The ten swords represent a mind that is out of control. The three lower swords pierce the red heart—the heart of the child. Attempting to manifest our thoughts in physical form on this earth is not easy. The mind can be our greatest saboteur by slaying the children of our creative thoughts and leaving behind only confusion, despair and ruin. The swords break from pressure and our thought forms become irrational. The vitality of the card, the sun's energy, is being directed into the negative aspects of the mind.

Symbols of the Disks Suit

Earth is the element associated with the Disks Suit, and it is through this element that primal life force manifests in physical form. At its best, it represents beautiful sun-filled days, starlit nights and clear pure water; every breath we breathe is a gift from Mother Earth. At its worst, the primal life force manifesting in physical form can wreak great devastation. The earth quakes, rivers flood and hurricanes blow. Mother Earth can nurture and care for you or destroy all you have created. If we allow the earth element to become out of balance in our lives, it will produce disturbing effects.

As we move from the Ace of Disks through the Ten of Disks, we experience the progression of primal life force into a three-dimensional earthly reality. Taking this infinite energy and solidifying it into finite matter is no simple task.

For example: The Ace of Disks represents the primordial power and sacredness of the earth; the potential to create heaven here on earth. You're inspired to build a house. Ace of Disks—Heaven at the moment is the image of building your own home. You start by mentally playing with design ideas, perhaps even sketching them out. With an architect, you begin to tentatively examine the different elements you want. Two of Disks (Change)—To move toward the final dream house, you must be flexible about making changes. There are many times when you will press the delete button and start over. Three of Disks (Work)—You persevere, however and devote many long hours to the project. In fact, you give it all you have. Four of Disks (Power)—You now have a solid plan to work from, and move forward into the construction phase. You get your permits, the foundation is laid, and the house is underway. Five of Disks (Worry)—Now anxiety sets in. Are you doing the right thing? Will this turn out as you dreamed? The construction site is a mess and everything is going so slowly. Yet soon the framing is going up, the plumbing is laid, the walls are being closed in . . . you begin to see tangible results. Six of Disks (Success)—There's a light at the end of the tunnel. You're feeling a sense of triumph. It's coming out so well that you begin to look for things to worry about. Seven of Disks (Failure)—The painter can't seem to find the right color, the kitchen cabinets haven't arrived— the initial passion is flagging. The day-to-day materializing of a dream is wearing you down. Eight of Disks (Prudence)—You will have to slow down and be more patient. You don't want to blow it now that you're so close. Nine of Disks (Gain)—Suddenly, the home is built. Moving day comes and you arrive with your all my possessions in tow. You put the key in the lock and open the door to the solid reality of your dream home. Ten of Disks (Wealth)— Reward on all levels: You think it's beautiful, you feel great about it. It feeds your soul and is a solid physical structure that will be home to you and your family.

Ace of Disks

The Ace of Disks symbolizes the primordial energy of the Material World and represents the power of the earth. The card is covered with angel wings, giving the appearance of the sacred energy present. The earth is a dynamic expression of the divine in physical form. The Earth Mother has been impregnated by the Spirit (Sun). As offspring of this new millennium, our purpose here on earth is to express this primordial power within the confines of the human condition. Crowley's signature *To Mega Therion* (Greek for the Great Beast—666) and personal seal are placed in the center of the card.

Two of Disks (Change)

Jupiter is in Capricorn. A snake is coiled in the figure eight, the symbol of the Infinite. For things to stay the same we must constantly change. Change is necessary if we are to express ourselves in physical form. If we become motionless and fixed on any level, we begin to decay. Two circles with the Yin/Yang symbols appear within the coiled snake and represent all life in harmonious motion, through the balance of opposites. Within creation there is always the dynamic of destruction; the status quo must be destroyed to give birth to the new. The golden crown represents that change itself governs the earth.

Three of Disks (Work)

Mars is in Capricorn. Three red wheels are behind a translucent pyramid. The red wheels signify the three *Gunas* (*Sattvas*, *Rajas* and *Tamas*) of the Hindu system of Fire, Air and Water, the forces that make the wheels turn. This card represents the great work we do on ourselves. Through a process of uniting mind, body and soul, we move in a state of integration that respects humanness and venerates one's spirit. The background is earthy green. Waves of energy move to the perimeter of the card as if propelled by the energy radiating from the wheels of change.

Four of Disks (Power)

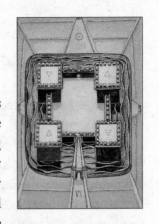

The Sun is in Capricorn. The four towers representing each of the four elements are part of a fortress with a moat surrounding it. There are other paths, but the narrow bridge across the moat seems to be the only way in. The fortress represents the physical plane. The earth is the way primal life force is able to manifest in physical form. It is mandatory to play by the rules and do what we do in an orderly way to feel secure enough to risk going beyond the walls. By working within these parameters, you come to realize that personal power exists in the ability to bridge the world of spirit and the material world.

Five of Disks (Worry)

Mercury is in Taurus. The gears are turning but the upside-down pentacle indicates that there's a wrench in the works. Beyond the dark gears, the card is bright yellow with red streaks trying to shine through. Things may look good from the outside, but inside there is doubt and uncertainty. Feelings of insecurity surface. Worry is causing physical anxiety. The instability of earth is taking its toll. You're worried that you won't be able to accomplish the manifestation.

Six of Disks (Success)

The Moon is in Taurus. The Six of Disks embodies the manifestation of the potential within the Ace of Disks. The card radiates the success of the moment. The six planets symbolize a formula for earthly success. *Moon:* listen to your intuition. *Mercury:* be willing to communicate your wants and needs to yourself and others. *Venus:* do what you love. *Jupiter:* think big. *Saturn:* structure, plan and organize your strategies. *Mars:* be willing to stay with it until you succeed (do battle to protect your vision when necessary).

Seven of Disks (Failure)

Saturn is in Taurus. This card is visually upsetting. It has gone past a state of chaos—in fact, everything is rotting. The overgrown vegetation appears spider-like and ominous. It represents a state of acquiescence and resignation. The symbols for Saturn and Taurus are on the disks. Saturn requires discipline and structure. Taurus is requesting tenacity and hard work. If the present apathy continues, all will be lost. Study the Six of Disks and rediscover the formula for success.

Eight of Disks (Prudence)

Sun is in Virgo. The bold plant dominating the card symbolizes the object of manifestation. We have obviously planted the seeds and now are happily watching them grow. Each of the eight flowers is dark pink and grows on a golden stem. Each blossom is protected by a large leaf, representing caution and patience. The sturdy stem is blue green; the background is yellow, with green earth beneath. These colors illustrate that everything is in our favor. All that can be done has been done. All we need do now is wait and see.

Nine of Disks (Gain)

Venus is in Virgo. The faces of Crowley, Lady Frieda Harris and Israel Regardie are pictured on the six disks. The symbols of the planets are overlaid on their images. They are the same six planets that are on the Six of Disks (Success): Saturn, Mars, Mercury, Moon, Venus, and Jupiter. Added to these are the three large disks in the center in the shape of a triangle. They represent the gain we experience within our mind, body and soul. Balance and harmony have returned in this card. Primal energy has manifested in form and has out of necessity become denser and slower. The material benefits abound.

Ten of Disks (Wealth)

Mercury is in Virgo. Ten yellow coins are in the positions of the Sephiroth of the Tree of Life. The process is complete; you have used all the energy you had to manifest your vision. Material success flourishes. If you're to accomplish more, you must return this energy to its original primal form. Something wonderful needs to be done with the fruit of your labor, as opposed to hoarding it. As you spread the wealth, the energy regenerates and returns to you tenfold.

Symbols of the Court Cards

The Court Cards represent the roles we play, the masks we wear and the talents we are developing. They can serve as a mirror of the internal world and reflect the qualities that we possess within but may be unwilling to express. In this way they characterize the shadow side of one's personality and act as a catalyst to growth. The Court Cards can also signify another person who has mastered the qualities of his or her Suit and who reflects to us the attributes we need to expand our own awareness.

Each of the figures in the Court Cards are illustrated with the special symbols of their Suits (Wands, Cups, Swords or Disks) to express their talents and abilities.

The Knight, as the Queen's defender, wears battle armor and is mounted on a horse. The Queen appears seated upon a throne. The Prince drives his chariot, which carries him into the world to prove himself. The Princess brings the nature of her Suit into physical form.

The Knight and Queen are more mature and possess more experience. The Prince is still in the adolescence of his development. He is active and trying to find himself; as a result he is constantly testing his boundaries. The Princess is the least mature, and still somewhat naïve. For that reason she is fearless in her pursuits; she's willing to move out into the physical world and attempt to express her traits in material form.

The Elements

To work with the Court Cards effectively, it will help you to understand the influence of the Elements. The four Elements that concern us now are Fire (Wands), Water (Cups), Air (Swords) and Earth (Disks).

Each suit of the Court Cards symbolizes the mastering of its specific qualities.

For example:

> Wands (Fire) represent mastery of *Will*
> Cups (Water) represent mastery of the *Heart*
> Swords (Air) represent mastery of the *Mind*
> Disks (Earth) represent mastery of *Matter*

Attributes of the Elements

FIRE: Primal life force energy expressed as *Will*. Fire embodies the energy of the Archetypal World (formless world—pure conscious energy). Fire is:

Intent	Masculine Energy	Charisma
Courage	Direction	Sexuality
Idealism	Desire	Lust
Virility	Creativity	Inspiration
Purification	Illumination	Initiation
Ecstasy	Sensuality	Enterprise
Optimism	Motivation	Spontaneity
Ambition	Drive	Strength
Change	Aggression	Growth
Movement	Passion	Activity

WATER: Primal life force energy expressed as *Heart*. Water embodies the energy of the Creative World. It exemplifies the unconscious from which life itself springs forth. Water is:

Understanding	Empathy	Meaningful
Emotions	Sensitivity	Transformative
Intuition	Feminine	Caring
Imagination	Adaptability	Compliance
Secrecy	Flexibility	Receptivity
Surrender	Transition	Nurturing
Feelings	Fantasy	Supportive
Tears	Illogical	Considerate
Compassion	Irrational	Open
Passivity	Holistic	

AIR: Primal life force energy expressed as *Mind*. Air embodies the energy of the Formative World. Air is:

Intellect	Organized	Astute
Thought	Logical	Judicious
Perception	Curious	Knowledgeable
Mental Awareness	Analytical	Gregarious
Communication	Clever	Humorous
Beliefs	Cunning	Diplomatic
Rational	Discriminating	

EARTH: Primal life force energy expressed as *Matter*. Earth embodies the energy of the Physical World. It is the pull toward manifestation. Earth is:

Material	Committed	Cultivated
Structure	Disciplined	Informed
Form	Stable	Systematic
Grounding	Serious	Methodical
Patience	Weighty	Refined
Self-Discipline	Value-Oriented	Sharp
Convention	Function	History
Tradition	Purpose	Self-Control
Caution	Shrewd	Conventional
Propriety	Reliable	Worldliness
Conservation	Practical	Restraint
Loyal	Innovative	

Elements that rule specific Court Cards

All Knights are Fire   *All Princes* are Air
All Queens are Water   *All Princesses* are Earth

The Wands Suit is ruled by the element Fire
The Cups Suit is ruled by the element Water
The Swords Suit is ruled by the element Air
The Disks Suit is ruled by the element Earth

Blending the Elements
of the Court Cards

Every Court Card is a combination of two elements, with one predominating. The influence of each element is expressed by the action taken.

For example: The Queen of Wands is the *watery part of Fire*. We know that all Queens are influenced by the element Water. We also know that all Wands are Fire. Therefore, we need to consider how the Water attributes of the Queen will be affected by the Fire element of her Wand Suit. To understand the nature of this card we must know what happens when fire meets water. As a Queen, she has access to her emotions, intuition and compassion (Water). The Fire element adds strength, action and courage. Combining Water and Fire makes the Queen a person of strong convictions and sensitivity, boldness and profound feeling. She can go deep within herself yet actively express her emotions. The Queen of Wands has a feminine nature expressed with masculine authority.

If we reverse those elements and look at the Knight of Cups, who is the *fiery part of Water*, we see a different picture. The Water element will be blended with the Fire element in a different way than in the Queen of Wands. In the Queen of Wands, where fire meets water, the water picks up energy; as the water boils, the energy increases. In the Knight of Cups, water meets fire, and the water diminishes the fire, eventually extinguishing it. The Knight may act swiftly with fiery conviction, but the passive yet persistent fluidity of water will prevail in the long run.

The Knight of Wands is the fiery part of Fire
The Queen of Wands is the watery part of Fire
The Prince of Wands is the airy part of Fire
The Princess of Wands is the earthy part of Fire

The Knight of Cups is the fiery part of Water
The Queen of Cups is the watery part of Water
The Prince of Cups is the airy part of Water
The Princess of Cups is the earthy part of Water

The Knight of Swords is the fiery part of Air
The Queen of Swords is the watery part of Air
The Prince of Swords is the airy part of Air
The Princess of Swords is the earthy part of Air

The Knight of Disks is the fiery part of Earth
The Queen of Disks is the watery part of Earth
The Prince of Disks is the airy part of Earth
The Princess of Disks is the earthy part of Earth

Fire and Air—Knight of Swords, Prince of Wands. This combination leads to high-energy people who take life as it comes. They don't necessarily want to contemplate—they want to take action. If Air is predominant, as in the Knight of Swords, they will be quick thinkers. If Fire is predominant, as in the Prince of Wands, they will be charismatic and opportunistic.

Water and Air—Queen of Swords, Prince of Cups. These combinations are tuned in to other people. Interested in relationship, they are tactful and exhibit social ease and competence. If Air predominates (Queen of Swords), they have a rational approach to reality and see things clearly. If Water predominates (Prince of Cups), they have a passionate desire for mystical union and interaction.

Earth and Air—Princess of Swords, Prince of Disks. Earth and Air combinations are inclined to theorize and meander in subjective reality. They also have a well developed sense of duty and responsibility. If Earth is predominant (Prince of Disks), they tend toward a single-minded focus that may isolate them. If Air is predominant (Princess of Swords), they have a greater sense of social awareness.

Water and Earth—Princess of Cups, Queen of Disks. These combinations are deliberate, stable and cautious. They have a strong desire to contribute to something that withstands the test of time. If Earth predominates (Queen of Disks), nurturing qualities are accentuated and there is a strong sense of integrity. For the Princess of Cups, with Water predominant, emotional sensitivity and imagination are more pronounced.

Fire and Earth—Princess of Wands and Knight of Disks. These cards signify strong focus and a lot of know-how. They represent a keen desire to manifest and abundant resourcefulness. If Earth is predominant, there is a decided need to understand and predict experiences (Knight of Disks). If Fire is predominant, there is a greater trust in one's innate abilities (Princess of Wands).

Fire and Water—Queen of Wands and Knight of Cups embrace a powerful vision for their lives. If Water is predominant, as in the Queen of Wands, her vision serves as an inspiration to others. If Fire is predominant, as in the Knight of Cups, there is a strong need to openly express one's vision with emotional intensity.

Knight
of Wands

Knight of Wands

He represents the fiery part of Fire. The Knight rides a black horse through fiery flames; even the horse's mane reminds us of flames. He is fire of Fire and for that reason is the purest representative of the element. Fire alters everything in its path. It purifies and transforms all levels of reality. The Knight is concerned with will and intent. Thus he needs continuously burning fires to transform himself and clarify the road ahead.

He is passionately fierce, impulsive and willing to use his talents to change and revolutionize both himself and the world at large. He wears complete body armor, ready to do battle at anytime. He is the forerunner who will lead the campaign and fight the good fight. However, with so much ablaze, he may burn himself out and not be there in the long haul. The Knight holds a torch of flames reminiscent of the Ace of Wands, and uses his burning passion to clear his path as well as burn down the structures of negativity, ignorance and lethargy. The Unicorn on his helmet signifies his highly perceptive nature and the clearness of his vision.

CARD SYMBOLS	INTERPRETATIONS
Element	Fire
Flames of fire	transformation, revolution, honesty, integrity, initiator
Leaping black horse	activity, strong instinctive forward motion, courage
Flaming torch	purification, clearing the way, focus, determined
Body armor	prepared to fight the good fight
Unicorn on helmet	highly perceptive, insightful, unity, single-minded focus
Colors	red, orange and yellow: fire of creativity, activity, warmth

Queen of Wands

Queen of Wands

S he represents the watery part of Fire. The Queen of Wands is sitting on a throne of fire, the source of her constant energy. The fiery flames feed her ability to communicate with her spirit and translate this energy into unambiguous intent, inspiration, and illumination. There is a transformational aspect to this card. The Queen resides within the fires of purification that lead to her transformation. Her crown is rayed with fiery flames, indicating a highly perceptive nature. The winged globe above her head represents connection with the archetypal world. She is such a brilliant light that she can illumine your path and help you connect with your own vision.

She wears armor made of fish scales with the symbol of Pisces on the breastplate. The Piscean symbol speaks to her sensitivity, depth of her feelings and her fluidity. The armor suggests that while her intentions are loving and kind, she will not tolerate opposition for she is committed to her truth and to the full expression of her spirit. The Queen is the epitome of feminine influence and authority. Her consort is a leopard; he contributes his power and strength to her convictions. His black spots will hopefully remind her of her dark side which includes uncompromising obstinacy.

CARD SYMBOLS	INTERPRETATIONS
Element	Fire
Fiery flames	transformation, primal spiritual energy
Crown of flames	extremely perceptive
Winged globe	connection with primordial world
Scaled armor	will not tolerate opposition
Symbol of Pisces	sensitivity, fluidity and depth of feelings
Wand with pinecone	transformation here on earth; the cone is representative of Bacchus
Leopard	strength, power
Long flowing hair	awareness, perception
Colors	red/yellow: healing fires of transformation; brown: work yet to be done

Prince of Wands

Prince
of Wands

He represents the airy part of Fire. The Prince of Wands is surrounded by flames which symbolize his relationship with the fire of spirit. His golden chariot is pulled by a lion and suggests the power and strength inherent within the creative process. The Prince's crossed legs form a number 4 to signify that spirit supplies the passion, motivation and inspiration needed to create in form. He holds the reins loosely to illustrate his trust in the creative process; this also denotes his need for unrestrained freedom of expression.

Flames are enclosed within the chariot, showing that the energy is contained and advances with direction and purpose. The green base of the flames in the chariot denotes the creative force that drives his passion. He is naked—trusting of the process and open to the inspiration that moves him forward. The Phoenix Wand in his left hand indicates the power and energy he puts into his creative endeavors. The rayed crown shows the enlightened state he works toward. His creative perspective is represented in the arched wings with the lion's head. The dark marks in the background of the card are reminders of the darkness he has come from and caution him to be aware of external influences. The sigil on the Prince's breastplate reads *To Mega Therion* and signifies Crowley's Mark of the Beast.

CARD SYMBOLS	INTERPRETATIONS
Element	Fire
Flames of fire	consumed by passion, ambition, drive, enthusiasm and optimism
Phoenix Wand	power and energy directed toward his goal
Cloak of fire	surrounded by primal spiritual force
Chariot	the creative process
Lion pulling chariot	power of the spiritual process, creative imagination
Reins loosely held	trusting the process, surrendering to one's passion
Rayed crown	moving toward enlightenment, strong will and intent
Wings with lion's head	creative perspective
Dark marks in background	remember where you have come from
Naked	openness
Body in number 4 position	builder, creator of form
Colors	yellow/red/orange: vitality, passion, inspiration

Princess
of Wands

Princess of Wands

S he represents the earthy part of fire. The Princess of Wands is herself
fuel for the fire. She is traveling in the energy current of the flame
carrying her out into the world. The flame generates the heat of her
passion, vitality and enthusiasm. She has a wand with a solar disk at
the top, signifying the primal life force of the sun empowering her to
action. She has the tiger by the tail, denoting that even though she
may be afraid, she courageously takes hold of her fears and continues
in spite of them.

Committed to liberation of the spirit within, the Princess moves
boldly into the world, walking her talk. The altar is covered with
roses in flames, embodying the changes she has gone through as well
as the sacrifices she has made. The ram's heads on the base of the
altar symbolize the energy of something new materializing. She is
totally naked, thus unencumbered, open and trusting. She wears a
headdress of large antennae denoting a high degree of perception.

CARD SYMBOLS	INTERPRETATIONS
Element	Fire
River of fire	energy, instinctual drive, ambition that moves us into the world
Tiger	fears and inner demons
Altar with flaming roses	using one's self to fuel the fire
Ram heads on base of altar	materialization of something new; pushing through resistance
Headdress with antennae	perception, awareness
Wand with solar disk	the passion that empowers us and moves us to action
Colors	red/yellow/orange: warmth, energy and healing of fire

Knight
of Cups

Knight of Cups

He signifies the fiery part of Water. The Knight of Cups represents the luminous glow of a wave as it unfolds on shore. He is the active part of water but remains passive by nature. He is on a beautiful white horse that symbolizes the purity of his intuition. He has a sense of immediacy that keeps his intuition and imagination moving and in the present. His feelings may not be long-lived, but they will be enthusiastic and fully expressed. He acts spontaneously and communicates from his heart; however, being in the moment, he is already moving on to the next hunch.

The wings sprouting from his armor indicate that he thrives on imagination and is uplifted by emotion. His red hair denotes the intensity of his imagination, intuition and sentiments. He is without a helmet, allowing himself to be vulnerable and open in expression. The peacock illustrates that the Knight can be a bit dramatic in his delivery. He raises a red cup with a crab above it which depicts the more assertive side of Cancer. The blue tones of this card speak to the fluency of the water element, and the green to the Knight's creative expression of the element.

CARD SYMBOLS	INTERPRETATIONS
Element	Water
White horse	purity of expression
Wings	flying high on imagination, intuition and emotions
Green armor	creative communication of feelings, intuition and imagination
Red cup	assertiveness, intensity of delivery
Peacock	dramatic execution, ego, flamboyance
Bare-headed	open, trusting and vulnerable, freewheeling intellect, sureness
Red hair	intensity of imagination, intuition and emotions
Colors	blue: emotional wisdom and intelligence; green: creative expression; red/orange: energy, intensity, vitality

Queen
of Cups

Queen of Cups

She represents the watery part of Water. The Queen of Cups has a dreamy, illusive quality and lives in the mysterious depth of the unconscious from which our intuition, imagination and dreams are born. She is enthroned on the mirror-like surface of calm water that reflects fantasies, dreams and intuition. Her own image on the water tells you that she herself reflects her environment without necessarily being affected by it. Swirling veils of water screen her, enhancing the sense of the Queen's illusiveness.

There are many layers to this Queen's personality—she may be something different to everyone she encounters. She holds the lotus of perfect love and devotion, and carries a shell cup with Neptune's trident above it, which illustrates the depth of her understanding, intuition and feelings. The two water lilies illustrate her ability to maintain a position of emotional neutrality. The stork corresponds to her capacity to nurture through her love, kindness and compassion those in her care.

CARD SYMBOLS	INTERPRETATIONS
Element	Water
Enthroned upon water	composed of her intuition, creative imagination and feelings
Watery veils	hiding behind a veil of illusion
Still water	reflective nature
Shell-like cup	feminine mysteries, holder of dreams, imagination and intuitive feelings
Neptune	depth of intuition, understanding and emotions
Lotus in right hand	love
Two water lilies	balance, neutral position
Stork	nurturing, compassion and understanding
Colors	blue: emotional wisdom and intelligence; yellow-gold: light of spirit coming through; green: creative imagination

Prince of Cups

Prince of Cups

He is the airy part of Water. The Prince of Cups sits upon a shell-like chariot that carries him swiftly over the water. He is pulled by a powerful eagle, which symbolizes that strong intuition and imagination direct his chariot. This is also shown in the eagle surmounting his helmet. His chariot skims over the surface of the water but does not touch it, suggesting that he keeps hidden what is deeply important to him. He has a cup at his chest with a snake rising from it, depicting the emotional transformations he experiences in his lifetime.

The Prince is naked and wears only his helmet—thus he is trusting of his feelings, but detached from his thoughts. The crashing waves in the background supply him with the emotional drive needed to re-create himself over and over again. He has an extremely passionate nature and is open to exploring his needs and desires. The lotus blossom in his hand faces down, showing that the Prince of Cups has difficulty in expressing the depth of his feelings to those around him.

CARD SYMBOLS	INTERPRETATIONS
Element	Water
Shell-like chariot	carried by intuitions and emotions
Eagle helmet / Eagle pulling chariot	driven by powerful emotions, intuition and imagination
Cup with serpent	emotional transformation
Naked with head covered	trusting of feelings, detached from thoughts
Still water	deep emotions, intuition and imagination
Chariot skims above water	prefers to keep deeper emotions hidden
Waves in back	emotional drive, volatility
Colors	blue: emotional intelligence; green: creative expression

Princess
of Cups

Princess of Cups

S he is the earthy part of Water. The Princess of Cups is a beautiful
young woman in a splendid rosy mantle that flows like gentle
ripples of water and indicates her tender loving nature. She has a
dreamy, romantic quality. The jewels on the hem of her garment
illustrate that she crystallizes her intuition, imagination and feelings
in a material way through acts of love, generosity and kindness.

There are many facets to her emotions and she openly expresses
them within her relationships. In her hand a large seashell has a
tortoise peeking out of it. They represent her commitment, strength
and reliability within relationship. Her hand lightly holds a lotus as
it moves with the flow of the water; the floating lotus symbolizes
that she loves without condition and with an open hand. The rose-
colored dolphin illustrates the power of the Princess' loving
communication. The water around her flows softly and gives the
card a sensual feel. The swan above her head with outstretched wings
depicts the materialization of spirit as love. She herself is the
expression of love in form.

CARD SYMBOLS	INTERPRETATIONS
Element	Water
Rosy mantle	gentle, loving nature
Jewels on gown	love, kindness, generosity materialized
Seashell	contains imagination, intuitions, dreams and feelings
Tortoise	longevity, commitment, loyalty, supportive
Lotus	love
Lotus loosely held	love without condition
Dolphin	loving communication, instinctively knows what to say and do
Swan	materialization of spirit as love
Colors	blue: loving wisdom; pink: innocence, beauty; green: creative expression of love

Knight of Swords

Knight of Swords

He represents the fiery part of Air. The Knight of Swords symbolizes the will and intent of the mind. The propeller-like wings on his helmet signify his capacity to look at a situation from every conceivable angle and change his mind easily if new data calls for a different conclusion. He allows thoughts to flow through his mind without becoming attached to any one in particular. He is aware that no single idea or belief is absolute—it is only relative. If he loses sight of that fact, his thinking can become rigid and he will be unable to make decisions.

He is able to discriminate between many alternatives and can help with understanding and analyzing options. People respect his opinions and admire his cleverness. If you need to know something, ask the Knight—he probably has the answer in his mental files. He puts forth his views with great authority and can back up what he says with facts. He sees things clearly and can have difficulty with people of a highly emotional nature; they don't get to the bottom line quick enough for him. He takes pride in his mind and does not like having his opinions questioned.

CARD SYMBOLS	INTERPRETATIONS
Element	Air
Four transparent wings	can move in any direction: mental emotional, spiritual, or physical
Six-pointed star in center of propeller-like wings	clarity, balance, flexibility
Sword	masculine logic
Dagger	feminine, flexibility, open, receptive
Golden armor	malleability prevents rigid thinking; intellect is always ready to do battle; can defend any position with vigor
Three birds	mind, body, and spirit moving in one direction
Horse	Knight's symbol of passionate intent (fire)
Speed of blue clouds	mind (air) moves quickly, with agility

Queen of Swords

Queen of Swords

S he represents the watery part of Air. The Queen of Swords symbolizes the rational, objective and intellectual mind. She has a sword in one hand and the severed head of an old man in the other. This shows she is able to separate the higher faculties of the mind (pure intellect) from the lower faculties (reactive mind) so that mind remains a pure and clear receiver of thought. It also illustrates that she has cut away the facade and sees clearly what is behind it.

She is not absolute in her thinking and as a result can allow things to just be. She is naked at her chest to show that her heart is open and that she really does understand. The Queen appears very relaxed enthroned upon the clouds . . . just sitting and observing what happens. The cherubic face and the crystals reveal a clear and open mind that entertains new thoughts with a child-like curiosity and crystal-clear perception. The blue sky depicts the serenity of the Queen's mind. The thunderhead clouds may threaten rain, which symbolizes that she has the potential to use the sword of her mind to cut right to the heart of the matter, and even cut you down to size if she so desires.

CARD SYMBOLS	INTERPRETATIONS
Element	Air
Sword	mind's cutting tool; cuts through the waste and penetrates to the issues
Severed head	a polluted mind that has lost objectivity, disconnected from reality; serving no master but itself
Old man's face	obsolete ideas; letting go of the old patriarchy
Child	new ideas, curious nature
Naked chest	compassionate, understanding, open at the heart
Crystals	seeing clearly, rationally and objectively
Enthroned upon cloud	sitting back to observe; able to detach
Blue sky	tranquility

Prince of Swords

Prince
of Swords

He symbolizes the airy part of Air. The Prince of Swords represents thinking for its own sake. His mind is full of ideas—each as good as the next. He holds a sword high in the air with one hand and a sickle in the other. The sword cuts through the confusion and a great idea emerges; the sickle, however, is close behind and slashes it down. The Prince's chariot is being drawn by three child-like, winged creatures who seem to be having great fun going in any direction they want.

Creative thought needs freedom and unlimited expression, but it also needs a creative focus to give it direction. Herein lies the paradox: if you hold the reins too tightly, freedom of thought is gone and creativity dies. If you hold them too loosely, your thoughts lack focus and direction. The Prince's green armor shows that he is prepared for battle and poised to find the balance needed to keep the chariot moving forward. The yellow spheres with pyramids inside illustrate the power of the inventive mind. The many crystals on this card represent the intellectual mind, full of thoughts and ideas.

CARD SYMBOLS	INTERPRETATIONS
Element·	Air
Green armor	fight to balance powers of mind and creativity
Reins in hand	loosely held to allow freedom of thought, and creative thinking to unfold without interference
Yellow spheres	thought
Pyramids inside spheres	power of inventive mind
Three winged figures	freedom of body, mind, and soul
Lines of constraint	moving through resistance; creating boundaries when necessary; learning to maintain equilibrium
Crystals in background	intellect, thoughts, ideas

Princess of Swords

Princess
of Swords

S he represents the earthy part of Air and symbolizes the process of
manifesting her ideas in the marketplace. The Princess holds a sword
in one hand, while her other hand rests on the throne. She appears to
be defending the throne. For that reason she can at times appear
defensive. The card's dark, sinister clouds indicate the struggle we
must undertake if our ideas are to bear fruit in the physical world.
The Princess must constantly cut through her moods as well as the
conflicts that normally surround the process of creativity.

She has the strength and courage to take on the job. She is
outspoken and will risk saying exactly what's on her mind. If she is to
counteract her anxiety, and offset the heaviness of the earth element,
she must remain active. Her sword is pointed down toward the earth,
illustrating the fact that she has the imposing responsibility of putting
her ideas into physical form. It's not an easy job—no matter what she
does, she feels as if it always falls short of her original idea. When her
thoughts become too depressing and the clouds too dark, she cuts
through them and just keeps trying. The yellow and green colors
indicate that when she gets past her moods, her creativity returns,
and she is up and running again.

CARD SYMBOLS	INTERPRETATIONS
Element	Air
Hand on throne	defends her position; protects her ideas
Dark clouds	struggle to bring ideas into the world
Sword	mind as a tool to cut through the darkness; outspokeness
Helmet with medusa crest	frightening process that takes a person of courage and daring to face
Colors	yellow: inspiration to penetrate the clouds; insights; seeing the light at the end of the tunnel; green: creativity that is being expressed; blue: ideas one is manifesting

Knight of Disks

Knight
of Disks

He represents the fiery part of Earth. The Knight of Disks doesn't appear to be ready for battle. He rides a plow horse with all four feet firmly on the ground. This represents an inclination toward convention, stability and hard work rather than going anywhere fast. With his head hanging low, this horse looks as if he's already done a full day's work. The Knight carries a flail pointed toward the earth, not raised for battle. He's more like the dying embers of a fire whose flame is returning to earth as ash. The surrounding wheat fields and rolling, grassy hills symbolize his connection with the fertile land. He has solid plate armor, yet his helmet is open and crested with a stag, illustrating preoccupation with physical reality.

It's not easy to take the fire of one's passion and materialize it. It calls for hard work and commitment. The Knight contemplates the fields cultivated by his labor and anticipates the bounty of his harvest. His sturdy body shows the ability to work hard and enjoy the fruits of life. The large solid disk (shield) in his hand is for protection. This is to remind him that success will come to him through his hard work and earthy instincts, not through abstract intellect.

CARD SYMBOLS	INTERPRETATIONS
Element	Earth
Plow horse	best for work, not speed
Horse with four feet on ground	stability, structure, tradition
Horse's head hanging down	exhausted from hard work
Flail pointed at the earth	not planning to do battle, except with planting and harvesting
Solid armor	protecting one's physical body through proper health and sustenance
Open helmet with stag	preoccupied with material world
Large disk in hand	understands the physical plane
Wheat fields	abundant harvest
Fertile hills	importance of food production
Colors	brown: earth, stability, fertility; green: creativity, growth, healing; golden yellow: sun as it relates to growing crops

Queen of Disks

Queen
of Disks

She represents the watery part of Earth. The Queen of Disks is
enthroned in a lush green oasis and looks back at the barren
wasteland she has traveled through to achieve her understanding.
Gazing back, she is able to see a river now flowing through the desert,
bringing abundance to the material world. She supports a globe in
her arm to indicate that she has a grasp of the physical world and
comprehends its workings. The goat poised on the sphere symbolizes
the importance of materializing divine energy through creating a
heaven here on earth.

The Queen holds a scepter with a cube containing a three-
dimensional hexagram, indicating that she is clear about what she is
doing and why she is doing it. Her helmet has spiral horns to signify
that she aspires to know the Great Work and take part in the process.
Her ability to materialize her spiritual energy is depicted by the chest
armor of coins and the long skirt of intertwined disks. She embodies
the abundance of Mother Earth and illustrates the prosperity available
to each of us.

CARD SYMBOLS	INTERPRETATIONS
Element	Earth
Enthroned in lush vegetation	natural abundance, prosperity
Desert	hard times
Flowing river	looking back she sees the abundance that she did not see before
Globe in her arm	she has a grasp on the world
Goat on sphere	importance of materialization
Scepter with Cube/Hexagram	sees clearly
Helmet with horns	aspires to understand more
Chest armor of coins	prosperity on all levels
Skirt of disks	Comprehends the physical world and how to work with its abundance
Colors	green: lush fertile creative environment; brown: Earth element, bringing to earth

Prince
of Disks

Prince of Disks

He represents the airy part of Earth. The Prince of Disks sits upon a steel chariot drawn by a powerful ox. It illustrates the Prince's potential and determination to reach his goals. The ox symbolizes the power of physical manifestation and the strength of the Prince's physical instincts. He is determined to succeed and unstoppable in his desire to surround himself with the beauty of this earth. The tapestry behind him suggests the fertility of the earth and the abundance available to each of us. We have only to work at its materialization.

The Prince is practical by nature and committed to creating what he intends. His chariot is filled with seedpods for planting and indicates his capacity to develop new things and help them grow. He wears a metal helmet but his face is uncovered, symbolizing that he neither restricts his thinking nor hides his intent. His hand resting on a large globe shows that he seeks his fortune in worldly arenas. In his other hand is a scepter with a globe surmounted by a cross, signifying that he is a crusader in the land of physical manifestation. Naked except for the metal helmet with the head of a winged bull, he is sensual and open to earthly experience of all kinds. He respects his body and his material possessions as part of divine expression.

CARD SYMBOLS	INTERPRETATIONS
Element	Earth
Steel chariot	power of physical manifestation
Ox pulling chariot	strong physical instincts
Large globe	the outer world
Scepter with globe and cross	crusader in physical expression
Tapestry	beauty of earth's abundance
Helmet without faceplate	does not hide intent, integrity, unrestricted thought
Winged bull	determined, steadfast, loyal
Seedpods	ready to plant and nurture new things, growth
Nakedness	sensual, open to all types of earthly experiences
Color	dark greenish black: fecundity

Princess of Disks

Princess of Disks

S he represents the earthy part of Earth. The Princess of Disks has been on a vision quest. The barren landscape behind her shows that it's been a long and trying journey. She has endured the struggle of creating form in this three-dimensional world. The ram on her headdress has given her the determination, strength and sure footing necessary to climb to great heights and bring her vision back down to earth. She carries a scepter with a diamond-shaped, pointed crystal emitting gold light. This symbolizes the crystallization of intent into matter and its return into the light source from which its journey began.

The wheat motif on the Princess' altar expresses the abundance and prosperity of earthly harvests. Her pregnancy illustrates giving birth to future manifestations. In fact, she gives birth to all possibilities. The disk in her hand is a large seedpod with the yin/yang symbol of perfect balance in the center. Around her neck is a large animal skin cape that suggests her strong physical instincts. Her long red hair represents the integrity and clarity of her thoughts and perceptions. The golden light behind her represents the light that heals the barren wasteland from which she has emerged.

CARD SYMBOLS	INTERPRETATIONS
Element	Earth
Barren landscape	long hard journey
Ram on headdress	strength, surefootedness, determination
Scepter with crystal pointed toward earth	crystallization of intent into matter
Wheat stalks on altar	prosperity, abundance, harvest
Pregnant	giving birth to future possibilities
Animal skin cape	human instincts
Holding disk of seedpods	planting of new seeds
Yin/Yang	perfect balance between one's feminine (receptive) and masculine (active) nature
Long red hair	integrity, clear perceptions
Colors	earth tones: earth, grounding, form
Roots of bare trees in golden light	light heals the barren wasteland

Section III

PERSONAL
GUIDANCE
CARDS

Personal Guidance Cards

Lifetime Cards

       Personality Card
       Soul Card
       Inner Teacher Card
       Challenge and Opportunity Cards

Growth Year Card

Lifetime Collage

All paths lead to the same destination, but each of us has a unique method of travel as we explore different landscapes, different lessons and different opportunities in this lifetime. Your Personal Guidance Cards represent the desire of your essence to seek experiences that expand your awareness and contribute to your spiritual growth. Together they create a profile of your true personality traits, talents and abilities. They explain your inherent spiritual, mental, emotional and physical makeup. They illustrate how you perceive the world and interact with it, as well as how you can make use of your talents and turn your weaknesses into strengths.

Guidance cards differ from those of a tarot reading because they are not selected at random but chosen for their astrological or numerical relevance. You might think of these cards as asking: What is the essence of my soul in this lifetime? What are the true elements of my personality? What comes easily to me? What may present some difficulty? Your Personal Guidance cards are selected based on your birth date, and read as a blueprint of your personal journey. The tarot cards that pertain to your life path supply the information you need to help to navigate the road ahead.

The Personal Guidance cards described here **are the same throughout your lifetime**, except for the Growth Year Card which you select every year on your birthday.

Guidance cards are chosen from both the Major and Minor Arcana. They are based on either their numerical value or astrological designation.

The tarot recognizes numbers as spiritual symbols of the portals of initiation into each distinct stage of our lives. Master numbers are 0 through 10 (also known as the decad), and simply stated are as follows:

0   Nothingness, Potentiality

1   Unity, Divine Spirit (Eternal Masculine Principle)

2   Duality, Divine Receptivity (Eternal Feminine Principle)

3   Divine Intelligence (Eternal Principle of Neutrality)

4   Stability

5   Disruption

6   Equilibrium

7   Expansion

8   Stability through Change

9   Foundation and Completion

10 Form

These numbers help to illuminate a specific phase of our development as well as reveal any opportunities or challenges in our path.

Most of us are familiar with our basic sun sign. The Chart that follows will help you determine the tarot card related to your sun sign.

Your astrological sun sign corresponds to your birth date. Its traits represent the filter through which you perceive the world, the lens through which you focus your behavior and the method you use to prioritize your values. We can read the astrological symbols of the tarot in a way that helps us to clarify our special talents and abilities, and thus, through our increased understanding, learn to use these to our utmost advantage.

Sun Sign and Corresponding Major Arcana Card

Birth Date	Sun Sign	Major Arcana Card
March 21 to April 20	Aries	The Emperor
April 21 to May 20	Taurus	The Hierophant
May 21 to June 20	Gemini	The Lovers
June 21to July 21	Cancer	The Chariot
July 22 to Aug. 22	Leo	Lust
Aug.23 to Sept. 22	Virgo	The Hermit
Sept. 23 to Oct. 22	Libra	Adjustment
Oct. 23 to Nov. 22	Scorpio	Death
Nov. 23 to Dec. 21	Sagittarius	Art
Dec. 22 to Jan 19	Capricorn	The Devil
Jan. 20 to Feb. 18	Aquarius	The Star
Feb. 19 to March 20	Pisces	The Moon

This section provides you with the meaning of your Personal Guidance Cards as revealed by the Thoth Tarot. Take time to draw these cards and refer to them often. You can even create a Lifetime Collage (instructions on Pg. 345) that renders a detailed picture of your lifetime map.

Personality Card (Major Arcana): Represents particular patterns of behavior that influence your thoughts, emotions and actions. These patterns create the "persona" (the face) you turn toward the outer world. This card emphasizes your talents and shows you how you express them.

Soul Card (Major Arcana): The Soul Card signifies the deepest essence of your nature. It depicts who you are *beyond* the personality you exhibit to the outer world. The Soul Card represents where your heart is, what you value, and what feeds your soul. It reflects what you need to feel fulfilled.

Inner Teacher Card (Court Cards): Visually depicts what you are committed to, what you value, where your priorities are—and in particular what drives you.

Challenge and Opportunity Cards (Minor Arcana): Illustrate the type of challenges you may encounter, the opportunities you will be given, and the resources (gifts and talents) you possess.

Growth Year Card (Major Arcana): This is the only Personal Guidance Card that changes. Selected yearly on your birthday, it portrays the opportunities and challenges ahead for the year. It will also list the special resources you will have at your disposal.

Lifetime Collage: This is a deeply meaningful spread that gathers all your Personal Guidance Cards, and depicts an overview of the inner workings and deepest qualities of your life. It can help you awaken to your purpose, make the most of challenges and opportunities, and gain mastery of the whole of your potential.

Personality and Soul Cards

Major Arcana

The Major Arcana illustrates the principal issues of your life as they pertain to both your spiritual and physical maturation. It reflects the possibility for internal development as well as external accomplishments.

Determine your Personality and Soul cards by using the simple method below. When you've gathered your specific cards, you can turn to the appropriate page in this section and read the text. This information helps you to recognize and reach your full potential with the Personality and Soul traits you've elected to work with during your lifetime.

Each description includes a definition of the card when it is *Ill-dignified*. *Ill-dignified* is what happens when we take the potential energy embodied in that card to immoderate extremes. For example: tenacity is a wonderful quality that allows us to remain steadfast long enough to accomplish what we set out to do. But excessive tenacity can become stubbornness, rigidity and obsession. What began as productive behavior has become nonproductive.

TO DETERMINE YOUR PERSONALITY AND SOUL CARDS, USE THIS FORMULA:

1. Add the numbers of the day, month and year of your birth.

   (day) _____ + (month) _____ + (year) _____ = (sum) _____

   Example: April 27, 1943

   4 + 27 + 1943 = <u>1974</u>

2. Add each individual number of this sum:

   ___ + ___ + ___ + ___ = _____

   This is your **Personality Card**.

   Example: 1+9+7+4 = 21

   21 is the Personality Card for this example.

3. Reduce the Personality Card number:

   ___ + ___ = _____

   This is your **Soul Card**.

   Example: Reduce 21: 2+1 = 3

   3 is the Soul Card for this example.

For your Soul Card, you reduce every double digit number up to and including number 22, in order to arrive at a single digit.

Exceptions to calculating your numbers:

There are two exceptions to determining your numbers:

1.) When the sum of your birth date is more than 22

2.) When the sum is 19

Exception #1: The sum of your birth date is more than 22.

Example: August 7, 1962 $8 + 7 + 1962 = \underline{1977}$

Add the numbers of the sum individually: $1+9+7+7 = \underline{24}$

There are only 22 Major Arcana cards, therefore you **reduce any number over 22.**

Example: The sum is $\underline{24}$. $2+4 = 6$

6 is the Personality Card for this example.

6 is also the Soul Card.

In this example, having both cards the same signifies that you are determined to understand the energy of the number 6 card (The Lovers card). It clearly reveals that your life lessons will always revolve around equilibrium and balance.

Exception #2: The sum of your birth date is 19. With this exception, you will always have *three* cards.

Example: January 2, 1951: $1 + 2 + 1951 = \underline{1954}$

Add the numbers of the sum individually.   Example: $1+9+5+4 = \underline{19}$

Next, reduce the number 19.   Example: $1+9 = \underline{10}$

Then reduce the number 10.   Example: $1+0 = \underline{1}$

You now have three numbers: $\underline{19}$, $\underline{10}$, and $\underline{1}$

19 is your Personality Card

1 is your Soul Card

10 is a Gift, being that the 10 card is the Fortune card (what a gift to be given!).

The only time this configuration occurs is with the number **19.**

Find your Personality and Soul cards with the corresponding numbers in the Major Arcana. (Note that The Fool card is considered number XXII for the purpose of determining these Cards.)

Major Arcana

I.	The Magus	XII.	The Hanged Man
II.	The Priestess	XIII.	Death
III.	The Empress	XIV.	Art
IV.	The Emperor	XV.	The Devil
V.	The Hierophant	XVI.	The Tower
VI.	The Lovers	XVII.	The Star
VII.	The Chariot	XVIII.	The Moon
VIII.	Adjustment	XIX.	The Sun
IX.	The Hermit	XX.	The Aeon
X.	Fortune	XXI.	The Universe
XI.	Lust	XXII.	The Fool

In the example, you will see that the Personality Card is 21 (the Universe card). The Soul Card is number 3 (the Empress card).

This means that you experience the *Personality Card* traits of The Universe—XXI—and would therefore turn to Page 321 in this section to read the text for The Universe card. Briefly, The Universe card reveals that your basic personality is one of loyalty and patience. You must respect your own thoughts and behavior to be at peace with yourself. You're non-judgmental, and allow people to be themselves. With The Empress—III—as your *Soul Card,* you would turn to the appropriate text in this section to discover the deepest essence of your nature. For The Empress soul, these gifts are your ability to nurture yourself and others, as well as the necessity to express your creative imagination. You will learn how important it is for you to address your tendency to give too much and spread yourself too thin.

The Personality and Soul Cards

Major Arcana

I • The Magus

You enjoy being number one and whenever possible want to be first in line. You have a way with words and always seem to have something to say. You know exactly how to put the resources you have to good use. You seem to be able to create something out of nothing, and leave people wondering just how you did that. You have an excellent sense of timing and seem to be in the right place at the right time. You're happiest when your life is full of activity and surrounded by people. You always have a smile on your face, have a first-rate sense of humor and are optimistic by nature. You enjoy life and take great pleasure in playing the game.

Ill-dignified: This card signifies that you can be cunning and deceptive, manifesting the traits of the con artist. You can lack discipline and self esteem.

II • The Priestess

You are self-contained, easy-going but sometimes appear aloof. You can be shy and hard to get to know, let alone to understand. You have a wonderful imagination and love to daydream. Appreciate it, because it's how you get some of your best ideas. You're fascinated by mysteries and like nothing better than to unravel them. You can be a bit secretive and always know much more than you let on. Trust your intuition—it has never steered you wrong. You really enjoy one-to-one relationships and tend to avoid crowds. You would rather work in the background than take center stage; from that vantage you can see everything that's going on. Because your feelings run deep, you often find it difficult to put them into words. Don't take it all so seriously; you will become overwhelmed by life if you personalize everything that happens.

Ill-dignified: You may make superficial judgments based on lack of understanding. You can be temperamental and lacking in imagination.

III • The Empress

You have a nurturing disposition; other people feel very comfortable being around you. You love to entertain and seldom find yourself alone. In fact, you love holding court and being the center of attention. You see the best in other people and will do all you can to encourage them to demonstrate their talents. You're so bright, and have so many good ideas, sometimes you suffer from creative overload. You need to periodically slow down, back off and focus on one or two things. When you spread yourself too thin, you're inclined to become irritable, and this should be your cue to do something nurturing for yourself.

Ill-dignified: You have the potential to get carried away and smother those in your care. You can be demanding and become a first-class pain in the neck.

IV • The Emperor

You're a leader by nature and radiate a sense of power and stability to those around you. People look up to you as an authority and seek out your counsel. You will always be seen out in front and aren't willing to take a back seat to anyone. There's a wonderful naiveté surrounding your actions. You never worry about falling short, you just jump! Surprisingly, you usually land on your feet. You are a confident person with a strong sense of integrity. You are up front and direct in your communication and assume everyone else is. This assumption has caused you a lot of trouble and disappointment in your life. You love being on the ground floor of a new project but will spend little time talking about it; you're more anxious to get started.

Ill-dignified: You may have a short attention span and not finish what you start. You can be a domineering bore with a temper to go with it. You can be impulsive and go "where wise men fear to tread."

V • The Hierophant

You take a conservative approach to life and are most comfortable operating within the structure of the establishment. You possess a deep sense of history and can be troubled by the changing times, particularly if life changes too fast. You would make a terrific teacher. With your practical nature, you learn best from your own experience and therefore prefer a hands-on approach. You have a strong sense of conscience and operate from your own integrity. You value your family and friends and give them unending support and loyalty. You have a deep regard for history, continuity and stability. You may change the form a relationship takes but the people themselves usually remain in your life. You have a deep appreciation for material comforts, but choose them for their functionality as well as beauty.

Ill-dignified: You can be narrow-minded, stubborn, lazy and opinionated. You may possess a rigid sense of moral superiority.

VI • The Lovers

You're a good mediator because you're able to see both sides of a situation and can therefore negotiate a truce. With personal challenges, however, you're always trying to take things apart and analyze the situation. When you finally arrive at a conclusion, you begin to second-guess yourself. You wish you could do less of it, but that's how your brain works. You instinctively know that sometimes one answer is as good as the next. Relationships are important to you because they are the vehicle by which you learn the most about yourself, so you tend to draw intense relationships into your life rather than superficial ones. You are a romantic at heart and love to shower affection on your significant other.

Ill-dignified: You have the potential to be fickle, untrustworthy and incapable of commitment. You may lose your identity within a relationship and believe you cannot live without it.

VII • The Chariot

It is extremely important to you that you're able to live your own life and be independent. Deep curiosity and a spirit of exploration are second nature to you. You're always on the move, looking for the next adventure—you would find it difficult to have a nine-to-five desk job. You are concerned about how you appear to other people and consequently will try to hide your insecurities. Until you make peace with yourself, you will find it difficult to feel secure, to be still and relax. You need to realize that what you're searching for is not outside, but deep within your very nature.

Ill-dignified: You can be a victim of extremes, constantly at war with yourself. You may appear cold and aloof. It's possible for you to be temperamental and anxiety-ridden.

VIII • Adjustment

You approach decision-making with caution and attempt to consider all aspects of a situation. Sometimes this process leaves you frustrated and undecided, because as soon as you reach a decision you see clearly that the opposite could also be true. People in your life need to respect this and give you the time you need to make a decision. You are an excellent mediator and are equipped to do well in any business venture you choose. You may even want to consider a career in some sector of law. You're a peacemaker, but have low tolerance for discord in your life. As a good-natured person, you'll listen to others. You're reasonable, sincere and care about people.

Ill-dignified: You can be fickle, superficial and hard to pin down. Thinking you know what's best for everyone, you may be severe in your judgments.

IX • The Hermit

You're always ready to offer help where it's needed. You're good at breaking things down to their basic components and eliminating extraneous data. You are broadminded, compassionate and understanding of others. You have a lively imagination and therefore a rich inner life. You take time to think through a situation before committing yourself. You insist on working at your own pace andnot being rushed. You would be a wise counselor and would excel in a position of public service. Since your mind is constantly processing information, you find that you need time alone to assimilate it. If you don't set this time aside for yourself, you can feel frustrated and totally burned out. Make it a priority to finish what you start. Tie up loose ends before moving on.

Ill-dignified: You may be over-critical, preoccupied with detail and unable to see the bigger picture. You can be secretive and devious, unwilling to look others straight in the eye.

X • Fortune

You have the capacity to adapt to change quickly—in fact you thrive on it. Without change in your life you feel frustrated at being stuck in a rut. You're happiest when you're fully engaged in the flow of life. You not only have the ability to hear opportunity when it knocks, but also the courage to get up and open the door. You can take a non-productive situation and turn it to your favor. This gift comes from the fact that you perceive that inherent in every problem is a creative solution. You understand that life brings ups and downs, but you've developed a system that helps you to ride out the downs and take full advantage of good fortune when it presents itself.

Ill-dignified: You can be addicted to living life on the edge. You can be an extremist. You may become materialistic, directionless, extravagant, always in debt.

XI • Lust

You are a warm, loving person with the ability to act with purpose and determination. You possess a lust for life, a need for creature comforts, abundant charisma and a strong sense of drama. You're basically an outgoing person who is physically strong and seldom ill. You don't tolerate anything that inhibits your self-expression. You have strong survival instincts and a need to be out in the world playing the game. You have an inner confidence that inspires others to put their trust in you—you would make a good leader. You have a love of romance and express passion easily. There are so many different aspects to your personality that other people find you fascinating.

Ill-dignified: You have the potential to be troubled with addiction. You may demonstrate an inflated sense of self, ruthlessness and opportunism. You can be arrogant, superficial and hedonistic.

XII • The Hanged Man

You will undergo significant transition in your life. You are a very sensitive person with strong psychic ability and a fantastic imagination. If you stay too long in uncomfortable situations, life will pull the rug out from under you. When the need to let go is imminent, you might find it easier to let go willingly rather than try to control the situation. It will be less wear and tear on you if you do. You have an abundance of resources available to you if you take the time to uncover them. In retrospect, can you see that every time you approach a difficult junction and work through it, your life seems to blossom? Learn to trust yourself at these times and know that in your life a crisis has always indicated a new awakening.

Ill-dignified: You may suffer from guilt and paranoia. There's a possibility of becoming a martyr, or a drug abuser. Unable to move into action, you may evade responsibility, be indecisive, or care only about yourself.

XIII • Death

You love change and have no problem shifting direction quickly and often. You continually surprise the people around you because they don't see it coming. You're committed to continuous introspection and love to unravel mysteries—yours or someone else's. You are broadminded and liberal in your thinking. You are a healer, a mystic, and extremely psychic. Your life will invite you to change course many times. You dislike routine constraints and prefer a job that lets you move freely, or at least work at your own pace.

Ill-dignified: You can be mentally or emotionally abusive. Your words can cut others to the bone. You may have a dark, brooding temperament and exhibit obsessive-compulsive behavior.

XIV • Art

You are a person of deep faith who has an innate optimism about life and believes in the goodness of others. Yours is a resilient nature and you don't accept defeat easily. You are a mediator and can resolve difficult situations in a way that pleases everyone. You're willing to speak out for social reform and will volunteer to carry the banner for a worthy cause. A champion of the needy, you will fight to revolutionize the system. You cannot abide mental, emotional or physical restriction and choose work that allows you freedom to explore new ideas and new ways of being in the world. Since your communication is swift and to the point, you may on occasion have to eat your words.

Ill-dignified: With this Personality Card, you can be opinionated, dogmatic, argumentative, and dishonest. You can lack patience and be a real know-it-all.

XV • The Devil

Like the goat, you are surefooted and capable of executing a high-wire juggling act. You are extremely patient and will persevere indefinitely. In spite of outside pressure, once you've made up your mind you are immovable. You're inherently honest, not from a sense of morality as much as from an inner sense of integrity. You literally cannot tell a lie without feeling physically uncomfortable. You don't like leaving much to chance and will take time to plot out your path, one step at a time. You have many associates but very few friends. People have to earn your respect before they enter your inner circle. Since you are shrewd and ambitious, you will usually be in the driver's seat. You enjoy the physical pleasures of life and will be the first one to the dinner table and the last one to finish the wine.

Ill-dignified: You have the potential to be manipulative and unethical. You can hurt others deeply because of your lack of sensitivity.

XVI • The Tower

You are a high-energy person, extremely motivated and determined to succeed. You have a tendency to be a bit rigid in your thinking, yet something always seems to come up unexpectedly to alter the course of your life and change your mind. You cannot be stuck for long. You process much of your frustration through your physical body and can suffer from problems of psychosomatic origin. You're strong-willed, extremely intelligent, self-aware and—when you put your mind to it—you can get everyone around you moving. You're independent by nature, assertive, and not one bit afraid to put yourself out there. You need healthy outlets for your energy and grab onto any new adventure or project that captures your interest.

Ill-dignified: You can fly off the handle easily. Just to feel alive, you may create chaos and discord.

XVII • The Star

You're a bohemian at heart. You seem to operate from a different reality map then the rest of the world. Yet, though your head might be in the clouds, your feet are firmly planted on the ground. You can find innovative ways to improve on the status quo, not hesitate to break rules to solve problems. You're idealistic by nature and see the good in everyone. You have great communications skills and love center stage so that you can express what's on your mind. You're always fighting for personal freedom—yours and others'. You are highly intuitive and extremely psychic. You are inherently loyal, idealistic, compassionate and inventive.

Ill-dignified: You can be irresponsible. There is a possibility of living on the edge, frequently challenging life and taking dangerous chances.

XVIII • The Moon

You may appear calm, cool and collected, but there's always a sense of anxiety and struggle beneath the surface. You can't just let things be; you want to uncover what's really going on and do something about it. You can tune in to those around you and easily lose yourself in their emotions. If they're feeling down, you start to feel depressed and wonder where those feelings came from. If you don't create boundaries for yourself, you become emotionally drained and physically exhausted. Listen to your body. It will tell you when you have spread yourself too thin. If you feel anxious, your body may be telling you that it's sensing danger and you should back off.

Ill-dignified: You can be an escape artist, living in a fantasy world and unable to commit to this one. There's a potential for illusiveness and deceit.

XIX • The Sun

You're outgoing and optimistic—when you smile you light up a room. You have an unlimited supply of energy and very seldom slow down. You seem to enjoy life no matter what's going on. You experience good health, a strong body and a positive outlook. You don't mind hard physical work and whenever possible prefer to be outdoors. You have the potential to be prominent within your community, you get along with everyone and seem to have been born under a lucky star. You're highly motivated, ambitious and extremely creative. You enjoy partnership and, surprisingly, are willing to share the limelight with other people. In fact, you're really not all that happy to be left out there alone.

Ill-dignified: You have a potential for being arrogant, self-indulgent and impractical. You can be selfish and uncompromising, finding little pleasure in life.

XX • The Aeon

You have the ability to appreciate every moment of your life. You possess a childlike wonder and enjoy doing new things. Because you seem ageless, you get along with diverse groups of all ages. You can have as much fun with a group of children as you can at the senior citizens' center. You have most likely learned to cope with outside criticism. Hopefully you haven't internalized this criticism and turned it on yourself. Your actions are well thought out, you tend to speak slowly as if you're weighing your words, you're cautious by nature and always trying to understand yourself and others. You would be excellent in any field that requires research because you love details and enjoy uncovering hidden information.

Ill-dignified: You can be finicky and judgmental, even extremely prejudiced. This card can indicate a personality that is thoughtless, insensitive and cynical.

XXI • The Universe

You are loyal, patient and hard-working. You do things in an orderly way and prefer to use a tried and true method to get the job done. Your early life may have been one of restriction. Self respect is of the utmost importance to you. If you want to change the world, you will do it from within the system (by running for office as opposed to being a radical). You're non-judgmental, allowing people to be themselves. You're sensual by nature and appreciate material comforts. You love being surrounded by beautiful things, yet have been known to give them away to someone who admires them.

Ill-dignified: This card shows a capacity for being ultra conservative, dull and lethargic. You can be stubborn, immovable, dense and demanding.

XXII • The Fool

You obviously march to the beat of your own drummer. In fact, if everyone is moving to the left, you seriously consider going to the right. You have an underlying wanderlust and travel a lot, either physically or in your fantasies. You're naturally spontaneous, and underneath it all you may choose to keep the childlike wonder alive within you. You make up your own rules and at times can appear inconsistent to those around you. You are not—they just don't think like you do and can't seem to understand you; in fact, they may never be able to. You don't always finish what you start. You may even choose to stop just short of success; if you lose interest, it's over. Being that your talents are so diverse and many possibilities are open to you—you would just as soon try something else.

Ill-dignified: You can lack discipline, be accident-prone, and irresponsible, keeping your head in the clouds . . . never coming down to earth.

Inner Teacher Card

Court Cards

The Court Cards illustrate what inspires you to create. They represent the traits you are mastering and the "type" of person you're striving to be when you grow up. The Inner Teacher Card is based on the astrological sun sign you were born under and is selected from the Court Cards. This card explains the path you've chosen to travel and represents the realm of your potential mastery.

For example: If your sun sign is Taurus, your Inner Teacher Card would happen to be the Prince of Disks. You would turn to the Prince of Disks in this section to find the Prince's inherent qualities, which are his practical nature and down-to-earth ability to operate in the marketplace of the world. He is an excellent businessman. If your sun sign is Gemini, the Knight of Swords is your Inner Teacher. You will read of his inherent ability to collect information and be a fount of knowledge. You will discover just how clever he *is* and you *can* be if this is your specific card.

Determine your Inner Teacher Card by finding your birth date or sun sign on the following chart.

Astrological	Your Birthday	The Court Card
Aries	March 21 to April 20	Queen of Wands
Taurus	April 21 to May 20	Prince of Disks
Gemini	May 21 to June 20	Knight of Swords
Cancer	June 21to July 21	Queen of Cups
Leo	July 22 to Aug. 22	Prince of Wands
Virgo	Aug.23 to Sept. 22	Knight of Disks
Libra	Sept. 23 to Oct. 22	Queen of Swords
Scorpio	Oct. 23 to Nov. 22	Prince of Cups
Sagittarius	Nov. 23 to Dec. 21	Knight of Wands
Capricorn	Dec. 22 to Jan 19	Queen of Disks
Aquarius	Jan. 20 to Feb. 18	Prince of Swords
Pisces	Feb. 19 to March 20	Knight of Cups

(The Princess Court Cards have no corresponding astrological sign)

The Inner Teacher Cards
Court Cards

Knight of Wands

He is a powerful, straightforward person who is not the least bit afraid to fight for what he believes in—which is freedom from oppression of any kind. He will tell you exactly what's on his mind. A natural gambler, he's not beyond playing the odds. The higher the stakes the better he likes it. He enjoys the attention he gets and uses it to further his ambitions. He is appalled at unfair situations and is inspired to balance the scales of justice. He's a leader who can inspire others to change the world. But he may not stay and help you—he has other battles to fight. He is an idealist with great faith in life. He is a storehouse of energy and is always ready to leap into the next adventure.

Ill-dignified: He may be a prideful, domineering presence whose fiery temper can clear a room. If his first efforts fail, just quitting is a viable option.

Queen of Wands

She is an attractive woman and knows how to use her allure to get what she wants. She is a powerhouse of energy who has seen the path clearly and will not be compromised. She is a loving, generous Queen, but doesn't appreciate opposition. She insists that things be done her way because she is confident about her vision and secure in her abilities. She knows how to recruit others to do her bidding and get the job done. Like a queen, she holds court with style and grace. She may invite you into her inner circle, but only on her terms. She has cat-like instincts: a good sense of timing and a sure, quiet way of going about her business. She is sensitive to what's needed in a situation, confident about her actions, and gets to the heart of a matter quickly. She is honest to a fault . . . a woman of courage, conviction and honor who can inspire you and connect you with your own vision.

Ill-dignified: She may be snobbish, self-absorbed, superficial, and insensitive. Her dark side may attack others where and when they are the most vulnerable. She bites.

Prince of Wands

He is inspired to take action and ready to stop planning and start doing. In fact, he's in a hurry to get into his life and move full speed ahead. He's a warm outgoing person who is extremely charismatic. The Prince of Wands is romantic and radiates a sensual relationship to life itself that seems to say *Here I am, world—take a look at me*. He is self-contained, self-centered. Because outside influences can easily throw him off course, he holds tight to his own position so he can do it his way. He is noble, virtuous and generous. He's always looking for ways to prove himself, so he takes more risks than most of us do. Since he's willing to take risks, in the long run he will be successful. He has strong passions and is willing to express his desires. He loves to say things he doesn't necessarily believe for the pure shock value, and to keep other off balance.

Ill-dignified: He may suffer bouts of rage and jealousy and regret it later. He can spend a lot of time fighting his own insecurities, and become intolerant as well as intolerable.

Princess of Wands

She is the liberated woman existing independently in the outer world. She's uninhibited, direct in her communication, goal-oriented and motivated to succeed. Unafraid of hard work, she'll do whatever necessary to get her ideas into the world. Her nature is bold, daring and courageous. If she feels fear, she certainly doesn't show it. This Princess has insatiable energy and never seems to tire. Her expectation is to win, and she'll keep trying until she does. She'll encourage you to seek expression for your own passion.

Ill-dignified: She may become irresponsible and reckless in her self-gratification. She can be impetuous, and insensitive, and strong-arm a situation a little too much.

Knight of Cups

He's able to express his emotions at the moment he is experiencing them and with the same intensity he feels them. His emotional expression is what makes him feel truly alive, so he finds it easy to tell someone exactly how he feels about him or her. He has a high degree of integrity in both his thoughts and emotions. He will permit himself to be approachable and completely vulnerable within his relationships. He is fundamentally a loving, kind and generous person that other people find attractive. He has a lust for life that can lead to over-indulgence and subsequent burnout if he's not careful. An enthusiastic romantic by nature, The Knight of Cups just loves being in love.

Ill-dignified: He can be defensive and insecure unless he's on his home turf. He may be guarded, aloof and secretive. He can use flattery to advance his own agenda.

Queen of Cups

Highly intuitive, The Queen of Cups enjoys a deep understanding of life. She is a gracious hostess and people are attracted to her and feel at ease in her presence. Like the other Queens, she is social and loves holding court as the queen bee, but she may be very difficult to get to know. In fact, because there are so many layers to her personality, everyone who knows her seems to know a different person. She reflects to others what they need while keeping herself hidden behind a veil of illusion. As an adept counselor, she inspires those she chooses to mentor. She is empathetic, compassionate and accepting by nature. If the circumstances in her life change she will adapt to the new situation seamlessly.

Ill-dignified: If not careful, she'll gossip and distort the facts. She may become impractical and get lost in her fantasies. She can be extremely irritable overly critical of others if she's not comfortable with herself.

Prince of Cups

He's extremely passionate about most things, but doesn't always express his emotions. When he does communicate his feelings, he may come across as too intense and be misunderstood. Sometimes people find it hard to know where he's coming from. He's committed to change and transformation, and has a strong desire to understand himself better. In fact, he knows himself well enough to know that he needs to develop a more emotionally balanced life. This dreamer will follow his visions wherever they lead him. He likes to live intensely each moment, as if it where his last. He is ambitious and motivated to succeed, but shouldn't go through life as if he has something to prove. If he appears to have a chip on his shoulder, instead of helping him, other people may try to knock it off.

Ill-dignified: He can be caught up in self-abusive behavior. He might even create chaos in his life just to live off the adrenalin rush. He has the potential to be emotionally brutal and hurt other people deeply.

Princess of Cups

She is a loving, creative and imaginative young woman. Sure of herself, she's willing to take a back seat, working from behind the scenes. She enjoys being a supporting player because she feels a bit vulnerable being out there alone. But there's considerably more strength in the Princess of Cups than may appear at first glance. She is secure in the knowledge of her own talents and abilities and poses no threat to the males in her life. In fact she likes being taken care of. She is an idealist, and the epitome of femininity, of beauty and of faithful companionship. She is the ideal helpmate and will support you in any venture you choose to embark on.

Ill-dignified: She can a lack a direction of her own and become overly involved with your life and dependent on you. She can use her femininity in an unfair way to manipulate a situation to her advantage and further her own agenda.

Knight of Swords

He's a walking encyclopedia and usually knows what he's talking about. He likes collecting information and takes great pride in his ability to assimilate new information. He thinks fast and talks fast and gets impatient with people who can't keep up with him. In fact, he'll finish their sentences for them if necessary. He researches every conceivable aspect of a situation before deciding how to proceed. He's subtle, clever and has a great sense of humor. He's not a great listener, not because he doesn't care, but because he's too busy thinking.

Ill-dignified: He can have a closed mind and act without thinking the situation through. At worst, he may try to go in four different directions at the same time.

Queen of Swords

She is a peacemaker by nature and has the potential for a calm, receptive mind. As a keen observer, she finds it easy to maintain a neutral position that gives her the ability to see beneath the surface and fully perceive what's happening. She inspires those around her and makes them comfortable. She loves holding court and surrounding herself with artistic, creative and intelligent people. Her empathy gives her an uncanny sense of timing. She can bear witness without becoming involved. She is an individualist who's happiest living in a rich, imaginative mental realm. She is sincere, gracious and just.

Ill-dignified: She lives with her head in the clouds and never comes down to earth. She has a sharp tongue that can be used to cut others down.

Prince of Swords

He likes expressing his ideas, beliefs and philosophies of the moment. The Prince of Swords can take any side of a discussion and run with it in a logical manner, then five minutes later argue the opposite position. He enjoys mental exercise and he is always full of ideas, one idea being as good as the next; his mind can make quick shifts. He seems to be constantly testing life and trying to create boundaries for himself, to move through life in a more balanced and consistent way. Inventive, an original thinker, a bohemian of sorts—he's able to cut through any restrictions that limit his creative expression. He's more comfortable with his thoughts than his feelings.

Ill-dignified: He has the potential to be self-absorbed, thoughtless and insensitive. He can lose focus and forget that he's involved in a discussion and move aggressively into a fierce argumentative stance.

Princess of Swords

She's a street-smart person willing to take on difficult tasks because somehow she always finds a practical solution to the challenges presented. She sees what needs to be done and knows how to do it. She risks saying what she thinks and has the courage to get out into the world and strive to put her ideas into physical form. She's idealistic enough to want the job, naive enough to think it's easy, hardworking enough to do it. Sometimes she can get a bit depressed and have to push herself to keep going. She has learned that physical movement helps to calm the turbulence of her mind. She'll be the first one up in the morning and the last one to bed at night because she doesn't want to miss one single moment of her life.

Ill-dignified: If she doesn't keep trying, it will be her undoing. If she allows dark moods to get the best of her, she will have difficulty going out into the world.

Knight of Disks

He is preoccupied with the material world, fully immersed in affairs of a practical nature. His concern is with tradition, convention and security. He is involved with watching things grow and being sure that the seeds he has planted have the opportunity to reach their full potential. He lacks initiative, but more than compensates for it through stability and endurance. You can count on him to be in the game for the long term. He doesn't believe in unnecessary motion and will sit back and relax until the time is right; then he 's unstoppable. He instinctively knows how to make money. He's extremely resourceful, a conservative investor, prudent in his dealings, who knows how to take care of business. He is community-oriented and well respected among his peers.

Ill-dignified: He is subject to suffering from constant anxiety, lacks foresight and may resist change. He can be corrupt in business dealings.

Queen of Disks

She is Mother Earth; stable, resourceful and hard working. She has created a life of physical prosperity and well being for herself and those in her charge. She allows the abundance of the universe to flow through her without distortion. She has a passive, quiet personality with a deep respect for all living things. She is sensitive to the needs of others and is always willing to help. A wise counselor in practical matters, she listens to her instincts and intuition and is able to prosper in the physical world. She does not separate her physical life from her spiritual life. She understands that they are one and the same thing. She recognizes that we are not humans searching for our spiritual nature, but Spirit expressing in the physical realm. Therefore, she has respect for her physical body and cares deeply for the sacred Earth she calls home.

Ill-dignified: She can be weighed down by a sense of duty and obligation so that all joy goes out of her life. She may lack common sense and have trouble keeping her checkbook balanced.

Prince of Disks

He is a planner, organizer and builder. He not only relies on instincts but has a good head for practical matters. He will bring new ideas into the world through traditional avenues and can be counted on to know as much as possible about a situation before acting. He'll be sure he has more than one back door before he begins a project. He likes to know that he has a way out if needed and that all his bases are covered. He's a man on a mission. Like the other princes, he has something to prove: that he can prosper in the physical world. He is a worthy opponent in negotiations and is bright enough to make you think he's made concessions, but when the dust clears you'll see that he's gotten exactly what he wanted.

Ill-dignified: He can be insensitive to the needs of others. It takes him a long time to get angry, and when he does it will take even longer to calm him down.

Princess of Disks

She is a woman of means willing to move out into the world and prosper there. She's full of wonderful ideas and is able to put these ideas into physical form. She constantly creates new avenues of exploration and has a natural curiosity that compels her to take these ideas into the marketplace. Because she is totally committed to being out in the world, her life is full of diverse experiences. She is resourceful, creative and willing to go it alone if necessary. She has high integrity and accepts full responsibility for her words and actions. She believes in herself and has the patience to stay with a project until it is completed and totally successful. She is beautiful, sensual and loving as well as bold, strong and courageous. What a combination!

Ill-dignified: She can be rough around the edges and seem a bit crude at times. She can become resentful and insensitive. She may lose initiative.

Challenge and Opportunity Cards

Minor Arcana

This section will help you to see the specific challenges and opportunities of your life path. Your cards will be taken from the Minor Arcana based on either the number of your Soul card or your *personal* astrological sun sign.

For example: If my Soul Card is III—The Empress—I would choose all the **threes** from the Minor Arcana. I would select the Three of Swords (Sorrow), the Three of Cups (Abundance), the Three of Wands (Virtue) and the Three of Disks (Work). These cards represent the *challenges and opportunities* that The Empress faces in her lifetime. The Empress is focused on giving form to intuition through creative imagination. With this card, I will confront my personal power (Virtue), surround myself with like-minded people (Abundance), seek balance between head and heart, and in so doing encounter a lot of mental pain (Sorrow), as I learn to put my mind, heart, and soul into everything I do (Work).

Use the following chart to find the cards that apply to you. (The formula for finding your Soul Card is on Page 311.) Add your sun sign cards from the next page, and explore the advice in the following Challenge and Opportunity cards.

Major and Minor Arcana Correspondence Chart

Soul Card from: Major Arcana	Minor Arcana Number from each Suit: Wands, Cups, Swords, Disks
I The Magus	All Aces. All Tens: Ruin, Satiety, Oppression, Wealth
II The Priestess	All Twos: Peace, Love, Dominion, Change
III The Empress	All Threes: Sorrow, Abundance, Virtue, Work
IV The Emperor	All Fours: Truce, Luxury, Completion, Power
V The Hierophant	All Fives: Defeat, Disappointment, Strife, Worry
VI The Lovers	All Sixes: Science, Pleasure, Victory, Success

VII	The Chariot	All Sevens: Futility, Debauch, Valour, Failure
VIII	Adjustment	All Eights: Interference, Indolence, Swiftness, Prudence
IX	The Hermit	All Nines: Cruelty, Happiness, Strength, Gain
X	Fortune	All Aces. All Tens: Ruin, Satiety, Oppression, Wealth

Astrological Sign and Corresponding Minor Arcana Card

Your lifetime challenges and opportunities are influenced by your astrological sign. To add to your knowledge of your life path, you can also select the three *Minor Arcana* cards that relate to your sun sign. For example: If you are a Taurus, you are an Earth sign, and would choose Worry, Success and Failure (5,6,7) from the Disks Suit.

Find the three astrological signs Minor Arcana cards that pertain to your specific sun sign in the following chart.

Wands Suit ~ Fire Signs

Aries	Dominion, Virtue, Completion (2, 3, 4 of Wands)
Leo	Strife, Victory, Valour (5, 6, 7 of Wands)
Sagittarius	Swiftness, Strength, Oppression (8, 9, 10 of Wands)

Cups Suit ~ Water Signs

Cancer	Love, Abundance, Luxury (2, 3, 4 of Cups)
Scorpio	Disappointment, Pleasure, Debauch (5, 6, 7 of Cups)
Pisces	Indolence, Happiness, Satiety (8, 9, 10 of Cups)

Swords Suit ~ Air Signs

Libra	Peace, Sorrow, Truce (2, 3, 4 of Swords)
Aquarius	Defeat, Science, Futility (5, 6, 7 of Swords)
Gemini	Interference, Cruelty, Ruin (8, 9, 10 of Swords)

Disks Suit ~ Earth Signs

Capricorn	Change, Work, Power (2, 3, 4 of Disks)
Taurus	Worry, Success, Failure (5, 6, 7 of Disks)
Virgo	Prudence, Gain, Wealth (8, 9, 10 of Disks)

The Challenge
and Opportunity Cards
Minor Arcana

WANDS

Ace of Wands   Create something new! Express your primal life force through physical manifestation.

Two of Wands: Dominion   Build personal freedom through self-mastery, by exercising the power of your will.

Three of Wands: Virtue   A strong sense of personal power gives you the ability to attempt something new.

Four of Wands: Completion   Completion releases your energy so that you can move on to the next step.

Five of Wands: Strife   When creative energy is temporarily blocked, the challenge is to learn to be patient with yourself and others.

Six of Wands: Victory   Relief from strife. Inner victory brings peace and equanimity into your life.

Seven of Wands: Valour   Be courageous and take a risk if necessary.

Eight of Wands: Swiftness   Master spontaneity. By staying in the present moment you are able to think and act quickly.

Nine of Wands: Strength   Everything in life constantly changes. Keep your sense of balance through moderation.

Ten of Wands: Oppression   You're being challenged to ask for help. You don't need to do everything yourself.

CUPS

Ace of Cups Open your heart to your creative intuition and you will live an inspired life.

Two of Cups: Love Trust in your relationships—they always serve you well.

Three of Cups: Abundance Surround your self with like-minded people. They will understand you and support your efforts.

Four of Cups: Luxury Keep emotional balance in your life, so that you can maintain a steady course.

Five of Cups: Disappointment Learn to work through your disenchantment and regret by letting go and moving on.

Six of Cups: Pleasure Celebrate the everyday beauty of life. Appreciate all you have been given.

Seven of Cups: Debauch Beware of overindulgence. If unchecked, it will be your undoing.

Eight of Cups: Indolence Set limits on your time, energy and resources.

Nine of Cups: Happiness Express joy every chance you get. You'll feel great and you'll make everyone around you happy.

Ten of Cups: Satiety Self-satisfaction is both an opportunity and a challenge. Enjoy, but don't become too full of yourself.

SWORDS

Ace of Swords Keep your mind clear, quiet and focused.

Two of Swords: Peace Mastery of the mind encompasses living in the present moment . . . where true peace resides.

Three of Swords: Sorrow Let go of past sorrow. What good does it do to drag it with you?

Four of Swords: Truce Discover the art of negotiation. Learn to create peace through compromise.

Five of Swords: Defeat Live in the present; don't let past defeats control you.

Six of Swords: Science   Stay objective. Do research and gather information you need.

Seven of Swords: Futility   Don't over-analyze. Cut the situation to a manageable size.

Eight of Swords: Interference   Stay out of your own way. Don't be part of the problem by obstructing your own path.

Nine of Swords: Cruelty   How you choose to think is entirely up to you. Change your mind and change your life.

Ten of Swords: Ruin   Trust the resources you have instead of being "Chicken Little"—fearful that the sky is falling.

DISKS

Ace of Disks: Life is a sacred experience. Use yours well.

Two of Disks: Change   Make the changes you know need to be made, and you can easily balance the many different aspects of your life.

Three of Disks: Work   Always give it your all. Put your mind, heart and soul into everything you do.

Four of Disks: Power   Stability, self-discipline, commitment and a conservative approach are the building blocks for material success.

Five of Disks: Worry   Worry could be your middle name. Give it up and do something constructive instead.

Six of Disks: Success   Enjoy the success of the moment. It feeds your soul and gives you the incentive to do it again.

Seven of Disks: Failure   Success takes courage because it changes your life. Have the audacity to risk success.

Eight of Disks: Prudence   Patience is golden. Let time take care of things for you.

Nine of Disks: Gain   Be grateful for your good fortune and more will come to you.

Ten of Disks: Wealth   Be generous. What you give will return to you tenfold.

Growth Year Card

Major Arcana

On your birthday, choose a card to represent the coming year. This provides guidance on what you can expect and how you can best work with the situations that will occur.

This year goes from birthday to birthday, not January to January. The Growth Year card is chosen from the Major Arcana.

The Growth Year Card is determined by adding the month and day you were born to the current birthday year. Note that if you haven't celebrated your birthday yet, you would calculate the *year* number as one less than the current year (see Example #2).

1. Add the numbers of the day, month and year of your birth.

    (day) _____ + (month) _____ + (year) _____ = (sum) _____

    > **Example #1:** Your birthday has already occurred in the current year:
    > You birthday is on April 27, 2006, and you're calculating on April 28, 2006:
    >
    > $$4 + 27 + 2006 = \underline{2037}.$$

2. Add each individual number of this sum:

    ___ + ___ + ___ + ___ = _____

    This will be your **Growth Year Card** from birthday to birthday for the year.

    > **Example #1:** $2+0+3+7 = 12$

12—The Hanged Man—is the example Growth Year Card. The Hanged Man would influence your year beginning April 27, 2006 through April 26, 2007. You would read the Personal Guidance Card text in this section for The Hanged Man and learn that for you this is a time to surrender fixed ideas and give up any illusion of control you may have. This is a year that you may have to yield to the current situation, and let time and patience do what needs to be done.

Example #2: Your birthday hasn't yet occurred in the current year. You birthday is on April 27, 2006, and you're calculating on February 28, 2006:

Use the same formula as above, except use 2005 for the current year. (Remember, your birthday hasn't occurred yet, so you're still in the Growth Year April 27, 2005 to April 27, 2006.).

You reduce any number over 22 so that you fall within the numbers of the Major Arcana.

Major Arcana

I.	The Magus	XII.	The Hanged Man
II.	The Priestess	XIII.	Death
III.	The Empress	XIV.	Art
IV.	The Emperor	XV.	The Devil
V.	The Hierophant	XVI.	The Tower
VI.	The Lovers	XVII.	The Star
VII.	The Chariot	XVIII.	The Moon
VIII.	Adjustment	XIX.	The Sun
IX.	The Hermit	XX.	The Aeon
X.	Fortune	XXI.	The Universe
XI.	Lust	XXII.	The Fool

The Growth Year Cards

Major Arcana

I • The Magus Year

The time has come to take full responsibility for the direction your life is going. Strive for your own independence this year. Depend on no one but yourself. Pay special attention to the script you've been working from. Remember: you're not only the script-writer, but the producer, director, actor and stagehand as well. Make whatever changes necessary to be more in alignment with your personal goals for the year. Use the resources you have available to further your vision. Allow magic into your life this year by opening up communication with your inner self, and with those around you. Settle all disputes by reason and logic. Pay attention to your self-talk: Does your internal dialogue sabotage you, or does it empower you?

II • The Priestess Year

Establish your independence this year by listening to your own inner wisdom. Don't waste time trying to figure out how you know—just follow your intuition because it's right on! This year whatever you need comes to you if you just sit back and be receptive to it. Soft-pedal everything you do this year. There's so much going on inside that you may be seeking even more alone time than usual. Friends may feel that you're acting very mysteriously and wonder what's going on with you. This is a year to use patience and diplomacy as your mantra.

III • The Empress Year

Give birth to something new. Surround yourself with beautiful things. Work on the environment. Beautify your garden. Plant a tree. Be social—throw a party and enjoy yourself. This is a good time to experience motherhood, and a good year to resolve issues with one's mother, sister or daughter. Don't push so hard; just relax and let things come to you. You needn't plan too far ahead: take each day as it comes, and get the most possible pleasure out of your life. Be creative.

IV • The Emperor Year

This is a good year to experience fatherhood, or to work out longstanding issues with one's father, brother or son. Take advantage of your eagerness to move out into the world by starting something new this year. Start building a reliable foundation for the rest of your life. This is your year for self-confidence and a passionate sense of purpose in life. You know where you really want to go. Therefore, take a proactive role and be willing to plant the seeds to get there. Whatever you have truly wanted to do—this is the perfect year to do it.

V • The Hierophant Year

This is a good year to re-establish family connections or learn more about your family heritage. You may experience tests and challenges this year, but hold the course because these experiences will be invaluable to you further on down the road. You'll look back and understand the importance of the knowledge you have gained. This is not a good year to be innovative and play the rebel, but rather a time for tried and true methods; those based on traditional structures will serve you well.

VI • The Lovers Year

This is a year for resolving relationships in general: beginning new ones, deepening old ones, and letting go of the ones that no longer work. It's an auspicious period for strengthening the rapport with your family, or with yourself for that matter. This is an appropriate time to be more self-absorbed. The most wonderful thing you can do this year is to begin a relationship with yourself. See it as a perfect time to recreate your self. You may want to consider a new self-image, a new way of seeing the world and playing your role in it.

VII • The Chariot Year

This is the year to prove yourself by showing the world what you're made of. Acquire a spirit of adventure and be willing to take risks you normally wouldn't take. It's a good time to travel or start a new venture. You might even consider changing your residence or starting a new career. This is a lucky year for you, and will allow you to feel like "the captain of your own ship, the master of your own destiny." Now is the time to take a chance on yourself. What do you want to be when you grow up?

VIII • Adjustment Year

This is a year to make a decision you've been putting off for a long time. You need to look at all sides of the situation and establish your own equilibrium in relationship to it. Then make a commitment you're willing and able to hold to. This is a good year for business negotiations—review your financial positions and adjust them accordingly. Make sure, however, that you're listening to yourself and not others' opinions. You have a good chance at success if you follow through on your own dreams. While moving forward, be aware of the legalities of your actions and attentive when signing contracts.

IX • The Hermit Year

This is a year to tie up loose ends and finish unfinished business, and not necessarily a good time to attempt new things. You need to examine your life this year so that you can weed out any problem areas. Have compassion, tolerance and understanding, particularly toward your self. Devote time to meditation and thinking about your life. Where do you want to go from here and what do you want to do in the future? Consider letting go of outworn ideas and attitudes so that you can move on to the next cycle of life unburdened by your past. Take care of your health this year . . . go on a diet, visit a spa, or take a well deserved vacation.

X • Fortune Year

Opportunity is knocking. This is a year for a major breakthrough. In retrospect, you'll see this year as a key turning point in your life. Be alert to the opportunities that cross your path and be willing to take a chance on yourself. You're able to see your life more objectively than in the past, and thus it will be clear to you what needs to be done. You'll feel motivated to manifest what you've long desired. Remember, your success depends on how well you work with the opportunities presented. It can be a year of good luck if you don't compromise yourself. A world of possibilities awaits you— get moving.

XI • Lust Year

This is a year of great creativity—a chance to find the strength and stamina needed for something you've wanted to do for a long time. You'll have the courage this year to take a risk and put yourself out there. Listen to what you feel passionate about, then act accordingly. This is a good year to address any addictive behavior that has been troubling you. Realize that you're not one single type of person. Your personality is made up of many facets. Take time this year to discover something new about yourself and run with it. It won't be difficult, because this year you will not tolerate anything that inhibits your self-expression.

XII • The Hanged Man Year

This year you need to surrender any fixed ideas or beliefs and be willing to look at alternative views. You might have to suspend some long-held expectations. The sooner you relax and let go, the sooner you'll be able to move on. Though you may feel your life is on hold and that you're out of the mainstream, realize that this only temporary. Factors outside of your control may play a large part in your life this year. This is a year of transition and transition is often rough. You need to be patient with others and with yourself as well. Hang in there and you'll see that in the long run everything will be okay.

XIII • Death Year

It's a year of change and transition followed by new beginnings. This will be nothing short of a major rebirth for you personally, and a regeneration of your entire life. First, you may need to get to the bottom of something that's been troubling you . . . perhaps let go of some outmoded ideas, beliefs, attitudes or relationships. You may even discover that you're not who you thought you were. Your wants and needs have changed dramatically. The time has come to let go—you can't put it off any longer. If unwilling to let go, you may feel you're experiencing your own death. Change can be difficult if we resist. Instead of a "slow death," why not opt for a quick and painless demise? Let go, mourn your loss and move on.

XIV • Art Year

This year you'll feel confident and blessed, so take advantage of it. Take time to look at new ways of using the resources available in your life. Determine the right combination of solitude and socializing, give and take— choose a moderate path that brings your life into balance. Be your own "art project" this year by redefining yourself. Who are you? This is a year to start communicating your thoughts. Give voice to the ideas you've kept under cover. Once you get the conversation going, you'll find it easy to express yourself. A trove of new information is coming your way: Monitor you dreams, pay attention to your inner guidance, start reading the signs—the synchronicities—in your day-to-day life.

XV • The Devil Year

This can be a year of internal conflict and struggle; it will help if you keep a sense of humor about you. You may want to re-examine the habits of "should" and "ought to" you've embraced. You have imprisoned yourself in a situation of your own making—now's the time to let yourself off the hook. Release the shackles that bind you so that you can lighten up your life and have some fun again. If you free yourself now, this could be a year of great personal accomplishments . . . a good time to come out of the shadows and do some things you've wanted to do. This may turn out to be a year that you have a grand old time.

XVI • The Tower Year

If you've done your homework the last couple of years and made small adjustments along the way, you may be able to sail through this year with a wonderful burst of energy. If not, you need to get down to business and do some major housecleaning quick. Take the initiative to make the necessary changes yourself rather than wait for them to occur on their timetable. If change occurs that's out of your control, roll with the punches and know that something good will come of it. If unexpected change has already disoriented your life, it will be best to take a well deserved rest this year. Pick up the pieces of your life and create a new picture. Things will be moving again soon.

XVII • The Star Year

Go after your dreams this year and get the recognition you deserve. This is a good time to acknowledge your particular talents and abilities. You've been through some difficult times lately. But it's over—take what you've learned and run with it. Make the time this year to put your ideas into words. The game is changing and you'll find you know more than you thought you did. You may discover that you're more resourceful than you imagined this year. Take center stage whenever you can so that you can get the word out there. Your intuition is at an all-time high. Try meditation and maybe even learn to read the tarot cards. Let your psychic ability surface. If you look at the ordinary with a new vision, you'll see the extraordinary this year. Lucky you!

XVIII • The Moon Year

You may feel emotionally isolated this year, as if you were dealing with something that no one else could possibly understand. There are some things we just have to go through alone. You may find yourself taking life very seriously through this time, trying to define yourself and your place in the world. You could be confronting past fears that have resurfaced again. You might even be thinking about your own mortality. What is life about? Where do I go from here? This is a year for contemplation, for meditation or just spending time alone. Take time for daydreams, and let them reveal your secret self. They will shed light on what is going on beneath the surface of your mind. This could possibly be a year that a karmic relationship resurfaces so that you can give it closure or rekindle it.

XIX • The Sun Year

This is a great year to enjoy your life. Get outdoors and have some fun. Let your inner child out to play. Create a partnership, get married . . . if not marriage, find a great body to curl up with. Go dancing. Exercise, learn a new sport, and lay in the sun. Your body will love it. Take a vacation. If you want to start and complete a new project this year—go for it, it will unfold effortlessly. This is a good year to "blow your own horn" for a change. Create new things and enjoy the process—you have the potential to experience success and a great deal of personal growth.

XX • The Aeon Year

This is a year to resolve any family issues that may need to be ironed out so that you can move on. This can be the beginning of a new life, a second chance, an opportunity to create a new identity for your self. Now is a time to forgive—both yourself and others—for past ignorance and misunderstanding. Ask forgiveness from those you've harmed, including yourself. Wipe the slate clean, break away from the past and start over without prejudice. Begin again. Learn to walk your talk. Take responsibility for your words and actions. Think before you speak. Keep criticism out of your language by choosing your words carefully. Give people a second chance.

XXI • The Universe Year

This year asks that you work within existing structures and in a more conventional way then you may be used to. An old cycle is being completed and you are beginning a new one. Be prepared for change; know, however, that you'll never be asked to do anything that you're not up to. Take full responsibility for the new life you're in the process of creating. Focus on completing what you've started by first cleaning up any unfinished business. Expand your horizons and become more global in your thinking. If you own your own business, think about expanding your market. Get a website. Help Mother Earth; work to protect the environment. Be part of the solution; make a difference. You'll have a strong desire to travel; if you cannot physically do so, use your limitations to work for you rather than against you. Read travel books, study geography, increase your knowledge of the planet—this information will be invaluable to you.

XXII • The Fool Year

This is a year to lighten up and have some fun. Be optimistic. Take a look at the possibilities you've been ignoring. Do something this year that you would normally label foolish. Try on a different persona, march to a different drummer, do something out of character. Take a road trip; just get in the car and go! Leave the itinerary at home. Rediscover the child within you and let her call the shots for a while. Go where the mood takes you. Trust your instincts this year. Be impractical and spontaneous for a change— you might enjoy it. This is a vitally creative year for you, so take a chance on yourself . . . the results will surprise you.

Lifetime Collage

Creating a Lifetime Collage is a wonderful way to reveal your particular talents and resources. As a kind of blueprint of the numerous aspects of your personality, it helps you envision a path toward your goals, and also flags any "potholes" in the road so that you can avoid them.

Your individual guidance cards supply snapshots of both your internal life (personal values, feelings, emotions and intuitions) and your external behavior (expressed ideas, beliefs and attitudes).

As you grow familiar with using the Thoth Tarot, you'll want to take the time to create a Lifetime Collage for yourself. You can fill in the blank Collage following this introduction, or you may want to copy the cards, and make a collage of them, to place where you can see them every day.

Once you've determined the cards for your Collage, refer to the Thoth Tarot cards described in this section (Personal Guidance Cards) to understand what inspires, motivates and fulfills you. You'll see more clearly where you naturally move through life effortlessly, and the areas in which you need to be more alert.

Studying this special blueprint reveals the inner workings and deepest qualities of your life. The Lifetime Collage can help you awaken to your purpose, acknowledge challenges and opportunities, and learn to participate with awareness in your life. As you continue with your readings, using the Tarot Advisor section, you'll gain even further understanding of the forces at work in the continuum of your destiny, and gain mastery of the whole of your potential.

Have fun with this section, because it's all about you!

Lifetime Collage

☐ **PERSONALITY**
Major Arcana

☐ **SOUL**
Major Arcana

☐ **SUN SIGN**
Major Arcana

CHALLENGE & OPPORTUNITY

☐ ☐ ☐   *Minor Arcana*
based on SUN SIGN

☐ ☐ ☐ ☐   *Minor Arcana*
based on NUMBER

☐ **INNER TEACHER**
Court Card based on SUN SIGN

☐ **GROWTH YEAR**
Major Arcana based on NUMBER

Cards for the Lifetime Collage

See the Example following this section.

1. Personality

- Determine your Personality Card in the Major Arcana and place it in the Collage.

2. Soul

- Determine your Soul Card in the **Major Arcana** and place it in the Collage.

  Personality and Soul Cards represent your potential destiny.

  The formula for your Personality and Soul Cards is on Page 311. The definitions start on Page 314.

3. Sun Sign

- Find your astrological sun sign card in the **Major Arcana** and add it to the Collage.
  This represents the major astrological influence of the particular constellation you were born under.

  Find your sun sign on Page 309. Refer to the definitions on Page 314, and also the Sun Signs in the Appendix, Page 366.

4. Challenge and Opportunity

- Next find the three **Minor Arcana** cards that relate to your sun sign, and include them in your Collage.
- Next find the cards in the **Minor Arcana** with the *same number* as your Soul card (one from each of the four suits), and place them in the Collage.

These cards reveal the resources you need to expand your awareness and move toward your destiny.

See the chart on Page 332 to determine your cards, and read the definitions starting on Page 333.

5. Inner Teacher

- Locate your Inner Teacher Card in the **Court Cards** and add it to the Collage.
  The Inner Teacher illustrates your area of potential growth and mastery.

  Find the Inner Teacher card by referring to the chart on Page 323. The Inner Teacher definitions start on Page 324.

6. Growth Year

- Determine your Growth Year card and place that in the Collage as well.
  This card shows you the challenges and opportunities in the year ahead.

  Calculate your Growth Year on Page 336, and read the definitions starting on Page 338.

Lifetime Collage
Example

Lifetime Collage

| 21 | **PERSONALITY**
Major Arcana | | 3 | **SOUL**
Major Arcana |

THE UNIVERSE   THE EMPRESS

| 5 | **SUN SIGN**
Major Arcana |

THE HIEROPHANT

CHALLENGE & OPPORTUNITY

| 5 | 6 | 7 | *Minor Arcana*
based on SUN SIGN |

WORRY   SUCCESS   FAILURE

| 3 | 3 | 3 | 3 | *Minor Arcana*
based on NUMBER |

VIRTUE   ABUNDANCE   SORROW   WORK

| P | **INNER TEACHER**
Court Card based on SUN SIGN
PRINCE OF DISKS |

| 12 | **GROWTH YEAR**
Major Arcana based on NUMBER
THE HANGED MAN |

Lifetime Collage *Example*

Here's an example of how to read a completed Lifetime Collage. Let's say your birthdate is **April 27, 1943.** You would select your cards for the Collage, and read each definition in Section III, Personal Guidance Cards.

Your **Personality Card** would be **The Universe** Card, revealing that you're a person who likes to operate within the confines of tradition and convention.

With **The Empress** as your **Soul Card**, you're able to take the seeds of creativity and nurture them into full manifestation. You see the best in everyone, and people are drawn to you because of your understanding and compassion.

Your **Sun Sign** is Taurus, therefore The Hierophant is your Sun card. This shows a strong practical nature that learns best from a "hands on" approach. You prefer continuity, and find frequent change troubling.

Your **Challenge and Opportunity Cards** are found by selecting the three Taurus cards from the Minor Arcana **Disks** suit: Worry, Success and Failure. Constant worry and fear of failure can sabotage your goals and interfere with your progress. But if you keep on track and overcome your tendency toward anxiety and uncertainty, the Success card comes into play and saves the day.

Complete the messages of your Soul card (number 3 of the Major Arcana) with the number 3 cards from the Minor Arcana, one from each suit. In this example, you would be blessed with the potential of Virtue, Abundance, and Work, and be challenged by Sorrow. You would know that you have a strong sense of personal power (Virtue), the potential to create a strong network (Abundance), and have the capacity to focus all your energy and materialize your dreams (Work). The Sorrow card shows your tendency to carry past distress, giving you the opportunity to create the mental tools to offset this inclination.

The **Inner Teacher Card**, also based on your sun sign, here is the **Prince of Disks**. The Prince of Disks tells you that you're a person with a strong sense of purpose, and that is to manifest your ideas in the physical world in this lifetime.

The **Growth Year Card** in this example is **The Hanged Man**. As a card of transition, he advises that, in this year, you're going to have to let go of fixed ideas and see things from an alternate view. But because Taurus thrives on constancy, and you tend to dig your heels in, this can be a rough year. *Yet your Lifetime Collage overall contains your guidance:* By having Sorrow, Worry, and Failure in your Lifetime Collage, you have already learned a lot about letting go and keeping faith in the bigger picture. If you follow the counsel of the Inner Teacher, and recognize the many talents and resources you have available—Virtue, Abundance, Work, and Success—you'll sail through the transitions of this year with flying colors.

END NOTES

Appendix I

Qabalah and the Tarot

Astrology and the Tarot

Alchemy and the Tarot

Patterns

Appendix II

Bottom Line Tarot Card Interpretations

A Quick Reference

to the Thoth Tarot Cards' Advice

The Qabalah, Astrology and Alchemy
in Relation to the Tarot

The tarot reveals profound aspects of your self that can result in a deeper awareness of the miracle of life, and thus living every day with more fulfillment and meaning. Qabalah, astrology and alchemy have a direct relationship and indeed interaction with the tarot. The Qabalah's Tree of Life, astrology's Zodiac and alchemy's Seven Phases, like the Thoth Tarot's cards, are all "schematics" in the sense that they illustrate the blueprint on which the universe was created and life as we know it unfolds.

The Thoth Tarot, through its images and symbols, tells the story of humankind's journey from The Great Unmanifest into physical existence.

The Qabalah reveals, in the Tree of Life, how our destiny is to experience our true nature through conscious unity with divine creation.

Astrology, via the Planets and Constellations, expresses in symbols the dynamic and powerful forces of nature that help to unlock the potential within us.

Alchemy, by means of its Seven Phases, illustrates the changes we undergo in our quest for the knowledge and wisdom of our true self.

This appendix gives a very brief, simplified overview of the Qabalah, astrology and alchemy as they relate to your Thoth Tarot readings. You can continue your exploration of these systems with books referred to in the bibliography.

1. Qabalah and the Tarot

The Qabalah is an ancient Jewish mystical system that teaches that all life, including animal, plant and mineral—everything that was, is or will be—comes from the One Universal Source. We all share the same origin, the same energy and the same destiny.

Some of our greatest thinkers have been students of the Qabalah, including Plato, Isaac Newton and Sigmund Freud, to name just a few. It's no wonder that Aleister Crowley, with his vast studies, saw that the configuration of the Thoth Tarot is a natural fit to that of the Qabalah's Tree of Life, and incorporated its wisdom into his cards.

This brief overview of the arrangement of the Thoth Tarot cards on the Tree of Life provides deeper aspects of tarot wisdom that you may wish to continue to explore.

In the diagram on page 357, you will see the Tree of Life, and the ten Sephiroth—divine attributes of consciousness. Through the Sephiroth, the Qabalah illustrates the way our universe came into being. The Tree of Life presents a "schematic" of how to live our lives as self-realized beings. It depicts how our universe began with the emanation of the Light Source as it descended through the ten Sephiroth into physical matter. A fully realized human life embodies all the attributes of the Sephiroth.

The descent of the Light Source begins with the first Sephirah, Kether (Crown/Pure Being). Kether is the state of "pure being"—it is the no-thing from which every thing is possible. As the "one," Kether divides into Chokmah (Wisdom—eternal masculine principle) and Binah (Understanding—eternal feminine principle). Together, Kether, Binah and Chokmah create the Supernal Triangle, or Holy Trinity, forming the basis for our journey into physical manifestation.

The Light proceeds to Chesed (Mercy), Geburah (Strength), Tiphareth (Balance), Netzach (Victory), Hod (Splendor/Glory), Yesod (Natural Instinct) and Malkuth (Physical Matter). As the primordial energy from Kether moves down the branches of the Tree of Life, it becomes more and more dense. Eventually it appears to solidify into physical matter in Malkuth. With the dissolution of matter, the Light Source is released and returns to Kether.

The Qabalah also depicts the existence of the *Four Worlds*—four distinct levels of reality represented in tarot by the four suits.

> *Atziluth*, the world nearest to Divine Wisdom, is called the World of Emanations (Divine Thought, Inspiration and Will). In tarot, this level of reality is symbolized by the Wand Suit. It is from this field of potentiality that Divine Intent starts the process of creation.
>
> *Briah* is the World of Creation (the Inner Spirit as Intuition, Understanding and Wisdom). The Cup Suit expresses this plane of reality. This is the world of Transcendent Awareness.
>
> *Yetzirah* is the Formative World (transmission of the higher mind). It is exemplified in the Sword Suit. It is in the world of Yetzirah that the intellect nurtures the potential for physical manifestations.
>
> *Assiah* is the Physical World (matter), portrayed in the Disk Suit. It is the world of action-reaction and emotion.

The last world, Assiah, is a very special realm because it is from this perspective that we are able to see the laws of manifestation laid out before us. On this level of reality the energy is denser, and the vibration of life force "slows down." Everything happens in the construct of time, a human-made illusion of this world, so that everything has a beginning, a middle and an end. It is in the physical realm that the energy of light slows enough for our nervous system to perceive it as fixed—therefore we can easily mistake matter as solid, when in fact the book you are reading, the paper it's printed on, as well the chair you're sitting on, constantly change form. Although thoughts move through our minds in kaleidoscopic instants, to materialize thoughts on this physical level takes time. Yet, because

Four Worlds of the Qabalah
in Relationship to the Tree of Life

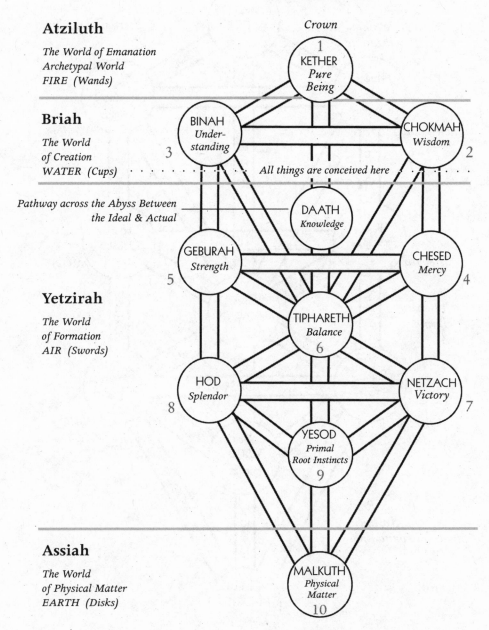

THREE VEILS OF
NEGATIVE EXISTENCE

Atziluth

The World of Emanation
Archetypal World
FIRE (Wands)

Crown

1
KETHER
*Pure
Being*

Briah

The World
of Creation
WATER (Cups)

3
BINAH
*Under-
standing*

CHOKMAH
Wisdom
2

· · · · · · · · · *All things are conceived here* · · · ·

Pathway across the Abyss Between ——
the Ideal & Actual

DAATH
Knowledge

5
GEBURAH
Strength

CHESED
Mercy
4

Yetzirah

The World
of Formation
AIR (Swords)

TIPHARETH
Balance
6

8
HOD
Splendor

NETZACH
Victory
7

YESOD
*Primal
Root Instincts*
9

Assiah

The World
of Physical Matter
EARTH (Disks)

MALKUTH
*Physical
Matter*
10

With dissolution of matter,
the Light Source returns to Kether

Sephiroth of the Tree of Life with Tarot Card Assignments

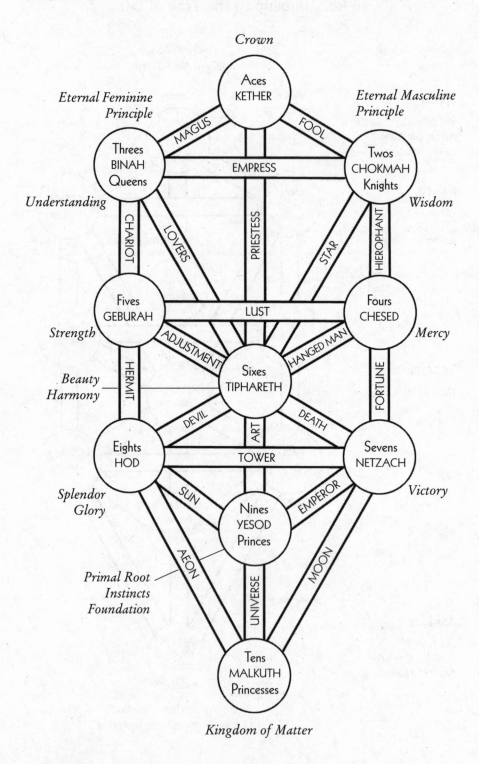

Kingdom of Matter

things move more slowly on the earth plane, it is easier for us to grasp the interplay between our thoughts, our emotions and our actions, and make conscious choices for ourselves.

Here on earth we have the opportunity to accomplish what Crowley (and others) call the Great Work—that of bringing about the union of our human nature and our divine spirit. The great gift of life in Assiah is being able to bear witness to this process of creation.

It is the work of the Qabalah, and the Thoth Tarot, to remind us of our grandeur and illumine our path. The deeply personal revelations of your Thoth Tarot readings are directly related to the divine attributes of consciousness symbolized in the Tree of Life.

To deepen your understanding of the cards you draw, refer to the Tree of Life on page 358. Consider the aspects of the Thoth Tarot cards in relation to their positions at each Sephirah or on the paths between:

The *Major Arcana* cards stand on the paths that connect each Sephirah, and represent a blending of the energies of the two Sephiroth they connect. For example, The Empress is shown on the path between Binah (Understanding) and Chokmah (Wisdom), and thus she embodies the balance between head "wisdom" and heart "understanding."

The forty small cards of the *Minor Arcana* are represented in the Ten Sephiroth of the Tree of Life. All the Aces are related to the Sephirah Kether, all the twos to Chokmah, the threes to Binah—all the way to the tens in the Sephirah Malkuth. Since the Aces correspond to Kether, the first/original, they are the "purest" sphere, and so each suit's attributes in the Ace will always be the purest expression of those traits. The Aces in Kether address the primal energy of each four suits. The Ace of Wands being the purest expression of will. The Ace of Cups the purest form of the spirit of understanding. The Ace of Swords the purest presentation of clear thinking. The Ace of Disks as the purest manifestation of physical life on planet earth.

The *Court Cards* are positioned on the Tree of Life as follows: The Knights (Father) in Chokmah indicate the wisdom that accompanies the strong sense of spontaneity, authority and ability to take action found in all four Knights. The Queens (Mother) in Binah point to the understanding and compassionate nature present in the Queens of all four suits. The Princes (Son) in Tiphareth underline the expression of primal root instincts as they influence the journey of each Prince. The Princesses (Daughter) in Malkuth show that the particular energy of each suit's Princess takes on a physical manifestation.

We all share the same destiny, and that is to find our way out of the darkness (reactive level) and into the Light (proactive level). Yet the majority of us, because we are unaware of our true nature, do not exercise our potential as conscious co-creators of the world. We behave like robots programmed by our culture, family structure and peers. Our lives are reactive.

In truth, our wakening is a kind of remembrance. Falling into the physical plane, we live in a cloud of uncertainty, having forgotten the nature of our true Self. But when we remember *what we are a part of*—and that is everything—we naturally, consciously ascend the path shown on the Tree of Life and experience a personal resurrection.

The wisdom of the Qabalah, as it is embodied in the Thoth Tarot cards, gives us a wide-angle lens to view the multi-dimensional worlds. Both the Qabalah and the Thoth Tarot reveal wisdom about the four worlds we live in and how best to consciously create the reality we desire; both champion a proactive life. They deliver not only a map of how to proceed from the merely reactive to the exultantly proactive, but the sentient experience of wakening to our spiritual nature.

2. Astrology and the Tarot

A study of the planets and constellations in astrology can help you develop a deeper understanding of the aspects of the Thoth Tarot because each card bears an astrological significance. The *planets* symbolize the primary energy, and the *constellations*—the 12 signs of the Zodiac—express how the energy is manifested.

As you become more comfortable with your tarot cards, you can deepen your readings by understanding the influence of the sun sign (constellation) or planet related to the card you're working with. The symbol of the sun sign is found on the Thoth Tarot's Major Arcana cards, as well as the Minor Arcana Small Cards.

When reading your cards, reflect on the Element of the card as well as the planet and sun sign symbols that rule the card you're working with. The Element of the card shows whether you're operating within the world of intent (Fire), emotions (Water), mind (Air), or the material world (Earth). Since the Elements need to mix with each other to create life as we know it, the Court Cards (Knight, Queen and Prince) each rule 20° of one sun sign to 20° of the next sign. The Princesses have no Zodiacal attribution.

Court Card	*Rules*
Knight of Wands	21st degree of Scorpio to 20th degree of Sagittarius
Queen of Wands	21st degree of Pisces to 20th degree of Aries
Prince of Wands	21st degree of Cancer to 20th degree of Leo
Princess of Wands	None
Knight of Cups	21st degree of Aquarius to 20th degree of Pisces
Queen of Cups	21st degree of Gemini to 20th degree of Cancer
Prince of Cups	21st degree of Libra to 20th degree of Scorpio
Princess of Cups	None

Knight of Swords	21st degree of Taurus to 20th degree of Gemini
Queen of Swords	21st degree of Virgo to 20th degree of Libra
Prince of Cups	21st degree of Capricorn to 20th degree of Aquarius
Princess of Swords	None
Knight of Disks	21st degree of Leo to 20th degree of Virgo
Queen of Disks	21st degree of Sagittarius to 20th degree of Capricorn
Prince of Disks	21st degree of Aries to 20th degree of Taurus
Princesses of Disks	None

The planet that rules the card you're reading reveals the type of energy that's being expressed. For example: the Sun is extroverted, the Moon introverted, Mercury is swiftness, Venus harmonious, Mars is assertive, Jupiter expansive, and Saturn challenging.

The sun sign affiliated with the card gives you even more information. For example: Aries has a "me first" attitude, Taurus is slow and steady, Gemini embraces duality, Cancer is the great ocean of receptivity, Leo is the fire of creativity, Virgo analyzes, Libra balances, Scorpio transitions, Sagittarius perceives, Capricorn is duty-bound, Aquarius exhibits an "I Know" stance, and Pisces, as the last sign, is closest to spirit.

When you study your Individual Guidance cards in Section III, you'll find that knowing the astrological significance of the cards is of benefit in understanding the diverse aspects of your Lifetime Collage.

For example: If The Priestess card is one of your Individual Guidance cards, you immediately know that, being ruled by the Moon, she will be illusive and highly intuitive. The Moon is a Water Element, therefore The Priestess will be passive and receptive by nature.

If The Priestess card appears in a reading, you're being shown that the endeavor itself may be illusive, and perhaps the only hope you have of gaining knowledge about the situation in question will be through your own intuition.

The following is a brief overview of the planets and constellations as they express themselves in the Thoth Tarot cards.

The Major Arcana has 12 sun signs (constellations) and 10 planets. The Minor Arcana's small cards show you the sun sign with a particular planet in that sign. For example: Aries rules the 2, 3 and 4 of Wands. These are Dominion, Virtue and Completion. Dominion has Mars in Aries which indicates the dynamically powerful energy that occurs when you fully focus your will and intent on a particular outcome. Virtue has the Sun in Aries, which indicates the extroverted, optimistic, and gregarious energy that inspires you to make a connection with others. Completion has Venus in Aries which tells you that you have completed or brought harmony and balance into a particular situation for which you felt great love.

Planets

Influence of the Planets on the Major Arcana Tarot Cards

Mercury	The Magus
Moon	The Priestess
Venus	The Empress
Jupiter	Fortune
Neptune	The Hanged-Man
Mars	The Tower
Sun	The Sun
Pluto	The Aeon
Saturn	The Universe
Uranus	The Fool

Moon (Water) symbolizes the darkness of night. It guards the gate to the unconscious so that the feminine mysteries are shielded from the fire of sunlight. The Moon represents the feminine, passive-receptive part of your nature; it supports your intuition and helps you to see in the dark. It rules your imagination, fantasy life and dream world. Keep in mind that the Moon can cast shadows that hide the road ahead and distort your sense of reason.

Sun (Fire) symbolizes the bright light of day as it represents primal life force energy. The warmth of the Sun brings courage, illumination, and idealization; in short, it brings everything into the light as all is revealed. It represents the masculine, active part of our nature, and supports expression through action. It encourages you to be optimistic, generous and fully visible in the outer world. However, if you spend too much time in the hot sun you can get burnt, losing contact with your inner life and therefore risking becoming superficial, dogmatic or authoritarian.

Mercury (Air) has been called the Messenger of the Gods. It signifies the lively, quick, mercurial part of our nature that gives your mind the capacity to process data swiftly. Mercury represents the power of transmission: the ability to talk, write, learn and teach. The fast pace of Mercury can be a liability if you hold on to information instead of integrating it and moving on. Your mind can move into a state of "circuit overload" and leave you feeling frustrated and overwhelmed. A state of conflict, struggle and futility follows.

Venus (Water) symbolizes peace, beauty and harmony. Venus is the goddess of love and rules all that is beautiful. She was born from the depth of the ocean and embodies the hidden mysteries of the feminine aspects of human nature. As a Water element, she brings the sensitivity that nourishes an artistic nature. Like the Moon, Venus has many phases that can express themselves as mood swings. She gives you social grace and elegance but can also contribute to excessive vanity and emotionalism.

Jupiter (Fire) indicates a dynamic expansion of energy. Bigger than life, Jupiter is the King of the Gods. It is the planet of faith, perseverance and enthusiasm. Jupiter is a benevolent planet and says "yes" to everything, so you want to be careful what you ask for. If you seek joy, Jupiter will bring greater joy than you can imagine. If you appreciate conflict and are addicted to it, Jupiter says "yes" and supplies you with an abundance of conflict.

Mars (Fire) is the Warrior God who is always pushing the limits of possibility. He rules new beginnings and generates the heat of passion, enterprise and courage, without which stagnation would occur. Mars is vital to life as we know it. The heat of desire can inspire you to achieve your goals through ambition, initiative and assertiveness. When you're ill, a physical fever (heat) will purify your body. Mars energy can destroy as well as heal. It can stimulate energy to purify body, mind and soul, and also run amiss and annihilate you through its aggressiveness.

Saturn (Earth) is a stern figure often referred to as Father Time. He is the disciplinarian who sets limits and time constraints. He represents tradition, convention and stability. Where Jupiter expands your world, Saturn compresses it. When Saturn crosses your path he brings tests and challenges to see if you're building your life on a firm foundation. If you haven't, the pressure he exerts will cause your world to crumble and you'll have the opportunity to start rebuilding from scratch. Saturn expects things to be done in the right way. He delivers self respect for a job well done and can be ruthless when it isn't.

Uranus (Air) is the higher octave of Mercury and depicts the higher mind. Where Mercury affects our intellect, Uranus portrays a mind unfettered by dogma and prejudice. Uranus brings hidden knowledge to the surface and evokes powerful change.

Neptune (Water) as the higher octave of Venus represents divine compassion and points toward the mystical realm. The mystical world is composed of the experiences that fall outside the normal parameters. It replaces words with symbols, and goes beyond mundane communication into a world that encompasses your divine intuition. Neptune can generate delusion as well as inspiration.

Pluto (Water) is the Lord of the Underworld. He brings your darkest feelings to the surface. Just when you think you've gone deep enough, Pluto demands that you go deeper yet. He is the planet of transcendence and revitalization. Pluto can produce obsession and destruction as it transforms.

CONSTELLATIONS

Sun Signs

The signs of the Zodiac are twelve in number. In the 360° circle, each sun sign or constellation "rules" 30° of the Zodiac. This means each sun sign influences the overall expression of energy in its respective section of the Zodiac, and the expression of energy in its related tarot card. For example, Scorpio, the sign of transition, represents birth, death and rebirth. The sign of Scorpio is found on the Death card. It influences the Death card by creating an atmosphere conducive to change.

Influence of the Constellations on the Tarot Cards

Zodiac Sign	Major Arcana	Minor Arcana	Court Card
Aries	The Emperor	2-3-4 of Wands	Queen of Wands
Taurus	The Hierophant	5-6-7 of Disks	Prince of Disks
Gemini	The Lovers	8-9-10 of Swords	Knight of Swords
Cancer	The Chariot	2-3-4 of Cups	Queen of Cups
Leo	Lust	5-6-7 of Wands	Prince of Wands
Virgo	The Hermit	8-9-10 of Disks	Knight of Disks
Libra	Adjustment	2-3-4 of Swords	Queen of Swords
Scorpio	Death	5-6-7 of Cups	Prince of Cups
Sagittarius	Art	8-9-10 of Wands	Knight of Wands
Capricorn	The Devil	2-3-4 of Disks	Queen of Disks
Aquarius	The Star	5-6-7 of Swords	Prince of Swords
Pisces	The Moon	8-9-10 of Cups	Knight of Cups

Attributes of the Sun Signs

Positive/Receptive • Cardinal/Fixed/Mutable • Elements

Positive and Receptive

The sun signs are divided into Positive and Receptive signs. The Positive signs will be outgoing, strong and active, which helps in expressing initiative and courage. The Receptive signs will internalize, nurture and be less active which brings the qualities of tenacity and convention to the forefront.

Positive	Receptive
Aries	Taurus
Gemini	Cancer
Leo	Virgo
Libra	Scorpio
Sagittarius	Capricorn
Aquarius	Pisces

Cardinal, Fixed and Mutable Signs

There are three aspects of energy represented in the Zodiac that express the cycles of life. These might be considered as: Initiation (Begin), Stability (Maintain) or Adaptability (Change). In astrology they are called Cardinal, Fixed or Mutable.

Cardinal	Fixed	Mutable
Initiation (Begin)	*Stability (Maintain)*	*Adaptability (Change)*
Aries	Taurus	Gemini
Cancer	Leo	Virgo
Libra	Scorpio	Sagittarius
Capricorn	Aquarius	Pisces

The Cardinal signs are active, assertive and constantly in motion. The Fixed signs are stable, slow and purposeful. They cannot be easily swayed from their positions. The Mutable signs are flexible and pliable. They see all sides and can adjust accordingly.

By determining which of the three aspects apply to the card you're examining, you'll gain a deeper understanding of the card's highly personal guidance for you. For example: Aries/The Emperor is a Cardinal Fire sign which tells you that The Emperor is easily able to *initiate* new behavior. Taurus/The Hierophant is a Fixed Earth sign and is therefore able to *maintain* tradition and convention. Gemini/The Lovers as a Mutable Air sign is fluid and flexible, readily able to *change* the situation through its ability to relate.

The Elements

The four elements of Fire, Water, Air and Earth speak to us through their influence on both the planets and constellations, and consequently have bearing on the tarot cards. The Fire element is the thrust of primal energy into form. Water brings understanding; Air communication, and Earth materialization and manifestation.

Fire	Water	Air	Earth
Aries	Cancer	Gemini	Taurus
Leo	Scorpio	Libra	Virgo
Sagittarius	Pisces	Aquarius	Capricorn

Each Thoth Tarot card contains aspects of Fire, Water, Air or Earth, so understanding the nature of each Element will enhance your insight into the card's meanings. For example: The Emperor (Aries), Lust (Leo) and Art (Sagittarius) cards are all Fire signs, so instantly you know that like fire itself, these cards are not shrinking violets but dynamic, assertive and powerful aspects of the tarot. Like water itself, the Water Element cards will be receptive and adaptable, with unseen depths below the surface. It is through the air waves that communication occurs, therefore the Air Element cards will be highly communicative, bright and witty. The Earth Element cards are "the salt of the earth," rooted in the material world, convention and tradition.

Signs of the Zodiac

Aries (Fire). Aries is ruled by the Sun and is the first sign of the Zodiac. Symbolized by the Ram, Aries represents the will to be—the first primal fire that produces the impulse to move out into life. The Sun's influence feeds the fire of youthful passion and encourages a fully lived life. Like the Ram, the tarot Emperor rules by divine authority and isn't afraid to take risks. The Ram just lowers his head to push through any obstacles in the path. If Aries energy is blocked, it can easily go from being open and good natured to sullen and insensitive.

Taurus (Earth). Taurus is ruled by Venus. Where Aries adventurously sows the seeds, Taurus gives them structure and form. Taurus' earthiness influences The Heirophant to bridge the world of primal energy with the material world. The process of materialization takes time but the Bull's determination and tenacity will see the situation through to its natural conclusion. Venus supplies Taurus' appreciation of beauty in the physical world. The Bull seeks peace and harmony and therefore will avoid conflict whenever possible. If backed into a corner, however, the Bull will come out charging. Its shadow can show itself as stubbornness, lethargy and greed.

Gemini (Air). Gemini is ruled by Mercury and so possesses an insatiable appetite for information. Gemini's main question is *why*, followed by *when, where* and *how*? The Gemini Twins represent both sides of the coin, so to speak. Appearing on The Lovers card, they depict the union of opposites. The Hermit also makes his appearance on The Lovers card to bless the process of integration. Conscious mind is a powerful tool that can process data at the speed of light. But if the information gathered isn't incorporated into one's knowledge, it becomes the fuel for indecision, confusion and unreliability.

Cancer (Water). Cancer is ruled by the Moon and is considered to be the Mother of the Zodiac. As mother, Cancer is the symbol of a nurturing womb which keeps everything within itself and reacts to life through its feelings. Expressed as the Crab constellation on The Chariot card, this sign feels emotionally exposed and vulnerable unless on familiar turf. When insecure it pulls into its shell and keeps everything hidden. The Moon influences the subconscious instinctive patterns of behavior. Like The Chariot, if it is to move ahead it must trust its instincts. When this Moon sign feels at risk it can be overly sensitive, and behave defensively.

Leo (Fire). Leo is ruled by the Sun and is considered to be the Father of the Zodiac. As father, the Lion is the protector and claims dominion over his world. It is the Sun's influence that gives Leo tremendous vitality and allows for an outgoing, warm and charismatic energy. The Lion can pound his chest in pride and roar with authority. Leo has a sense of drama that commands attention. Leo represents strength, romance, and passion. As in the Lust card Leo is driven by creative energy and will not tolerate anything that obstructs its expression. If repressed, the Sun's energy can become morose, cynical and tyrannical.

Virgo (Earth). Virgo is ruled by Mercury, and therefore constantly analyzing and integrating new information. Mercury supplies the keen intellect and precision needed to do the job. The Virgin holding a shaft of wheat symbolizes the season of harvest—the time when the information we need is gathered. Virgo's desire to serve mankind is illustrated in The Hermit card. By uncovering new ways of being in the world, The Hermit is able to light the lantern that shows the path to others. The shadow side of Virgo can contribute to an overly critical nature that breeds low self esteem.

Libra (Air). Ruled by Venus, Libra seeks beauty and harmony in life. In the Adjustment card we see the Scales of Justice that continually weigh the pros and cons of each situation so balance and equilibrium are maintained. Libra possesses a strong sense of justice and is always fair in dealings with others. Relationship is an element crucial to Libra's life path, therefore Venus supplies the charm, grace and gregarious nature found in this sign. If the Scales of Justice are out of balance, Libra's expression can become superficial and indecisive.

Scorpio (Water). Scorpio is ruled by both Pluto and Mars. Pluto demands that Scorpio remains totally committed to self-knowledge. The momentous energy of Mars keeps Scorpio in a constant state of transformation. The symbol of the scorpion signifies the lowest level of awareness; it changes into a phoenix to symbolize the more aware levels of consciousness, and culminates in the eagle at the highest stage of development. The Death card is attributed to Scorpio and points out that life is in continual flux, a cycle of birth, death and rebirth. There is a depth and intensity of passion that influences Scorpio's thoughts, emotions and deeds. If this energy becomes too intense (which can occur when undergoing deep transformation), Scorpio can deliver a sting not only to another but to itself as well.

Sagittarius (Fire). Sagittarius is ruled by Jupiter and concerned with expansion. The fiery energy of Jupiter accounts for the tendency to take risks and engage fully in every life experience. The Centaur with his bow and arrow requires as much personal freedom as he can command to experience the myriad wonders of life. As seen in the Art card, Sagittarian energy is philosophical and idealistic by nature, and tends to encourage expression from the depth of one's being without restraint. The shadow appears when Sagittarius, feeling constrained or confined, is pushed to fire poisoned arrows at others or himself.

Capricorn (Earth). Capricorn is ruled by Saturn and this gives him a strong sense of purpose. The Goat is positioned on the mid-heaven, which illustrates its tenacity and sure-footedness. The Devil card depicts the Goat as determined, goal-oriented and duty-driven to make the precarious climb. This energy is committed to leaving nothing to chance. Capricorn plots and plans, and is willing to work long and hard to reach the goal. This energy pattern has a strong sense of propriety and self-protection about it and can keep emotions locked up inside. If this energy is repressed for too long, carelessness and disorganization will result.

Aquarius (Air). Aquarius is ruled by Saturn and Uranus. Uranus imparts the desire for liberation, Saturn the need for limitation; in short—freedom through discipline. It represents the power of the inventive, forward-thinking mind. The Star card represents the bohemian, the crusader of ideas and defender of one's right to express these ideas. Restricting the natural flow of Aquarian energy can cause complete disassociation from emotion, and even brutal insensitivity to others.

Pisces (Water). Pisces is ruled by Neptune. Neptune is the higher octave of Venus and brings Venus's love of beauty and harmony to the level of divine compassion. The Two Fish (one swimming upstream and one downstream) symbolize the personality and the soul. Pisces, as expressed in the Moon card, continually tries to balance the needs of this worldly life with the needs of the soul. Fish are highly sensitive to their surroundings and express a deep sense of intuitive ability. Pisces is a mystic, seer and psychic. Fish live in a state of empathy and can relate to your deepest needs and emotions. Because of this Pisces must be vigilant to be able to discriminate between personal feelings and those of others; if not, healthy boundaries are lost and invasiveness or overreaction result.

3. Alchemy and the Tarot

Alchemy was a medieval science concerned with the study of chemical elements and compounds, especially the conversion of base metals into gold by subjecting the raw material to progressive stages of burning, cleansing, separating and solidifying. Yet it was only partly a natural science of chemical substances and reactions. Alchemy was also an occult religious-mystical system that dealt with humanity's search for the highest knowledge: an eventual unity with God.

Alchemy had its heyday from the ninth century until around 1700, when it became the basis of modern chemistry. In Arabic, alchemy meant "matter of Egypt" (from Khemennu, "Land of the Moon," an old name for Egypt). The Arabs thought alchemy was invented by the Egyptians; medieval Christians also believed that it originated with the Egyptian god Thoth, or Hermes, as the Greeks called him. Although long of interest to mystics and psychological explorers, it is Carl Jung who can be credited with our current approach to alchemy and the profound relationship between alchemy's ancient, secret processes and the struggle of human beings to evolve to our highest state.

We are born into this world a *whole* being that possesses spirit and soul as well as a physical body. Spirit is the dynamic primal force (masculine) that energizes our life with action, wisdom and reason; soul is the passive (feminine) chalice of receptivity, understanding and intuition. In our natural state, spirit and soul are in balance within our essence, contained in the vessel of the body. In this balance, one is experiencing, learning and growing in the full magnificence of the human state, as an individual and a participant in planetary life. Spirit keeps you out in the world, maneuvering intent into a desired physical form, while your soul supplies meaning to that manifestation. Your soul allows you to follow your feelings as you seek to creatively express yourself in the world. Without spirit, human beings go nowhere; without soul, the journey would be meaningless.

As you mature, adaptation to the outer world becomes a full-time job and you begin to compartmentalize your essence as well as your life, gauging who you are and how you act according to culturally acceptable behavior. When you do that, eventually both spirit and soul suffer; you begin to see life as something that happens to you, something you have to "deal with." Bereft of wholeness, you are left feeling lost and diminished. Alchemy presents you with a path toward rediscovering the congruency and balance that brought joy and bliss into your life.

The Thoth Tarot uses alchemical symbols to illustrate the changes you undergo mentally, emotionally and physically throughout your lifetime. The richness of these references are typically Crowley and distinguish the Thoth Tarot from other decks, so further study of alchemy will add depth and revelation to your tarot readings.

The following is a brief description of the Seven Phases of Alchemy as they relate to the tarot. The Thoth Tarot with its use of alchemical symbols gives you insight into the development and spiritual evolution that occurs within your personal as well as transpersonal (beyond individual survival and self interest) environment. You can follow your individual development through the seven phases of alchemy.

The first four phases are called Calcination, Dissolution, Separation and Conjunction. They relate to your personal ego self—who you think are you in the three-dimensional material world. The last three phases—Fermentation, Distillation and Coagulation—deal with a greater sense of being that includes a multi-dimensional self and answers the question: Who am I *really*?

Tarot, like alchemy, concerns itself with the synthesis of opposing forces: active/passive, good/bad, male/female, conscious/unconscious. By accepting this dual nature and realizing that you have the potential for action and passivity, for good and bad thoughts, you're able to balance these dualities within your consciousness and function with greater awareness and fulfillment.

The Seven Phases of Alchemy

1. Calcination
2. Dissolution
3. Separation
4. Conjunction
5. Fermentation
6. Distillation
7. Coagulation

Calcination

Calcination is purification by Fire. Fire is the most powerful force of transformation and readily reduces the ego to ashes. When your ego-identity has overpowered your soul, Calcination must occur if you are to grow and evolve. For example: You realize that lately you've made "everything" about you. You're too full of yourself, so you make a conscious choice to reel in your ego and deflate it yourself. That'll work. Or Calcination can simply appear to *happen to you*, as shown in The Tower card of the Thoth Tarot. For instance: you feel stuck in a career you're unhappy with. However, you stay because you feel duty-bound since others are depending on you. You've often wondered—what else could I do? When your life becomes too rigid and doesn't allow for change, the alchemical Fire-Breathing Dragon of the card will blast you out of your self-centered ivory tower and toss you to the ground. In other words, the company you work for suddenly downsizes and you lose your job! The result is that you wake from your ego-trance and begin the process of Calcination that eventually returns you to wholeness.

The Wand Suit is aligned with **Calcination** in that it expresses, through Fire, the will and intent of spirit.

Dissolution

After the Fire of Calcination has done its job, the phase of Dissolution begins. This process is the dissolving of the remnants of ego. As your ego surrenders itself to the humbling experiences of life, the emotions that have been buried deep within your unconscious will surface. This emotional flood, symbolized by the Element Water, will dissolve whatever is left of your ego and what remains will be a small seed of the True Self. The Star card of the Thoth Tarot captures this profound transformation: the Waters (understanding and feelings) flow through your life, washing away the debris of Calcination.

To continue with the previous example: when you lost your job, buried emotions surfaced. Your insecurities, anger, and frustrations bubbled up from the unconscious. You realize how the job had angered and frustrated you—tears flow as feelings of betrayal surface. Your commitment to your company was rewarded with dismissal. This emotional release begins to wash away the familiar responses, and causes you to reach deeper into yourself to find the will to keep going and make the changes you've wanted to make. This phase could have been self-generated if you would have acknowledged your need for change and moved on willingly. Either way, it's important to dissolve the hardened emotions if you're to release your True Self.

Dissolution can also occur with the progression of physical illness. Disease will wear you down until all that is left is for you to surrender to your tears and release repressed feelings. When you cry and express your emotions, you always feel better.

The Cup Suit is aligned with **Dissolution** in that it expresses the dissolving of emotions through Water.

Separation

Once the dross of the rigid state has been burnt away, and water has dissolved the ashes, the process of Separation can begin. Separation is the phase in which you decide what works in your life and what doesn't work. When you are able to bear witness to your life in an objective way, new insights occur. The Adjustment card portrays this phase of Separation, with its large sword cleaving apart the different aspects of being (such as your likes and dislikes, what sustains you and what damages). To follow the previous example further: Once you acknowledge the emotions that have surfaced, you contemplate what will now provide a fulfilled existence, or return you to being a frustrated employee. You need to segregate these choices before you can know what to let go of and what to keep. Perhaps there isn't much you enjoy about your career and desire a completely different one. Maybe there were parts of the job you liked and want to keep those.

This phase gives you the opportunity to discover what is really important to you, what you value and what type of life you want to live and what kind of person you want to be.

The Sword Suit is aligned with **Separation** in that it expresses the divine will in thought comprised of two separate aspects: our masculine reason and feminine intuition.

Conjunction

When you've undergone the alchemical phase of Separation you're ready to experience, through Conjunction, a reuniting of your spirit with your soul (action with meaning). This union of the masculine and feminine principles within you is depicted in The Lovers card. Your spirit and soul work in conjunction with each other, and through their "marriage" a new belief system is formed. In the Thoth Tarot, the Knights are the masculine spirit (will, intent and wisdom) and the Queens are the embodiment of the soul (understanding, feelings and intuition). They join forces to empower each other. The Knight (your spirit) appears in the outer world as a dynamic expression of creative energy and the Queen (your soul) gives purpose and meaning to the creative force.

To continue the example: You're at a crossroads in life, faced with opportunities to re-invent yourself as you search for a more rewarding career. You've learnt what's important to you in the Separation phase and now you need to reassemble your life, so to speak, in a way that gives equal voice to both spirit and soul. You'll want to listen to your feelings and intuition to determine the direction you wish to go. Your spirit comes into play by empowering you to take the actions necessary to get there. As the alchemical process continues with Fermentation, it will now take you beyond the personal, to a transpersonal level.

The Disk Suit is aligned with **Conjunction** because they deal with the physical body as the vessel for expression of both spirit and soul.

Fermentation

Beginning with the process of Fermentation, you are moving into the next octave of consciousness. Fermentation carries you from a limited personal awareness to a transpersonal view of life that will include the recognition and acceptance of your True or Higher Self. In short, your essential self adjusts to encompass a multi-dimensional understanding of life. Where the first four alchemical phases uncovered the personal unconscious, these last three phases (Fermentation, Distillation and Coagulation) will bring you into contact with the "collective unconscious."

Fermentation itself has two aspects. *Putrefaction* is the first aspect and *Imaginatio* is the second.

Putrefaction occurs when you are the most "lost" in life. The very structure of your world is decomposing and you feel as if you're losing your mental, emotional and physical perspective. In the Thoth Tarot, the Death card illustrates this phase of Fermentation. It depicts the psychological death of the remains of your ego. Like the skeleton on the Death card, you feel as if neither you nor your life has any substance. What brought fulfillment in the past looks empty and shallow now; you're living day-to-day on automatic pilot. At the same time, your interests become more philosophical. You begin to wonder about the meaning of life. What is my purpose here? Who am I *really*?

The second phase of Fermentation is *Imaginatio* (Active Imagination), defining Imagination as will and intent. It is the process of consciously, deliberately letting go, clearing the mind so that you can plant the seeds of the new images that will bloom in your consciousness in the days to come. This can be done through contemplation and meditation. When Fermentation is complete, you will be ready to receive, through your Imagination, new dreams, hopes and visions for the future.

Distillation

Distillation is the rendering process that distills the new from the old and allows for innovative ideas, new feelings and fresh physical awareness to surface. At this stage of the alchemical process, your awareness will include a strong sense of spirituality. In the Thoth Tarot, the Art card is a prime example of Distillation. The card depicts a two-headed figure that is actually a fusion of the figures in The Lovers card. We see the King and Queen standing over a cauldron of boiling water (blending of Fire and Water). From the rising vapor, new droplets of Water (emotions, feelings, understandings) form and become the basis of your new essence. Here the ego-self is once again heated in the cauldron of experience over the Fires of life and the result is a new you—a deeper, more philosophical, and much wiser you.

At first you may feel disoriented because you're accustomed to looking to the outer world for support. Distillation results in an alternative world view that requires you to look deep within yourself for the support you need to continue your life with an expanded consciousness.

Engraved on the Stone of the Art card is the alchemical dictum *"Visita Interiora Terrae Rectificando Invenies Occultum Lapidem"* which means "Visit the interior parts of the Earth (go deep within your self) and through Rectification (making things right) you will find the Hidden Stone (your spiritual essence)." The Philosopher's Stone, as it's been called, holds the key to your immortality.

Coagulation

Coagulation is the final, longed for union of the spirit, soul and body. In this fusion, the body becomes more ethereal and the spirit becomes more corporeal. In tarot an androgynous figure, with both male and female characteristics, is the image for this union. The Aeon card symbolizes the Coagulated union of primal male and primal female energy expressed in one being. It is the resurrection of the True Self with conscious appreciation of the infinite intelligence of which it is a part. The Great Work is not the destruction of ego, but the ascension of "ego" into the Transpersonal Self that is expressed in the Trinity of Spirit, Soul and Body. This Work is the main focus and purpose of our life here on earth.

With that said—what does Coagulation look like in your life? It looks like a person who "is in the world but not of it." The Universe card illustrates the completion of The Great Work: YOU, as a unified being, returning to your day-to-day life as a perfected spiritual entity in a physical body, one who understands and embraces the full magnitude of existence—ultimately, a person who demonstrates his or her divine aspect while living that existence here on earth.

4. Patterns

When doing a tarot reading, it's helpful to notice any patterns that occur in the cards you select. Drawing a high proportion of a particular suit, number, astrological sign or Element is not a coincidence! An extra dimension of guidance is being made available to you when, for instance, you see a predominance of Wands, Cups, Swords or Disks in a spread of several cards. Or perhaps you find a number or group of numbers that appear more than others. Are certain astrological sun signs more prevalent? What about the Elements— are there more Fire, Water, Air or Earth element cards in the spread? Below are groups that may appear as patterns in your readings. Take note of the added depth of meaning in the Thoth Tarot.

Predominance of Suits

Wands: You're more than likely dealing with your will and intent to create something new in your life.

Cups: Your feelings and intuitions are making themselves known and require your immediate attention.

Swords: Something is definitely on your mind, and your mental powers are focused on analyzing your situation, integrating the information and ironing out any mental conflicts.

Disks: Your focus is on the mundane world, and it's important that you look at the overall reading through the lens of physical manifestation.

For example: You lay out the New Year's Spread on Page 22 and look up the individual cards in the Advisor Section. You also notice that of the seven positions in the spread, you've pulled four Wands, two Swords and one Disk. Those four Wands strongly indicate a primary focus on creating something new and important in your life. This desire is paramount on your mind (Swords) and you are determined to express it in the physical world (Disk). The lack of Cups may indicate that your feelings and intuition are secondary. At the moment you're more likely to move full speed ahead, based on your mental determination.

Predominance of Numbers

Aces: You are experiencing an explosion of energy as your raw potential begins its journey toward manifestation.

Twos: You're becoming aware of your will and intent.

Threes: Creative, formative energy is being generated in the situation.

Fours: The core energy is taking form as it moves from primal force into physical manifestation.

Fives: Disruption is occurring, but it will lead to further progress in the matter.

Sixes: Balance has been restored.

Sevens: The desire for expansion is renewed.

Eights: The changes you're experiencing will ultimately help things stabilize.

Nines: Here is the foundation upon which you will build the ultimate manifestation.

Tens: These signify that the situation is locked into its physical manifestation at this point.

Predominance of Astrological Symbols

Aries: The stage is set to take the initiative and just do it.

Taurus: View the situation through the lens of convention, stability and determination.

Gemini: Take care to consider all aspects of the situation.

Cancer:	Here the concern is with nurturing your feelings and expressing them.
Leo:	Focus on your strengths and protect your boundaries.
Virgo:	New information calls for careful analysis and judicious integration.
Libra:	Equilibrium and harmony are the ruling factors.
Scorpio:	Transitions are the focus of your spread; roll with them.
Sagittarius:	Take more risks, and your life expands.
Capricorn:	A strong sense of purpose dominates in the spread.
Aquarius:	Liberation is the overriding aspect.
Pisces:	The focus is on empathy and compassion.

Predominance of the Elements

Fire:	Become more in tune with your internal desires; be bold and energetic in following your passion.
Water:	Be receptive to your feelings and open to your intuition.
Air:	Consider being more communicative—use your head and analyze, synthesize and integrate the facts.
Earth:	Root your action in the material world, attending to your finances, relationships, career and family, etc.

Bottom Line
Tarot Card
Interpretations

A Quick Reference to
the Thoth Tarot Cards' Advice

THE MAJOR ARCANA

THE FOOL

Curiosity, spontaneity and a spirit of adventure will lead you toward success. When people say it can't be done, show them how wrong they are by doing it!

THE FOOL INVERTED

You've made some foolish choices lately. If you want to realize your goals, keep your commitments—pay attention to details and complete what you start.

THE MAGUS

Don't get hung up on just one way of doing this. You may have to revise your plans several times before you reach your goal, but when all is said and done—you will succeed.

THE MAGUS INVERTED

You create what you can imagine; therefore, think positively and then act creatively. What have you got to lose?

THE PRIESTESS

If you continue to seek advice from other people, you risk the chance of being misled. Trust your own intuition because at the moment, you are your best counsel.

THE PRIESTESS INVERTED

There's a lot more going on here than meets the eye. Before reaching a conclusion, take some time to learn more about your situation.

THE EMPRESS

Take a deep breath, slow down and relax. People want to help you if you'll just let them. Be gracious, delegate authority, and you'll get exactly you want.

THE EMPRESS INVERTED

If you want to succeed, stop trying to manipulate the circumstances and let the situation evolve at its own rate.

THE EMPEROR

Whatever you have wanted to do—now's the time to do it! If you're willing to jump, you'll land on your feet.

THE EMPEROR INVERTED

Get organized. You've been wasting valuable time spinning your wheels. If you put a plan in place before you act, you'll increase your chance for success.

THE HIEROPHANT

Now is NOT a good time for innovative strategies. Stick to a more conservative approach and go with what you know will work.

THE HIEROPHANT INVERTED

You're drowning in SHOULD and OUGHT TO. Rely on your own experiences. Trust yourself; do what you want to do and need to do, not what you think you should do.

THE LOVERS

You'll have a new relationship, or the deepening of a relationship in which you are currently involved. This is an opportunity to come to know yourself far better than you do now.

THE LOVERS INVERTED

If you're unwilling to change the structure of your relationship, or work to allow for new growth, the union or situation will become brittle and break under the strain.

THE CHARIOT

Your struggle is over and a new adventure is about to begin. Your hard work has guaranteed a successful outcome—why not just sit back, relax, and enjoy the ride?

THE CHARIOT INVERTED

This situation is unpredictable and can easily get out of control. Ask yourself: "Does my present behavior move me toward my goal, or further away from it?" Then act accordingly.

ADJUSTMENT

Postpone making any further plans until you've examined the pros and cons of this situation. Be sure you're on firm ground before you act. Check out the legalities.

ADJUSTMENT INVERTED

You may temporarily be caught in an unjust situation. In the short term, there's nothing you can do. However, in the long run, justice will prevail.

THE HERMIT

Stop and tie up the loose ends before you continue. Keep what is important to you and discard the rest. It will be easier to move forward unencumbered by the past.

THE HERMIT INVERTED

The time has come to confront your past and resolve any conflicting issues. If you can make peace with your past, you'll have a brighter future. Go ahead—you won't regret it.

FORTUNE

You've reached a major turning point in your life. This is a period of good fortune—so get up off the couch and meet your destiny.

FORTUNE Inverted

Opportunity is knocking but you're not opening the door! Hurry up and get going—it may choose not to knock twice.

LUST

Your determination gives you the stamina you need to work through any obstacles in your path. If you follow your passion, it will carry you to victory.

LUST Inverted

Why so cynical? If you want to succeed you need to find out what happened to your initial enthusiasm. Without it you will lack the staying power necessary to be successful.

THE HANGED MAN

This situation is temporarily beyond your control. In this specific situation you may have to yield in order to overcome.

THE HANGED MAN Inverted

Stop hitting your head against the wall. For the sake of progress, why not try a new approach?

DEATH

Everything is changing for the better; celebrate it. These changes will allow you to revitalize yourself and your situation.

DEATH Inverted

You're being warned if you continue to ignore the need for change, your situation will stagnate. These changes are choreographed to liberate you and make way for new and exiting times.

ART

Your life is full of new possibilities; however, you may have to be patient before they materialize. A delay at this time can only benefit you or your endeavor

ART Inverted

Exerting pure willpower will not get you the results you want; however, compromise, negotiation and moderation will.

THE DEVIL

You're taking yourself and your situation too seriously. You feel trapped—yet there are no locks on the door. Lighten up. You need to find out: What happened to your sense of humor?

THE DEVIL Inverted

You're in denial and denial is a no-win state of mind. Level with yourself and you'll know instinctively what you need to do next.

THE TOWER

The very foundation of this endeavor is crumbling. It's a blessing in disguise. The course of events eventually levels the playing field and provides you with the opportunity to go back to square one.

THE TOWER Inverted

To avoid misfortune you need to get your head "out of the clouds." Your talent for selective seeing and hearing has complicated the situation. Get real.

THE STAR

The spotlight is on, so go ahead and take center stage. It's time that you act like the true star you are!

THE STAR Inverted

A lack of self-confidence interferes with your success; get over it. Take a chance on yourself and you're sure to be pleased with the results.

THE MOON

Postpone making any decisions until you understand what's really going on. Like all cycles, this too shall pass and you'll be able to see clearly what needs to be done.

THE MOON Inverted

One of the most difficult phases of your life is over; relax. All you need to do is to tie up the loose ends and move on.

THE SUN

Celebrate the fact that each moment of your life is a new beginning. The sun is on the horizon; therefore, go ahead and prepare yourself to reap the rewards of a new day.

THE SUN Inverted

Of course there are challenges to overcome, but success will eventually be yours. Look at the brighter side—you're doing much better than you thought you were.

THE AEON

You're being given a second chance. Take responsibility for your actions and "walk your talk." Weigh your words before you speak, so you don't have to take them back later.

THE AEON Inverted

> You've been afraid to make the wrong choice, so you've made no choice at all. From now on, call your own shots; you'll be pleased with the results.

THE UNIVERSE

> Be patient with this project or situation because it needs time to develop. If you remain committed to your goals and stay the course, you'll create the outcome you want.

THE UNIVERSE Inverted

> Don't expect the situation to be resolved quickly. No matter how difficult it seems at the moment, stay with it until you succeed—and succeed you will.

THE MINOR ARCANA

THE SMALL CARDS

Wands Suit

ACE OF WANDS

> You can approach your present situation with a renewed sense of ambition—or embark on a totally new venture. Anything is possible for you if you're willing to get into the game.

ACE OF WANDS Inverted

> If you're not willing to look at your circumstances honestly, it will be difficult for you to succeed. Don't rush things. Back off until you have a better idea what's going on.

TWO OF WANDS (DOMINION)

> There's no better time than the present to take charge of your life. Trust your own insights and creativity because at this particular moment everything depends on you.

TWO OF WANDS (DOMINION) Inverted

> Instead of giving up and giving in—why not try harder? Desire will push you toward the goal, but it will not carry you there. However, your hard work and determination will.

THREE OF WANDS (VIRTUE)

Don't restrict yourself to the present area of exploration—broaden your horizons. Expand your venture to encompass the full scope of your talents and resources. Think big!

THREE OF WANDS (VIRTUE) Inverted

Because your energy is low, this isn't a favorable time to begin a new venture or expand a current one. Take a sabbatical. Then when you feel up to it, dig in again.

FOUR OF WANDS (COMPLETION)

A successful completion to your task is in sight. Keep the momentum going by taking one step at a time, and you'll achieve the goal.

FOUR OF WANDS (COMPLETION) Inverted

Stop dragging your feet. To regain lost momentum, it's important you take one step at a time, and finish what you start. Then the wheels of progress will turn in your favor.

FIVE OF WANDS (STRIFE)

Frustration with this project or situation is only temporary; therefore, don't allow it to undo all the good work you have done. You're just having a little difficulty going the last mile.

FIVE OF WANDS (STRIFE) Inverted

The path to your goal is not always a straight line. Thus your endeavor must be adaptable enough to withstand frustration and undergo frequent change.

SIX OF WANDS (VICTORY)

You're on your way to achieving the goals you've set for yourself. The struggles that have plagued you will come to an end and you will receive the recognition you deserve.

SIX OF WANDS (VICTORY) Inverted

Be forewarned: victory may elude you unless you're willing to stop questioning your talent, dig in your heels, and give it your best shot.

SEVEN OF WANDS (VALOUR)

Don't compromise; hold steadfast to your current position. If you want to win, look your fears in the face until they back down. Nothing short of total commitment is called for.

SEVEN OF WANDS (VALOUR) Inverted

Don't be so quick to abandon your dreams. You're allowing fear and anxiety to control your life. If you're willing to take a chance, you have far more to gain than to lose.

EIGHT OF WANDS (SWIFTNESS)

Don't waste time beating around the bush; say what you need to say. When you're ready to speak out, your words will be met with acceptance, understanding and appreciation.

EIGHT OF WANDS (SWIFTNESS) INVERTED

Unless your actions are more assertive, you'll continue to miss the mark. In the end you'll create only superficial changes and find yourself going nowhere fast.

NINE OF WANDS (STRENGTH)

Keep your sights on your goals while everything around you is the process of change. If you follow a path of moderation, you're less likely to be thrown off balance.

NINE OF WANDS (STRENGTH) INVERTED

You've allowed your present circumstances to throw you off balance. You need to keep your eyes on the goal rather than reacting to every little thing that happens.

TEN OF WANDS (OPPRESSION)

You're taking on too much responsibility. What may have once been a pleasure has now become a burden. Ask for help before the project or situation gets bogged down.

TEN OF WANDS (OPPRESSION) INVERTED

You're tired of feeling responsible for everything and everybody. Let others pull their own weight. Then when success arrives, you won't be too tired to savor it.

Cups Suit

ACE OF CUPS

There's never been a better time to promote yourself, your ideas or your situation. Open your heart to this endeavor and you will be motivated to put your best effort forward.

ACE OF CUPS INVERTED

Your inability to connect with your emotions has you feeling isolated. You need to reconnect with your true self before you'll be able to come together with anyone else.

TWO OF CUPS (LOVE)

If you're not yet involved in a mutually supportive relationship, you can expect to be very soon. Any partnership that is created on this level is surely destined for success.

TWO OF CUPS (LOVE) Inverted

Be receptive to the situation at hand. If you close yourself off, misunderstanding can easily occur. When you're open to it, what you need will come to you.

THREE OF CUPS (ABUNDANCE)

To achieve your goals, seek out like-minded people, and network. Talk about your ideas to anyone who will listen. People will support you if they know what you have to offer.

THREE OF CUPS (ABUNDANCE) Inverted

Give up trying to do this alone. Develop a support system. Friends are an asset so why are you avoiding the very people who are trying to help you?

FOUR OF CUPS (LUXURY)

Stop and examine where your feelings are taking you. If you can bring emotional balance back into your life, something new will be offered to you.

FOUR OF CUPS (LUXURY) Inverted

You've buried your feelings about this situation and now feel cold and aloof. Free up your energy because it helps you to motivate yourself and start things rolling again.

FIVE OF CUPS (DISAPPOINTMENT)

The loss of what you hoped for has been a shock to you. Give yourself time to mourn. Then start picking up the pieces because the new always rises from of the ashes of the old.

FIVE OF CUPS (DISAPPOINTMENT) Inverted

It's time to brush yourself off and get back into the game. Life is asking you not to close your heart, but to open it to the wonderful possibilities that await you.

SIX OF CUPS (PLEASURE)

The project or situation is unfolding according to plan. Take time to enjoy the process itself and it will be easier to maintain the energy needed to stay at the top of your game.

SIX OF CUPS (PLEASURE) INVERTED

You've begun to feel as if life is passing you by. Find a way to take pleasure in the process itself, otherwise it's an uphill climb. Start by having some fun again.

SEVEN OF CUPS (DEBAUCH)

Examine your options carefully before you commit to a specific direction. At present, it's necessary for you to look at practical solutions that will help you to get real.

SEVEN OF CUPS (DEBAUCH) INVERTED

Stretch yourself, put reason aside and follow your heart. When you're willing to express your feelings, you'll be able to accomplish anything you desire.

EIGHT OF CUPS (INDOLENCE)

Look after yourself so that you have the energy and resources you need to fulfill your own dreams. It's great to help others, but never do so if it means giving yourself away.

EIGHT OF CUPS (INDOLENCE) INVERTED

A balanced life has returned, and your feelings of vitality will soon follow. Enjoy yourself as you welcome in a new phase of your life.

NINE OF CUPS (HAPPINESS)

You're able to complete a long cherished dream and will be left with a sense of happiness and contentment. This is a period of peace and goodwill—so enjoy.

NINE OF CUPS (HAPPINESS) INVERTED

The situation itself is full of possibilities. However, you need to cooperate by changing your attitude. If you lighten up, you can create the results you desire.

TEN OF CUPS (SATIETY)

Success is inevitable—but don't rest on your laurels. Begin to lay the foundation for your next venture.

TEN OF CUPS (SATIETY) INVERTED

Your project will succeed if you can rediscover your original passion for it. Be willing to push the limits and take more chances. Don't accept "no" for an answer.

Swords Suit

ACE OF SWORDS
Your situation has been clouded in confusion; as the uncertainty lifts, you'll be able to see the light beyond the darkness—the path to success will be illumined for you.

ACE OF SWORDS Inverted
Your thinking is unclear. You need to wait until the dust settles before you act. Clarify your goals and carefully think out a plan to accomplish them before you proceed any further.

TWO OF SWORDS (PEACE)
You need to get off the fence and make a decision. Choose a direction you're willing to commit to—and then don't second-guess yourself, but just roll straight ahead.

TWO OF SWORDS (PEACE) Inverted
Don't be pressured into making a decision you're not ready to make. Sometimes doing nothing is the best decision of all!

THREE OF SWORDS (SORROW)
You're holding your breath waiting for the worst to happen. It will not. This is a time of new beginnings, a time to confront your past mistakes, learn from them and move on.

THREE OF SWORDS (SORROW) Inverted
The "soap opera" has ended and from this point on life will get easier for you. Go ahead with your plans because you will succeed.

FOUR OF SWORD (TRUCE)
You need a break. You've been trying to push a square peg into a round hole. Negotiate a compromise and back off for awhile. You'll know when it's time to try again.

FOUR OF SWORDS (TRUCE) Inverted
You're making too many concessions in an effort to keep the peace. Create a plan of action based on your needs and let others accommodate you for a change.

FIVE OF SWORDS (DEFEAT)
You're shooting yourself in the foot with your pessimistic attitude! If you want to accomplish something, your desire to succeed must outweigh your expectation of failure.

FIVE OF SWORDS (DEFEAT) Inverted

The first step in turning a loss into a win is to refuse to accept defeat. Don't let pride stand in the way of your trying again.

SIX OF SWORDS (SCIENCE)

Do your research and get all the information you can before you jump to conclusions. You need to see things as they really are—not how you want them to be.

SIX OF SWORDS (SCIENCE) Inverted

You've limited yourself to one point of view—yours. Admit you don't know everything. Give others a chance to speak instead of assuming you know what they have to say.

SEVEN OF SWORDS (FUTILITY)

You're overwhelmed at the moment and need to get the facts straight before you proceed. Keep the situation manageable by creating short term goals. Then relax, it will be okay.

SEVEN OF SWORDS (FUTILITY) Inverted

This endeavor is full of challenges. You're up to it—if you can set aside your doubts. Don't let your mind defeat you. When self-doubt speaks, you can choose not to listen.

EIGHT OF SWORDS (INTERFERENCE)

What we believe is possible to achieve can limit what we will achieve. Negate non-productive thoughts—choose to see the possibilities.

EIGHT OF SWORDS (INTERFERENCE) Inverted

Nothing will stop you reaching your goals unless you choose to stop yourself. Your steadfast belief in yourself helps you sail through opposition on your voyage toward success.

NINE OF SWORDS (CRUELTY)

How you think and feel about yourself is up to you. Lately you've been putting yourself down at every opportunity. Don't make decisions in this state of mind. Lighten up!

NINE OF SWORDS (CRUELTY) Inverted

Stop seeing yourself as a victim. If you want to change your situation, you need to change your mind and adopt a more positive attitude toward this endeavor.

TEN OF SWORDS (RUIN)

You're looking for trouble where there isn't any. Before you act, make sure you know what's actually going on—not what you imagine is happening.

TEN OF SWORDS (RUIN) Inverted

Don't waste time worrying about everything that could go wrong. With a more positive attitude, you'll take more risks. If you take more chances, the more likely you are to succeed.

Disks Suit

ACE OF DISKS

Be sure your endeavor is built on a firm foundation so that it can withstand the winds of change. From this solid stance, your spirit will be free to soar as you bring your dreams to life.

ACE OF DISKS Inverted

Gather the resources you need before attempting to move this project or situation forward. Take your time and be sure you've established a firm sense of trust in yourself to build on.

TWO OF DISKS (CHANGE)

You may have to juggle your time, energy, or money to achieve your goals. Nonetheless, these shifts and changes will bring you the results you desire.

TWO OF DISKS (CHANGE) Inverted

At the moment your life is like a juggling act; you might as well make the best of it. If you loosen up, you're less likely to drop the ball.

THREE OF DISKS (WORK)

This venture requires not only commitment and determination but hard work as well. Use a down-to-earth approach and good things will start to happen for you.

THREE OF DISKS (WORK) Inverted

To move ahead with this endeavor, remember that growth and expansion will be found by coming out of your retreat position and taking the bull by the horns. Total commitment is necessary.

FOUR OF DISKS (POWER)

Through your own effort, you've accomplished a lot to this point. However, the time has come to update your plan. You need to enlarge your vision as you once again test your limits.

FOUR OF DISKS (POWER) Inverted

You've started out with a bang, but don't seem to have a clue about how to continue. It is through planning, setting priorities and hard work that you will get what you want.

FIVE OF DISKS (WORRY)

Don't let worry get you down—either the foundation of your circumstances will be restructured, or you'll develop a totally different approach. Either way—you will win.

FIVE OF DISKS (WORRY) Inverted

All your worrying hasn't helped a bit. In fact, it's hindered your progress. Success is on your horizon, even if you don't see its light yet.

SIX OF DISKS (SUCCESS)

You're well on your way to victory. Remember it takes courage to accept success, because it changes your life. Are you ready for the changes about to occur?

SIX OF DISKS (SUCCESS) Inverted

You're overwhelmed. But no matter how difficult things seem at the moment, you're being asked to hold firmly to your path and continue to believe in this venture.

SEVEN OF DISKS (FAILURE)

You're dooming yourself to failure. Create a belief system that includes your ultimate success and prosperity—and you'll have a much better chance to reach your goals.

SEVEN OF DISKS (FAILURE) Inverted

Failure is not an option. It's time you took control of this situation. Determine what the end results will be—then make it happen.

EIGHT OF DISKS (PRUDENCE)

Be patient. Time itself will nurture your situation and create the growth and expansion you desire. Everything will work out when the time is right—not one moment before.

EIGHT OF DISKS (PRUDENCE) Inverted

Take one step at a time so this situation doesn't overwhelm you. Waiting for someone to do this for you will not work. The burden for success is on your shoulders.

NINE OF DISKS (GAIN)

To see your dreams materialize you must keep your priorities straight. Take time to tie up any loose ends now, while keeping focused on your goals—and the trophy is yours.

NINE OF DISKS (GAIN) Inverted

You're losing ground because you're cutting corners. For this project or situation, "good enough" is not good enough! To succeed, put your whole heart into it.

TEN OF DISKS (WEALTH)

This is the time to collect on your hard work. Abundance and prosperity will be yours. Enjoy what you've accomplished and share your good fortune with others.

TEN OF DISKS (WEALTH) Inverted

You desire prosperity but interfere with it at the same time. You need to give your thinking process a major overhaul and open your mind to receive if you're going to reach your goals.

THE MINOR ARCANA

THE COURT CARDS

KNIGHT OF WANDS

Persevere. Be willing to make changes quickly. Be honest and straightforward in your actions. Communicate your desires openly and everything will work out well for you.

KNIGHT OF WANDS Inverted

You need to adapt to the changes that are occurring. Everything must change—nothing stays the same. Even these hard times will pass and good fortune will follow.

QUEEN OF WANDS

Intuitively you know what to do, but you don't have to play "first fiddle" in this situation. Start by listening, and letting other people help you. You may even get it done on your terms.

QUEEN OF WANDS Inverted

When confronted with opposition, set aside the queen bee attitude. Soften up by opening your mind to new possibilities instead of closing down and becoming defensive.

PRINCE OF WANDS

Trust your sense of confidence and adventure, and move full speed ahead. When challenges appear, use them as opportunities to demonstrate just how much you can accomplish.

PRINCE OF WANDS Inverted

You're stalled in stagnation and indecision. You'll never know what you can do if you don't get out there and try. What would you do if you knew you couldn't fail? Now, go do it.

PRINCESS OF WANDS

Move forward with this endeavor despite your anxieties. You're empowered to act with inspiration and vitality, so trust your insights, and don't be afraid to question authority

PRINCESS OF WANDS Inverted

If this situation is as important to you as you say it is, you're going to have to work a lot harder than you have been willing to. Stop sulking, take the tiger by the tail and get on with things.

KNIGHT OF CUPS

Be assertive; at this point playing the "wallflower" won't help. You need to truthfully communicate your feelings about this situation, at least to yourself, so that you can see where you stand.

KNIGHT OF CUPS Inverted

You're having a problem expressing yourself. If you keep your feelings bottled up, you risk undermining the situation. You won't get anywhere pretending you don't feel as you do.

QUEEN OF CUPS

The situation may be elusive, if you rely on outer circumstances to guide you. You'll be on the right track if you listen with a quiet mind to what your intuition tells you.

QUEEN OF CUPS Inverted

This is not a time to chase rainbows, but a time to establish a practical, no-nonsense plan of action. Do your homework for this endeavor. The more you know, the clearer your path to success.

PRINCE OF CUPS

Listen to your heart and let your passions guide you. Keep your thoughts and feelings moving in the same direction, and you can accomplish anything you desire.

PRINCE OF CUPS Inverted

Surface appearances are not to be trusted. Be realistic about what's happening, and be sure you're not more attached to your fantasy than to the reality of your circumstances.

PRINCESS OF CUPS

If you're content being the power behind the throne, this situation will offer you a chance to demonstrate your talents and abilities. If it's recognition you desire, you may come up short!

PRINCESS OF CUPS Inverted

You want recognition for your talent and effort. However, you're afraid of putting yourself out into the world. Bravery is nothing more than acting in spite of your fears.

KNIGHT OF SWORDS

More than conjecture is needed before you proceed. If you can suspend judgment until you have looked deeper into the situation, you'll know exactly what to do next.

KNIGHT OF SWORDS Inverted

Stop and determine what the ultimate purpose of your endeavor is. Otherwise you're at risk of chasing your tail indefinitely. Then develop a plan of action you can live with.

QUEEN OF SWORDS

Don't let emotional attachment color your judgment. Put your feelings aside for the time being and think with your head, not your heart. Use your intellect to cut the situation down to size.

QUEEN OF SWORDS Inverted

To succeed you need to look at the situation more realistically. Set aside anger and resentment. You've been letting the past influence the present; wise up.

PRINCE OF SWORDS

Be prepared—before reaching your goals, you're going to encounter a few obstacles. If you have a well thought out game plan, it will help you stay focused.

PRINCE OF SWORDS Inverted

Misconceptions have clouded your thinking and confused the issue. You need to assume you know nothing about the situation and start over with an open mind.

PRINCESS OF SWORDS

Stop talking about your ideas and start acting on them. The best thing you can do for yourself right now is to put your ideas on the line and do what others only dream of.

PRINCESS OF SWORDS Inverted

If you want recognition for your ideas, you need to get a grip on your fears and move your ideas out into the marketplace. If you're willing to give it a try, you will succeed.

KNIGHT OF DISKS

You'll soon be able to relax and reap the profits of your hard work. However, at the moment you need to stay focused on your goals and use your good old fashioned common sense.

KNIGHT OF DISKS Inverted

All the worrying in the world won't help you now. Instead, adopt a well-structured, sober plan of action. You need to dig in and focus your energy, talents and resources in one direction.

QUEEN OF DISKS

You've experienced a dry spell lately, but soon your life will open up again. From here on out, if you continue to follow your instincts, very little effort on your part will achieve the goal.

QUEEN OF DISKS Inverted

If you quit now, you won't get to enjoy the fruits of your labor. It may not seem that way now, but you're too used to struggling. Take a deep breath; all will be better for you very soon if you persevere.

PRINCE OF DISKS

Leave your emotions out of this. You need to be cool-headed so you can think clearly. Investigate the situation, gather information and get the facts straight before you act.

PRINCE OF DISKS Inverted

Don't expect quick results. If you take a conventional, established approach to this situation it will simplify your life and conserve your resources.

PRINCESS OF DISKS

It takes courage to launch your dreams out into the world and take a chance on yourself. Stand tall; the world is looking at you and is impressed by what it sees.

PRINCESS OF DISKS Inverted

You've spent a lot of time dreaming about what you want. Now's the time to re-energize, dispel your fears—and start living those dreams.

Bibliography

Alli, Antero. *Angel Tech: A Modern Shaman's Guide to Reality Selection*. New Falcon Publications, 1987

Alli, Antero and Sylvie Pickering. *The Verticle Oracle: A Modern Divination Device*. Vertical Pool, 1996

Arrien, Angeles. *The Tarot Handbook: Practical Applications of Ancient Visual Symbols*. Jeremy P. Tarcher, 1997

Arrien, Angeles and James Wanless, editors. *Wheel of Tarot: A New Revolution*. Merrill-West, 1992

Arroyo, Stephen. *Astrology, Karma and Transformation: The Inner Dimensions of the Birth Chart*. C.R.C.S Publications 2nd Revised Ed., 1992

Bandler, Richard. *Using Your Brain for a Change*. Real People Press, 1985

Bandler, Richard and John Grinder. *Reframing: Neuro-Linguistic Programming and the Transformation of Meaning*. Real People Press, 1982

Booth, Martin. *A Magick Life: The Biography of Aleister Crowley*. London: Hooder & Stoughton, 2000

Campbell, Joseph. *Myths to Live By*. Penguin Books, 1972

_____. *The Hero With a Thousand Faces*. Princeton University Press, 1949

Campbell, Joseph, editor. *The Portable Jung*. Penguin Books, 1971

Cockren, A. *Alchemy Rediscovered & Restored*. Book Tree Publishers, 1998

Crowley, Aleister. *The Book of Thoth: A Short Essay on the Tarot of the Egyptians*. London: O.T.O., 1944. The Equinox III (5) Facsimile edition: Samuel Weiser, 1991

_____. *The Confessions of Aleister Crowley*. London: Penguin/Arkana, 1989

_____. *The Book of the Law*. Samuel Weiser, Inc., 1976

_____. *Magik*. Red Wheel/Weiser LLC, 1994

_____. *Eight Lectures in Yoga*. New Falcon Publications, 1998

DuQuette, Lon Milo. *Understanding Aleister Crowley's Thoth Tarot*, Red Wheel/Weiser, 2003

_____. *The Magick of Thelema*. Weiser Books Inc., 1993

_____. *The Chicken Qabalah*. London, Ernest Benn Limited, 1976

_____. *My Life With the Spirits*. Red Wheel/Weiser, 1999

Fortune, Dion. *The Mystical Qabalah*. Samuel Weiser, 1957

Gilchrist, Cherry. *The Elements of Alchemy*. Element Books, 1991

Graves, Robert. *The Greek Myths*. Penguin, 1993

Greer, Mary K. *Tarot for Your Self: A Workbook of Personal Transformation*. New Page Books, 2nd Ed. 2002

Hauck, Dennis William. *The Emerald Tablet: Alchemy for Personal Transformation*. Penguin Compass, 1999

Hubbard, Barbara Marx. *Conscious Evolution: Awakening the Power of Our Social Potential*. New World Library, 1998

Huber, Cheri. *There is Nothing Wrong with You*. Keep It Simple Books, 1993

____. *The Fear Book: Facing Fear Once and for All*. Keep It Simple Books, 1995

Jung, Carl. *Man and his Symbols*. Doubleday, 1964

____. *Psychology and the Occult*. Princeton University Press, 1997

Kaplan, Stuart. *The Encyclopedia of Tarot*. U.S. Games Systems, 1990

Kaczynski, Richard, Ph.D. *Perdurabo: The Life of Aleister Crowley*. New Falcon Publications, 2003

Murphy, Michael. *The Future of the Body: Explorations into the Further Evolution of Human Nature*. Jeremy P. Tarcher, 1992

Nichols, Sallie. *Jung and Tarot: An Archetypal Journey*. Samuel Weiser, 1980

Newcomb, Jasper Augustus. *The New Hermetics: 21st Century Magick for Illumination and Power*. Weiser Books, 2004

Roberts, Richard and Joseph Campbell. *Tarot Revelations*. Vernal Equinox Press, 1979

Rosengarten, Arthur. *Psychology and Tarot: Spectrums of Possibility*. Paragon House, 2000

Rudhyar, Dane. *The Astrological Houses: The Spectrum of Individual Experience*. C.R.C.S Publications, 1986

Ruiz, Don Miguel, M.D. *The Four Agreements*. Amber Allen Publishing, 1997

Sutin, Lawrence. *Do What Thou Wilt: A Life of Aleister Crowley*. St. Martin's/ Griffin, 2000

Wang, Robert. *An Introduction to the Golden Dawn Tarot*. Samuel Weiser Books, 1978

Wanless, James. *New Age Tarot*. Merill-West, 1986

____. *Intuition @ Work*. Red Wheel/Weiser, 2002

____. *Strategic Intuition for the 21st Century: Tarot for Business*. Merill-West, 1996

____. *little stone: your friend for life*. Booksurge Publishing, 2005

Wolf, Fred Alan, Ph.D. *The Spiritual Universe: How Quantum Physics Proves the Existence of the Soul*. Simon & Schuster, 1996

____. *Parallel Universes: The Search for Other Worlds*. Simon & Schuster, 1989

Wolinsky, Stephen. *The Dark Side of the Inner Child*. Bramble Books, 1993

____. *Trances People Live*. Bramble Books, 1991

Von Franz, Marie-Louise. *On Divination and Synchronicity: The Psychology of Meaningful Chance*. Inner City Books, 1980

Ziegler, Gerd. *Tarot: Mirror of the Soul*. Red Wheel/Weiser Books, 1988

ACKNOWLEDGEMENTS

My thanks to:

Patricia Selin for believing I could do it.

Alicia O'Neill for her professional input.

Mimi Sullivan for reading and re-reading this manuscript.

Alan Reade for his suggestions.

Ephran Younger for encouraging me to complete the project.

. . . and friends and students who cheered on this venture.

Special thanks to:
Kedron Bryson who through the magic of her editorial skills
brought this manuscript to life.

ABOUT THE AUTHOR

P. C. Tarantino has studied the Thoth Tarot and Aleister Crowley's writings for twenty-eight years. Her interest in philosophy and Jungian psychology first drew her to Crowley's compelling but complex work, a rich and mystical tapestry of Eastern and Western mythologies, the Qabalah, numerology, astrology and alchemy. Her own writings and instruction embody her straightforward, practical approach to using Thoth Tarot for self-awareness and transformation: "I can't help myself. I'm a Taurus. I keep Mother Earth in view most of the time. The Thoth Tarot has direct, firmly grounded guidance for our everyday affairs as well as our life path."

P. C. lives on the Central Coast of California, surrounded by books and in the good company of poodles Mollie and Maggie.